Case Studies in
Social Psychology

Case Studies in Social Psychology
Critical Thinking and Application

Thomas Heinzen
William Paterson University

Wind Goodfriend
Buena Vista University

Los Angeles | London | New Delhi
Singapore | Washington DC | Melbourne

FOR INFORMATION:

SAGE Publications, Inc.
2455 Teller Road
Thousand Oaks, California 91320
E-mail: order@sagepub.com

SAGE Publications Ltd.
1 Oliver's Yard
55 City Road
London EC1Y 1SP
United Kingdom

SAGE Publications India Pvt. Ltd.
B 1/I 1 Mohan Cooperative Industrial Area
Mathura Road, New Delhi 110 044
India

SAGE Publications Asia-Pacific Pte. Ltd.
3 Church Street
#10-04 Samsung Hub
Singapore 049483

Acquisitions Editor: Lara Parra
Associate Editor: Lucy Berbeo
Editorial Assistant: Zachary Valladon
Production Editor: Olivia E. Weber-Stenis
Copy Editor: Gillian Dickens
Typesetter: C&M Digitals (P) Ltd.
Proofreader: Jennifer Grubba
Indexer: Sheila Bodell
Cover Designer: Anupama Krishnan
Marketing Manager: Katherine Hepburn

Copyright © 2019 by SAGE Publications, Inc.

Printed in the United States of America

Library of Congress Cataloging-in-Publication Data

Names: Heinzen, Thomas E., author. | Goodfriend, Wind, author.

Title: Case studies in social psychology : critical thinking and application / Thomas E. Heinzen, William Paterson University, New Jersey, Wind Goodfriend, Buena Vista University.

Description: First Edition. | Thousand Oaks : SAGE Publications, [2018] | Includes bibliographical references and index.

Identifiers: LCCN 2017045423 | ISBN 9781544308913 (pbk. : alk. paper)

Subjects: LCSH: Social psychology. | Critical thinking.

Classification: LCC HM1033 .H4558 2018 | DDC 302—dc23
LC record available at https://lccn.loc.gov/2017045423

This book is printed on acid-free paper.

SFI label applies to text stock

18 19 20 21 10 9 8 7 6 5 4 3 2 1

Contents

Preface: To Students and Their Teachers

●●

What do we mean by a "case study"? When most people hear the term *case study*, they think of strange medical situations, where only a few people in the entire world have a particular problem. A medical case study might describe an individual's symptoms, family history, and the treatment the doctor used.

In this book, we use a broader definition of case studies as a teaching tool, closer to the approach used in the graduate program at Harvard Business School. We have selected nonfictional, real-world examples of how social psychological principles have played out in people's lives. The case studies we have selected represent the scientific backbone of social psychology. They convey the "take-home messages" about scientific values that psychology teachers have in mind for their students. Those values include critical thinking, the value of skepticism, the diversity of methods, the social relevance of scientific reasoning, the rich history of social psychological research, and the everyday applicability of social psychology.

Debate and discussion are expected as you read about personal interviews of participants in famous and controversial psychology experiments, the historical connection between the women who wrote the first computer program, or the human relevance demonstrated by social cooperation between whales and vampire bats.

We have several teaching purposes in creating this book, but they all support our larger mission: connecting social psychological theories to real-life data. We have three pedagogical paths to that goal; they all require that we focus on communicating

1. a comprehensive exposure to the content of social psychology by matching the content domains of a traditional textbook;

2. memorable stories about the successes, failures, and compromises of applying the scientific method to social psychology; and

3. the experience of belonging to the family of scientists who value social psychology.

This collection is a fraction of the stories available to all of us. The availability of so many case studies signals a healthy science. Flyvbjerg (2006) observed that a scientific discipline without case studies is not producing exemplars of its core insights. Social psychology's backstory is teeming with case studies, and this collection gives just some of those voices a chance to be heard. However, the origins of those stories required that we sometimes play fast and loose with the boundaries of social psychology.

We have thieved, for example, a story about correlations from its origins in public health. We also have connected self-fulfilling prophecies to sociology, documented aggression from film studies, and demonstrated the dangers of confirmation bias within the history of medicine. Both of your authors love social psychology, but real life doesn't know or care about the precise boundaries of our academic disciplines, and neither do we.

Each case study is well documented and minimizes speculative asides. However, some interpretation is unavoidable, especially when we identify specific social psychological theories that the actors in these dramas did not have a name for and perhaps never considered as an explanation. We understand the historian's reluctance to be misled by presentism (misperceiving the past by looking through the lens of the present). However, case studies, by definition, have already occurred. So we (perhaps too shamelessly) take advantage of the hindsight bias (interpreting events based on what we know already happened) to connect theories to data that only seem obvious in retrospect.

We have three defenses for flaunting the sin of presentism. Our first (serious) defense for daring to learn from history is that it's fun to apply current theories and key concepts to the data in case studies. Second, historical case studies allow students to observe apparent connections between theory and data—and then to critically assess those connections. Third, although we still don't enjoy the experience, we don't mind being proven wrong. Failing forward is how science works; it's a team effort.

In some important ways, it is far more difficult to both teach and learn social psychology from a case study perspective (as compared to a traditional textbook approach). It demands more critical thinking from students. From professors, the case study approach requires more personal creativity, filling in the blanks, and professional judgments—and the ability to guide a discussion about particular case studies. On the other hand, teaching and learning will be more engaging, be more organic to real life, and provide a more authentic frame for social psychological theories. Most teachers of social psychology recognize the power of a timely, well-constructed story—and like to tell them. The incompleteness of any collection of case studies creates room for personal discovery of the relevance of social psychological theories.

Each selection has specific teaching purposes guided by our underlying purpose: connecting theory to data. Connecting theories to case studies recognizes that students are hungry to discover something about which to care. Case studies as a teaching tool are a magnet by which we hope to attract, retain, direct, and fulfill our students' best ambitions.

Why Case Studies?

This collection of case studies introduces you to the discipline of social psychology. Like an introduction between two people, almost anything might happen. There may be a polite smile and a name quickly forgotten (after you get through this book, you might never think about it again). Or they might get married 4 weeks later and live happily ever after (you might fall in love with social psychology and dedicate your career to it). Or, 15 years later, one person might be in a position to hire the other for an important job (you might remember a few important ideas and apply them later when they become useful). With every introduction, the imagination is free to roam and the possibilities are wide.

The same wonderful uncertainty exists as we use case studies to introduce you to social psychology. Four weeks from now, you might be explaining to a journalist why you alone in a group of strangers came to the aid of a car crash victim. Or, 15 years from now, you might find yourself resisting the peer pressure of 11 other jurors. At least one of the case studies in this book should be appealing enough to move you from introduction to a somewhat deeper conversation about social psychology.

Psychological Science Needs Case Studies

The masterful scientific storyteller and neuroscientist Oliver Sacks (1970, pp. xii–ix) traces the origin of the "case history story" to Hippocrates (c. 450–c. 380 B.C.E.), an ancient Greek man who is now credited as being one of the founders of the medical field. Hippocrates noticed that a disease was structured like a story. Diseases had a beginning, a middle, and an end "from their first intimations to their climax or crisis, and thence to their happy or fatal resolution." The first obligation of case studies is that they discover and tell authentic, evidence-based stories.

Scientific storytelling often has directed the path of psychology (see Rolls, 2010). Alexander Luria told a long story about one man who could not forget. Kitty Genovese's tragic murder has itself become a case study about the hazards, possibilities, and controversies of case studies. The 42-inch iron rod that passed through Phineas Gage's brain may have changed his personality, but it did not prevent him from handling a four-horse stagecoach and telling entertaining stories to his nieces and nephews. Each of these stories has prodded science forward.

Flyvbjerg (2006) asserts that case studies signal a healthy science. Any scientific discipline needs to produce demonstrations of its core insights—and if social psychology can't be used to explain real-life events, then the field isn't doing its job. Case studies are the steel mesh embedded in the concrete of psychology's broad foundation, the network of observations that holds all that hard research together. By that measure, Figure 0.1 tells us that modern psychology is a healthy science; the term *case studies* (and similar phrasing) is (conservatively) projected to appear in approximately 4.64% of the (rapidly increasing) PsycINFO database by 2010 to 2019.

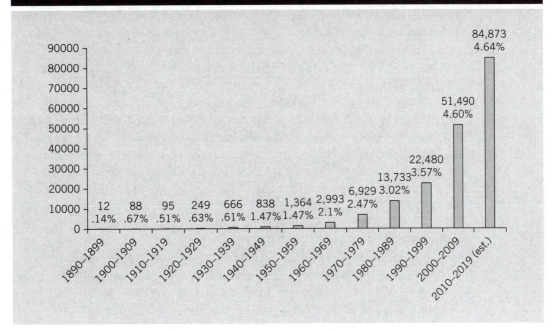

Figure 0.1   From 1890 through a projected 2019, the number of times the terms *case study, case studies, case report,* or *case reports* appears in psychological articles or books listed in the PsycINFO database has increased from almost nothing to about 4.64%.

Two Types of Case Studies

Case studies can be organized into two groups, based on their purposes: research case studies and teaching case studies. Case studies are not limited to exploratory, ethnographic, or participant-observation research. Those are merely data-collecting techniques, often used to build a case study—not to represent the boundaries of case studies. For example, a story about decision making can be a case study—so can stories about "individuals, organizations, processes, programs, neighborhoods, institutions, and even events" (Yin, 2009, p. 17). A summary of Yin's (2009, p. 18) definition of a research case includes four elements.

Case studies for research

1. are empirical inquiries that investigate a complex, real-life phenomenon in depth;

2. investigate a phenomenon in which there are many relevant variables or phenomena to consider;

3. seek multiple sources of converging evidence; and

4. are guided by theory.

Case studies for teaching are typically brief and intended to provoke discussion and critical thinking. For example, Martha Nichols (1993) presented Harvard MBA students with a case study that could be summarized in just one sentence: "A U.S. clothing manufacturer discovered that ten year-old girls were sweeping the factory floors of their Pakistani contractor." That sentence is loaded with real-life conflict.

The case study discussion promotes a conversation that models the complex, multivariable world that MBA students are about to enter. Should the clothing manufacturer, for ethical reasons, stop doing business with the contractor? Isn't it better to provide any employment rather than no employment? What if the press discovers their use of child labor? How will any decision affect future economic relations between Pakistan and the United States? Harvard MBA students will study about 500 such case studies because "we believe the case study method is the best way to prepare students for the challenges of [future] leadership" (Harvard Business School, 2014).

Future leaders likewise will benefit from social psychology's many insights and the theories that will help them remember and apply those insights to novel situations. We hope that you find the case studies presented in this book to be engaging, insightful, thought-provoking, controversial, and exciting.

CHAPTER 1

Introduction to Social Psychology

1.1 Does Corruption Corrupt?

"Power tends to corrupt, and absolute power corrupts absolutely. Great men are almost always bad men." This famous quotation, from the historian and politician John Dalberg-Acton (1887), presents an interesting idea. Does power always lead to corruption—and does corruption lead to more corruption?

We each answer this question, personally, whenever we observe someone getting ahead by breaking the rules. If you see a driver getting around a traffic jam by driving on the shoulder, will you then also drive on the shoulder? Or are you the kind of person who will pull onto the shoulder just enough to block other "cheating" drivers from getting ahead? Are you more likely to cheat in a class if you know other students cheated and received higher grades? Do you think, "If cheating works, then I am being played for a sucker by not cheating." And does your answer change if you know the class is being graded on a curve (say, for example, only the top 5% of students in class receive an A), such that anyone with a score higher than yours actually makes your score even worse?

These ethical questions illustrate two phenomena in social psychology. The first is **social norms**. Defined fully within the theory of planned behavior, social norms are your perception of what most people around you are doing or thinking. If you believe that several other people in your class are cheating—and getting away with it—then the social norm is actually to break the rules. The second social psychological principle involved in the question of whether power corrupts may be a **self-fulfilling prophecy**. If politicians enter the world of politics assuming that it's a corrupt system and that compromises will likely have to be made to get ahead, then it's more likely that those individuals will, indeed, make ethical compromises.

Consider the following interesting ethical questions:

1. Would you cheat in a sport by taking performance-enhancing drugs (PEDs)?

2. Would you offer a bribe to a police officer to get out of a much more expensive traffic ticket?

3. Would you be more likely to say yes to either question if you thought that everyone else was breaking the rules in this way and getting away with it?

These questions come from two relevant case studies, one from the real-world context of high-stakes athletics and one from scientific research. The first case study is the famous example of cyclist Lance Armstrong, who won the Tour de France a record seven times in a row. Heralded by many as a brave hero who overcame cancer to achieve this amazing feat, Armstrong became internationally celebrated as his "Live Strong" campaign made millions of dollars. When accused of using PEDs, Armstrong denied the charge for many years, making statements such as "that's crazy. I would never do that. No. No way" (Orjoux, 2005).

However, in a famous interview with Oprah Winfrey in 2013, Armstrong finally admitted that he had been using PEDs in all seven of his Tour de France wins. He admitting to lying about the drugs and to falsifying drug tests. In a crucial example of social norms, however, when Winfrey asked Armstrong whether he considered taking the PEDs cheating, he responded, "No . . . I viewed it as a level playing field" (Calamur, 2013). In other words, if other competitors were going to be using PEDs, then he should do it as well. If athletes enter the world of ultra-competitive sports assuming they will make this kind of decision, it becomes a self-fulfilling prophecy.

The question of whether social norms and self-fulfilling prophecies can be seen in scientific studies was tested in a large survey-experiment of 4,200 households in Costa Rica (see Corbacho, Gingerich, Oliveros, & Ruiz-Vega, 2016). The central hypothesis was that if people perceive that corruption is increasing in their society, then willingness to participate in corruption should increase as well. To test this, some participants were randomly assigned to see a flier discussing the increasing rates of corruption in Costa Rica. Other participants (a control group) saw a flier that was still negative about Costa Ricans but focused on the government's seeming inability to deal with crime in general. Everyone in the study was then simply asked to either agree or disagree with the statement, "In order to avoid paying a traffic ticket, I would be willing to pay a bribe to a police officer" (Corbacho et al., 2016, p. 36). People who saw the flier about increasing corruption were 28% more likely to say they would participate in corruption themselves, compared to the control group.

It appears that from both the Armstrong case and the scientific study described here, people are more willing to say they would make ethical compromises if they believe others are doing the same thing.

DISCUSSION QUESTIONS

1. Are there individual differences in how much someone's decisions will be affected by social norms—meaning some people will be more affected by social norms than others? Are there, in other words, people who conform to social norms more than others—and does it matter whether the norms are positive (such as helping others) versus negative (such as cheating or bribing)?

2. Imagine a culture at work, such as politicians, police officers in a large city, or accountants for millionaires, in which most people working in that setting assume (1) other people in this context are probably corrupt or breaking the rules in some way and that (2) I'm likely to do the same, at least on some small level. What might be done to change the culture and social norms and therefore the self-fulfilling prophecy? What actual interventions could be done within professional organizations or within local communities of employees to stop this cycle?

3. In the research study described here (Corbacho et al., 2016), the authors admit that responses to their major survey question about willingness to bribe a police officer might not result in honest responding from participants, a problem called **social desirability**. Is social desirability a problem within *any* research on ethical dilemmas? How could a particular study's procedure increase honest responding?

4. A central question in this opening case study is whether power corrupts. Choose a side of this debate—that power either inevitably corrupts everyone, or it doesn't necessarily—and identify three examples of real historical or contemporary figures that support your side of the issue. In other words, choose three people whom you believe were corrupted by power, or three people who resisted corruption, despite being powerful. Use them to explain and support your view on this question.

KEY TERMS

Self-fulfilling prophecies 1   Social desirability 3   Social norms 1

1.2 An Error of Intuition: Bloodletting and Purging

Can we trust a theory based on **intuition**?

There is a great deal to admire about Dr. Benjamin Rush. In addition to being a signer of the U.S. Declaration of Independence, Benjamin Rush is considered the father of modern psychiatry. In addition, Rush "served tirelessly as an advocate for many social reforms including temperance, women's rights, and humane treatment of the mentally ill . . . women's education and the abolition of slavery" (Toledo, 2004, pp. 61–62). In many ways, Rush was a product of the Enlightenment and, at least in the United States, often decades ahead of his time (see Shryock, 1971). But his story demonstrates why even a fine person, well-educated and sincere, can still be victimized by placing too much faith in his intuition. Rush believed in a theory that made intuitive sense—but it turned out to be dangerous (see Shryock, 1971; Toledo, 2004).

The Theory of Heroic Medicine

Dr. Benjamin Rush was a firm believer in a medical theory that he had never bothered to test. Why no experiments? Because his theory was intuitively obvious. If something inside your body is causing you illness, then the best chance for a cure is to get that something outside of your body. That's why he believed in bloodletting (the release of blood from the body) and purging. The idea was that disease is caused by an imbalance of substances in the body. To Rush, the obvious evidence that his theory and method of application were correct could be seen in the lives of his patients: Many of his extremely ill patients did not die. Their survival was proof enough that his theory-driven approach was sound.

The theory that Rush believed in so deeply was called "heroic medicine" and followed the central tenet that a drastic medical condition required a drastic treatment. The first step in this "proven" treatment was bloodletting as a way to rebalance the diseased body. Toledo (2004) described a common approach: "Typically, Rush would 'relieve' his patients of eight pints of blood over two or three days"—and if that did not work, Rush would administer "another round of bleeding and purging." Purging involved inducing vomiting and elimination. Get all that bad stuff out of your system!

Rush demonstrated his own personal heroism by bravely applying his theory to the sick people struggling through Philadelphia's contagious yellow fever epidemic. But an intuitively appealing theory combined with personal heroism still did not make his treatment effective. "Without doubt," Toledo (2004) concluded, the "brand of heroic medicine initiated and propagated by Rush cost thousands of Americans' lives including his own." Rush died of typhus fever in 1813.

Think of intuition as a way of knowing without knowing how you know. It is an automatic hunch or **heuristic** that leads you to behave in a particular way—a gut feeling, in some ways the opposite of careful, logical thought. Benjamin Rush's hunch about heroic medicine had big consequences. But many hunches are about small, relatively inconsequential decisions. For example, sometimes you will approach a door and it is unclear whether it is a push or a pull door. You don't stop to analyze the situation; you rely on your intuition without knowing where that intuition came from. Life is full of small ambiguities that require intuitive decision making. Intuition often feels good—and going against it often feels dangerous—but can we trust intuition? This is one of the central questions guiding the subfield of social psychology known as **social cognition**.

DISCUSSION QUESTIONS

1. Does the story of Benjamin Rush support both (a) Kurt Lewin's idea that "there is nothing so practical as a good theory" (Lewin, 1951, p. 169) and (b) there is nothing so dangerous as a bad theory? How did Rush's theory of "heroic medicine" lead to both good and bad application?

2. The intuitive appeal of bloodletting and purging was that if something inside your body is making you ill, then the cure is to get that something out of your body. Describe two other specific situations in which intuition or "going with your gut" is not always a wise choice and when relying on logical thinking probably leads to wiser decisions.

3. Describe with examples how these relatively routine but ambiguous situations require you to use your intuition—and how you respond when you are wrong:

   a. Doors that don't obviously indicate whether you should push or pull them

   b. Light switches that don't indicate which light they turn on

   c. Stove knobs that don't indicate which burner they will operate

   d. Road signs that seem to contradict themselves

   e. Your own unique example

4. What intuitive theories do you believe about each of the following—and why do you believe them? Do you think your theory would hold up to scientific testing?

   a. Gender differences

   b. Anger management

   c. Who falls in love with whom

KEY TERMS

Heuristics 4

Intuition 3

Social cognition 5

1.3 Decision Making: Sex and the Power of the Situation

Which is more influential in your thoughts and behaviors—your personality or the environment?

Many great teachers don't teach, at least in the traditional sense. Instead, great teachers follow the same impulse as great game designers (see Schell, 2014) by creating an experience—and then letting the experience do the teaching. It could be a well-designed lab, a class exercise, a field trip, an in-class demonstration, activities with other students, or even a great lecture. But when it works, you remember it for a lifetime, recalibrate your life and career, and eagerly tell other people the story about your experience.

The Theater of Social Psychological Experiments

Many of social psychology's classic experiments are also carefully designed experiences. For example, in Stanley Milgram's famous obedience experiments (see Milgram, 1974), ordinary people suddenly found themselves facing an unexpected decision: whether to deliver an electric shock to an innocent person, just because they were being ordered to do so. The level of shock "required" each time quickly escalated into what were presumably dangerous or even life-threatening levels.

If someone were reluctant to keep going, then Milgram created a situation that made it difficult not to obey. A firm scientific authority figure told the experimental participants that they had no choice; the *experiment required* that they continue. Most people (about 65%) continued to deliver potentially lethal levels of electric shock to innocent people. It's not surprising that Stanley Milgram was so good at designing experiences—he had a background in theater, music, and set design; he had tried his hand at writing Broadway-style musicals (see Blass, 2004). Milgram seemed to recognize that a reliable experimental procedure was like producing almost the exact same theatrical effect, night after night, across different people and participants.

Other classic experiments in social psychology rely on inducing the same experience over and over again and pit personality versus the situation at hand. Solomon Asch's (1951) line judgment experiments created another odd but reliable experience. A college student was set up to participate in a deliberately boring experiment about which of three lines in a display was the longest. The boredom vanished into an experience that was, for some, a sudden perceptual nightmare of self-doubt. Why? Everyone else in the room suddenly reported that the longest line on display was not the longest line—and they were serious! Everything you previously had trusted about your perceptions was suddenly up for grabs. It was an exquisitely designed peer pressure moment, and it delivered a whopping experience.

Social psychology's founder, **Kurt Lewin**, came to recognize the importance of the immediate experience when he was a foot soldier in the trenches of World War I. He observed otherwise civilized soldiers burning fine furniture to get through a cold night. Why would they do such a thing? Their decision to behave in this uncivilized way was the product of two factors: (1) their immediate experience (they were *really* cold) and (2) how people construed, or understood, the immediate situation (the cold night could be life-threatening). The situation led them to do things they normally wouldn't have done. Lewin famously noted that behavior is the result of the **interaction** between personality and the situation.

Decisions About Sex

We can see the power of the immediate situation when people are making decisions about sex. People sometimes make solemn promises to themselves about sex, such as this one: No unprotected sex. To say that this is a matter of life and death is more than playing with words. Sex without the protection of a condom or some other method really might produce a new life—and also could lead to a sexually transmitted disease, some of them deadly.

So, here's a hypothetical case study: A young couple suddenly find themselves in an appealing but unplanned romantic situation—and without any possibility of protected sex. As they become aroused, they both find that the power of the immediate experience is starting to overwhelm their resolve not to have unprotected sex. How much will their personalities and previously made decisions or perceptions about themselves matter in what happens? And, how much will pressures of the situation, perceived pressure from the other person there, social norms, and so on influence their decision?

DISCUSSION QUESTIONS

1. Lewin's famous equation, predicting that behavior is a function of both personality and the social environment or situation, is a well-known foundational idea in social psychology. Does this question—personality versus the situation—seem as important or interesting as another classic question, "nature versus nurture"? Which question matters more or should get more research attention, and why? Are both questions simply **false dichotomies**?

2. When you consider your own decision making, identify two specific examples of times when your personality or self-concept mattered more than situational pressures (you went against what most other people seemed to be doing) and two specific examples of times when you went along with the crowd, despite doubt on some level that it was the "right" decision. Can you identify what differentiates when you follow your personality versus when you follow demands of the situation?

3. People sometimes conform to a situation despite their inner nature by engaging in a behavior (such as the participants in Milgram's study who thought they sent deadly shocks to someone else). In other cases, sometimes people conform to a situation by *not* engaging in a behavior (such as not sticking up for a bully victim because no one else is doing so). Which type of situation—action versus inaction—leads to more regret, and why?

KEY TERMS

False dichotomy 7

Kurt Lewin's equation: $B = f(P, E)$ 7

Interactions 7

CHAPTER 2

Research Methods

2.1 Gang Leader for a Day: There's More Than One Way to Know

"How does it feel to be Black and poor? Your answer options are: Very bad, somewhat bad, neither bad nor good, somewhat good, very good."

When Sudhir Venkatesh (2008) looked at his clipboard and read those questions to a Chicago gang member, he was behaving like a statistically minded survey-oriented social scientist. He was still just an eager young graduate student at the University of Chicago, but he could tell this wasn't going to be a productive way to gather meaningful data. By the time that particular gang member answered his question, Venkatesh was on his way to adding **ethnography** to his skill set. The ethnographic approach is one step beyond **naturalistic observation**. While naturalistic observation passively records what happens while trying to be as unobtrusive as possible, ethnography gains knowledge by directly observing and participating in a community and its culture.

Statistics and ethnography are both necessary, potentially valid ways of knowing. This case study explores how the ethnographic approach helped Venkatesh understand Chicago race relations, supportive communities, the relative generosity of poor people, the economics of drug dealing, the organizational structure of street gangs, how to access emergency health care, and much more. You can find the more complete story of this case study in Venkatesh's (2008) book, *Gang Leader for a Day.*

The Making of an Ethnographer

Before he began his short-lived survey work, Venkatesh was running for exercise in a public park near the University of Chicago campus on the south side of Chicago. He began chatting with six park regulars, older men who began explaining race segregation in Chicago. Venkatesh (2008, pp. 5–17) reported that the men

> congregated there every day—playing cards, drinking beer, fishing for
> bass and perch in the lagoon. I sat and listened to them for hours . . .
> I had had little exposure to African-American culture at all, and no
> experience whatsoever in an urban ghetto.

Venkatesh started getting research advice from these gentlemen that he probably had never heard from his professors. He recounted some of those conversations:

Leonard Combs: Never trust a White man, and don't think Black folk are any better. . . . We live in a city within a city. They have theirs and we have ours. And if you can understand that it will never change, you'll start understanding how this city works.

Venkatesh: You mean you don't have *any* White friends?

Combs: You have any *Black* friends? And you may want to ask your professors if *they* have any. . . .

Born in India but raised in Southern California, Venkatesh is the son of a professor and an academic product of the beautiful beachfront campus of the University of California, San Diego. He tried to include the small group of men in his survey, but they gave him better advice. "You should probably speak to the people who you really want to talk to—young men, not us. That's the only way you're going to get what you need." So he traveled to the soon-to-be-demolished Lake Park housing projects to conduct his survey. He wrote,

> Customers were arriving, Black and White, by car and on foot, hurrying inside to buy their drugs and then hurrying back out. . . . Young men stood and crouched on plastic milk crates, a couple of them stomping their feet against the cold. . . . As I turned, a hand grabbed my shoulder.
> "What's up, my man, you got some business in here?"
> Suddenly some more people showed up, a few of them older than the teenagers.
> One of them . . . grabbed my clipboard and asked what I was doing. "Who do you represent?"

They assumed that Venkatesh was a member of a rival Mexican gang on a scouting trip, preparing for an attack on their drug territory. One showed Venkatesh his gun; another waved a knife in front of him. They kept asking him if he spoke "Mexican."

> The guy with the too-big hat who had taken my clipboard looked over the papers and then handed everything back to me. He told me to go ahead and ask a question.
> "How does it feel to be Black and poor?" Pause. "Very bad, somewhat bad, neither bad nor good, somewhat good, very good."
> "F—you. You've got to be f—ing kidding me."

That's when the local boss of the group, J.T., entered the stairwell and into Venkatesh's life. What was Venkatesh doing there?

I explained that the project was being overseen by a national poverty expert with the goal of understanding the lives of young Black men in order to design better public policy. . . . I read him the same question that I had read the others. He didn't laugh, but he smiled. . . . Then he leaned in toward me and spoke quietly.

"How'd you get to do this if you don't know who we are, what we're about?"

J.T. suddenly disappeared with instructions to the young men to keep an eye on Venkatesh. Some started planning on how to position themselves in various apartments against the attack they imagined that Venkatesh was part of. But they also offered him a beer while they waited. And when J.T. returned a few hours later, he brought more beer, some advice, and a few social science questions of his own.

"You know you're not supposed to be here. . . . You're not from Chicago. You should not be walking through the projects. People can get hurt."

J.T. started tossing questions at me. What other Black neighborhoods was I going to with my questionnaire? Why do researchers use multiple-choice surveys like the one I was using? Why don't they just *talk* with people? How much money can you make as a professor?

"I had a few sociology classes. In college."

I was astounded at what a thoughtful person J.T. appeared to be. It seemed as if he were somehow invested in my succeeding, or at least considered himself responsible for my safety. I got up and headed for the stairs. One of the older men reached out and offered me his hand. I was surprised. As I shook his hand, he nodded at me. I glanced back and noticed that everyone, including J.T., was watching.

Sudhir Venkatesh was becoming an ethnographer.

What You Can't See With Statistics

You can see things with statistics that you can't see in any other way: population trends, voting patterns, the sources of an epidemic. However, some other critical observations cannot be seen with statistics—and that's why Venkatesh started hanging out with the leader of a drug gang in Chicago.

He went back to the housing project—to the surprise of J.T. and his crew. But this time, the clipboard and questionnaires were left behind. Instead, Venkatesh asked about oil changes, fancy hubcaps, and whatever else was occupying the rotating shifts of drug dealers when they were not transacting business. He would wonder at the openness of it all and the lack of a police presence, but he let those questions wait for another day.

During one visit, J.T. had been in one of the buildings and suddenly came out shouting to the crew, "Okay! They're ready, let's go over there." Venkatesh had no idea what he might be talking about, but he wanted to go along. J.T. looked at Venkatesh, smiled, and said, "Why don't you meet me here next week. Early morning, all right?" Then the entire crew jumped into their cars, drove away, and left Venkatesh standing alone wondering where they all had gone and why.

It took Venkatesh 4 years and some serious discussions with his professors to realize that what he was seeing as an ethnographer also might create legal trouble for himself and the university (pp. 185–186). He mentioned to a couple professors about

> how J.T.'s gang went about planning a drive-by shooting—they often
> sent a young woman to surreptitiously cozy up to the rival gang and
> learn enough information to prepare a surprise attack—my professors
> duly apprised *me* that I needed to consult a lawyer.

Venkatesh needed a lawyer because if he learned of a plan to harm someone, then he had a legal obligation to tell the police. He could talk with the gang after a fight, but he could not go to any planning meetings. There was, at least in Illinois at that time, no such thing as a researcher-client privilege such as journalists and lawyers have with their clients. J.T. introduced Venkatesh to soul food and they spent long hours in restaurants where J.T. did his version of paperwork while Venkatesh read textbooks and prepared for class. J.T. ran a large organization, and since he

> didn't want to generate tangible evidence of his enterprise, J.T. didn't
> write down very much, but he could keep innumerable details straight
> in his mind: the wages of each one of his two hundred members, the
> shifts each of them worked, recent spikes in supply or demand.

The culture and community that Venkatesh had entered was often starkly different from the stereotypes he had developed about gangs and housing projects and drug trafficking. The gangs were structured like corporations and, like many corporations, the really big money—"if you lived to see it," J.T. cautioned—flowed to the few at the top. J.T. wasn't there yet. But he was getting close.

One day, J.T. sent some of his workers to pick Venkatesh up at a bus stop and drive him to a park for a party. Walking there would not have been safe, J.T. warned him. But when he arrived at the park, Venkatesh found himself at a large barbecue of some 50 people there to celebrate the birthday of 1-year-old Carla, complete with balloons and a large cake.

> "Is this the young man you've been telling me about?" said an older woman putting her arm on my shoulder.
>
> "Yes, Mama," J.T. said between bites, his voice as obedient as a young boy's.
>
> "Well, Mr. Professor, I'm J.T.'s mother."
>
> "They call her Ms. Mae," J.T. said.
>
> "That's right," she said. "And you can call me that, too." We forged a bond immediately . . . Carla, the birthday girl, was a one-year-old whose father and mother were both in jail for selling drugs. The adults in her building had decided to raise the child. This meant hiding her away from the Department of Child and Family Services, which would have sent Carla into foster care. Different families took turns keeping Carla. . . .
>
> Ms. Mae talked about how teenage girls shouldn't have children so early, about the tragedy of kids getting caught up in violence, the value of an education, and her insistence that J.T. attend college.

To Venkatesh, it all sounded so unexpectedly . . . normal: balloons and birthday parties, a community pulling together to help a child with absent parents, proud mothers insisting that their children go to college, peace-building community parties with barbecue, basketball, and card games—stereotypes that he didn't even know he had were smashed with every conversation.

The Bigger Story

The bigger research story for students of social psychology is easy to understand: There is more than one way to know about human social behavior. It's not that one way is better than another. Statistical, empirical, quantitative studies are not inherently better than case studies, and you can't assume that ethnography and naturalistic observation is more meaningful than controlled experiments. We humans are complicated people; we need to use *all* of these methods if we are to understand one another and, perhaps, create a more just world.

Although some reviewers of *Gang Leader for a Day* have expressed concern that Venkatesh sensationalized parts of the world he entered, most social scientists have approved of Venkatesh's ethnographic approach. Psychologist Robert Sternberg (2008) wrote that "Venkatesh's book is a model for how one can use ethnographic methods to study the practical intelligence of populations that are out of reach for most behavioral scientists" (pp. 730–731).

DISCUSSION QUESTIONS

1. What kinds of information was Venkatesh able to gather and understand because he used an ethnographic approach, instead of a more traditional survey or experimental approach? On the other hand, what are two disadvantages that this study has due to the ethnographic approach?

2. The book *Gang Leader for a Day* is a well-written, entertaining book that is full of both drama and insight. Does the drama mislead the reader by creating sympathies that are really the bias of the writer? In addition, discuss how experimenter bias may have been involved in Venkatesh's writing and conclusions.

3. One goal of research is to predict future patterns and possibly change them to improve individuals' lives. Make a prediction about J.T.'s life. What do you think happened to him? What do you predict happens to young men in gangs as they get older? What about Carla's life? What future do you see for this 1-year-old growing up in a community?

4. How does ethnography apply to your life? If an ethnographer were studying you as a case study, what patterns might emerge? What would an observer find most interesting, surprising, and troubling about your life? Which approach would allow the researcher to get to know you better?

KEY TERMS

Ethnography 9

Naturalistic observation 9

Statistics 9

2.2 The Pump Handle Affair: Correlations Can Be Clues

Superstition and science are struggling with each other for supremacy over our thoughts. But they are not struggling over *what* we think; superstition and science are struggling over *how* we think. The following case study describes a famous battle that was a turning point in the ancient war between superstition and science. We'll call it the Battle of the Cholera Epidemic of 1854.

The Opening Attack: An Accident

Like many battles, this one was started by a combination of accident and ignorance—so blame cannot be laid at the feet of Sarah Lewis. She and her husband Thomas, a London police officer, were new parents and probably felt fortunate to be living at 40 Broad Street. Their home was close to the cold, clear, good-tasting water from the Broad Street well in London's Golden Square neighborhood.

For the first time in her short life, the Lewis' baby had gotten seriously ill with diarrhea—another good reason to be glad that they lived so close to a ready supply of fine water. While Sarah Lewis waited for the local doctor, she accidentally started an epidemic by rinsing a cloth diaper in some warm water and emptying the bucket in the cesspool in the basement.

Emptying soiled water into the cellar or throwing it out the back window was how everyone got rid of their waste. Sometimes the waste became several feet deep, but there was nowhere else to take it. And yes, the stench was terrible. But if you needed to work in the big city, then you put up with the stench—and the risks. Cholera was the biggest health risk of all in midcentury England. The 1833 cholera epidemic in England had killed about 20,000 people. The epidemic of 1848–1849 had killed about 50,000. The start of the cholera epidemic of 1854 was far more severe than either of those disasters. "Imagine," wrote Stephen Johnson (2006) in *The Ghost Map,* "if every time you experienced a slight upset stomach you knew that there was an entirely reasonable chance you'd be dead in forty-eight hours" (pp. 32–33).

Sarah Lewis could not know that *Vibrio cholerae* was rapidly reproducing in her daughter's small intestine or that the now-contaminated cesspool in their cellar was seeping into the Broad Street well. She could not know that emptying that bucket of waste had started an epidemic that would kill not only her own baby but also her husband, three other people in their building, and—in just 2 weeks—about 700 of her friends and neighbors. At the start of previous epidemics, cholera had killed as many as 70 people, but it took a few months. This was considered the most vicious attack of cholera that the United Kingdom had ever experienced. The diaper that Sarah Lewis had rinsed was the beginning of the battle over *how* we think about cholera—and superstition was winning.

Superstitions and Illusory Correlations

Cholera was a fear-generating mystery that spawned superstitious explanations and crazy cures. No one knew what caused cholera or how it was transmitted from one person to the next. It might skip over one house, kill one or two in a neighboring building, and wipe out all the residents in the next. Ironically, the idea of a real but invisible world of tiny germs was too strange, even for people who fervently believed in angels, demons, and other supernatural creatures. Germ theory would just have to wait for better ways to communicate scientific evidence. It was the apparent randomness of who lived or died that confused people. There was a secret pattern to the disease, but it could only be seen through the lens of statistics. What looked like randomness was a particular statistical concept: a **correlation**.

Superstition is an excessive belief in something that cannot be true. Some of the incorrect explanations for cholera had some basis in facts; others were just sloppy thinking. Superstition usually starts as an **illusory correlation** (perceiving connections that do not really exist). It was easy to believe—but wrong—that cholera was carried through air so polluted that it was difficult to breathe. Once perceived, an illusory correlation can easily settle into a **confirmation bias**. Confirmation bias occurs when we only notice and remember evidence that confirms what we already believe while ignoring evidence that contradicts what we believe. The most dangerous superstitions may be the subtle ones that infiltrate our thoughts and beliefs with assumptions that we never bother to challenge.

For example, if you looked for evidence that knocking on wood prevents bad things from happening to you, then you can find lots of evidence that appears to support that idea. In fact, if there is any wood nearby, go ahead and knock on it right now . . . did anything bad just happen to you? Probably not, so the data from your experience—all honestly collected and accurately reported—appear to confirm the "knock on wood" **hypothesis**. The data have no meaning unless they are housed within some kind of experimental design. Remember this as you go forward with your psychology degree: Design precedes data.

Hypotheses and Hypothesis Testing

The strangest hypothesis of all turned out to be the right one—but it was only confirmed after several others turned out to be wrong.

One explanation for the 1854 cholera outbreak was the *divine retribution hypothesis*. Preachers implied, and sometimes declared, that the sins of the people had grown very great. As in the days of Noah and his supposed ark full of every possible animal, God had grown so disgusted with humanity that it was time for some serious housecleaning. Cholera was divine judgment.

The same *bloodletting hypothesis* that Benjamin Rush believed in (see Case Study 1.2) was a popular medical approach intended to cure victims of cholera (and many other diseases). This one made a little more sense than the divine retribution hypothesis. The reasoning was that if the disease was inside your body, then the cure would mean getting it outside of your body. Bloodletting was a way of letting the disease leave your body.

However, the dominant hypothesis in 1854 was the *miasma hypothesis*. Miasma referred to disease traveling through the air. In a large city where people emptied their waste in their basements and backyards, it just *felt* right to blame cholera on the "bad air" (as in "mal-aria"). The stink was constantly rising from all those backyard cesspools and stinking cellars.

A fourth hypothesis was generally ignored by everyone but the local physician, John Snow: the *waterborne contagion hypothesis*. The cholera was being spread through exposure to contaminated water. That's why John Snow would recommend to the local authorities that they could stop the epidemic by simply removing the handle of the pump, forcing people to get their water from an uncontaminated source. The first three hypotheses made intuitive sense—but the waterborne contagion hypothesis was regarded at the time as sort of crazy. It was such a simple, startling idea that the local authorities would not accept it even after John Snow demonstrated that it was the only remaining explanation that made sense of all the data.

According to Johnson (2006), at some point, London residents had to choose between believing the cholera was being spread either by air (miasma) or by water. This decision became vitally important when deciding whether or not to drink a glass of water from one of the many wells in the Golden Square neighborhood. For people who believed in the airborne hypothesis, confirmation bias could be strong because they could point to the fact that some people were drinking the local water and not developing cholera.

But there is something to be learned about hypothesis testing from that observation: Hypotheses must be specific. The source of the contagion was not just local water from *any* well; it was specifically the water from the Broad Street well next to the house where Thomas and Sarah Lewis lived with their small child.

But no one had any data, no one even knew how to collect such data, and the formula for the correlation coefficient did not yet exist. This desperate, dying world didn't know it, but they were waiting for a creative statistician who knew how to (a) design a study and (b) count observations (collect data). Design and data.

The Correlation Confusion and Confirmation Bias

How many times—and in how many different ways—do we need to be reminded of this life-saving insight? Correlation does *not* imply causation.

During the Battle of the Cholera Epidemic of 1854, the correlation confusion was killing hundreds of people because they insisted that their intuitive and illusory correlation—that miasma was correlated with deaths from cholera—had to be correct. People continued to die at an alarming rate because citizens, ministers, and public officials were all confusing correlation with causation. Part of the difficulty, of course, was that Francis Galton had not yet invented a mathematical understanding of a correlation. That was still 30+ years in the future. So it is even more astonishing that the local physician John Snow was able to apply the concept of a correlation properly before there was even a language or a formula to express it.

John Snow didn't need words or a formula, but he did need a visual display of data. He plotted dots on a map showing the local neighborhood and the locations of all of the water wells. Then, on the same map, he added a dot to represent each death of cholera and where the person lived. The death dots were clearly clustered around one well in particular—the Broad Street well next door to the home of Sarah and Thomas Lewis. There was a strong, positive correlation between how close people lived to the Broad Street well and how likely they were to die of cholera.

John Snow's map did something very important: It *communicated* this victory of science over superstition. It feels awkward, of course, to think of an event that started out by killing "only" 700 innocent people as a victory. But the viciousness of this particular outbreak and the tens of thousands of lives lost in previous epidemics suggest that it was a victory that saved lives and slowly liberated people from the fear of cholera as well as the actual disease. An upset stomach was no longer cause for existential alarm.

DISCUSSION QUESTIONS

1. What do the authors mean by "design precedes data"? Explain this idea in your own words. Include a discussion of why interpreting patterns after they are known (instead of hypothesizing in advance) might lead to hindsight bias.

2. To convince people that his hypothesis was correct, John Snow had to provide both data in support of his idea and arguments against other, alternative hypotheses. Discuss how the idea of ensuring that a hypothesis is **falsifiable** matters in this type of context, in which several possibilities are considered simultaneously.

3. How are scientific findings communicated in psychology? Who are the critical audiences for science communications? How could psychological scientists become better communicators to the general public?

4. Where are we in the current battle against cholera? Find a report of a recent cholera outbreak and describe why it occurred, even though we know that clean water is the only thing needed to prevent it.

KEY TERMS

Confirmation bias 16
Correlations 15

Falsifiable 19
Hypothesis 16

Illusory correlations 16

2.3 The Experimental Impulse During the Salem Witch Trials: Why Procedures Matter

During the Salem witchcraft trials, the magistrate John Hathorne tried to apply an experimental procedure called a **single-blind** experiment.

Hathorne had the right idea, but he didn't know how to do it; the innocent woman accused of witchcraft was hanged a few days later. If he had used a **double-blind** procedure, then she might have lived. In fact, the entire tragedy of the Salem witchcraft trials might have ended with a bad case of social embarrassment rather than the deaths of about 30 innocent people, 19 of them by public hanging.

Procedures matter.

The Experimental Impulse

Novelists, playwrights, and filmmakers have avoided or misled audiences about a key point during the 1692 Salem witchcraft trials: Everyone had doubts. Even the accusers and the magistrates had doubts about whether the witches (in the form of specters) were real. But to the social psychologist, those doubts—and how people reacted to their doubts—are the most compelling parts of the story. Doubt eventually helped end the Salem witchcraft trials—it just wasn't strong enough to prevent the first 30 deaths or the torture of innocent children and their parents. However, things could have gotten much worse. The terror ended when devout Puritans started listening to the stubborn voice of skepticism.

Doubt needs sound procedures. If sound legal procedures are violated, then justice is denied. If surgical procedures don't go right, then the patient can die. Failing to follow sound procedures for assembling a child's bicycle the night before a birthday can lead not to joy but to disappointment the next morning—and maybe even a lifetime of snarky comments from family members. During the Salem witchcraft trials, flawed procedures influenced what judges believed, who would hang, who would die of neglect, and who would continue to live.

One of the accused, 65-year-old Lydia Dustin, was acquitted of witchcraft. But legal procedures kept her in prison until she could pay her prison maintenance fees. Of course, she could not earn the money needed to pay those maintenance fees because she was in prison and accumulating even more fees. She still was in prison when she died the following spring. She was killed by bad procedures. These abuses slowly exhausted themselves in Salem, Massachusetts, but the proper procedures would not have allowed the situations to develop in the first place.

Is Spectral Evidence Valid?

The Puritans of Salem Village and Salem Town, Massachusetts, did not doubt that witchcraft was real or that certain people had privately turned away from God to follow Satan. However, they did have doubts about the spectral "evidence" that was the basis for most accusations. Even the preadolescent girls who made most of the accusations of witchcraft had their doubts.

Specters were witches' images of themselves that they could send to do their evil bidding. Specters were how witches could be in two places at the same time, how they could fly about on sticks while simultaneously stirring the soup at home, and why some people could see them but others could not. Sometimes painfully funny situations evolved out of believing in specters. They were painful because they were so terrifying at the time and only funny in hindsight more than 300 years later.

For example, Betty Hubbard saw the specter of the accused witch Sarah Good lying on a table with naked breasts, feet, and legs. The man of the house, Samuel Sibley, reported taking action to kill the specter by striking it with a staff; Betty Hubbard confirmed that he hit her across the back hard enough to almost kill her (see Norton, 2002, p. 28).

In another case, Abigail Williams and Mercy Walcott saw the specter of Deliverance Hobbs biting another girl on the foot. When Benjamin Hutchinson struck at the apparition with his sword, the two girls declared that he had successfully stabbed Hobbs on the side. The two girls later saw so many apparitions that "the roome was full of them." Once again, brave Benjamin Hutchinson fought to protect the girls by continually thrusting his rapier in the air. At last, the girls exclaimed that he had killed a "greet Black woman . . . and an Indian that come with her for the flore is all covered with blod."

It seemed to be a great victory over the devil. Grown men were bravely slashing the air as they battled their most terrifying enemy, Satan. But they could never know whether their blows had landed without the help of two young girls who vividly narrated the unfolding battles. It's hard not to wonder whether, at some level, these preadolescent girls—already working hard labor at the lowest rung of the Puritan social ladder—were having the time of their lives manipulating these gallant men into defending them from a terrible fate.

If You Ask Liars If They Are Lying . . .

Trusting spectral evidence presented an important logic problem to Puritans: They were asking liars (the specters speaking through the girls) if they were lying. Their courtroom procedures had no way to unravel this conundrum. Some people in Salem also doubted the validity of spectral evidence because they reasoned that a powerful Satan might send the specter of an innocent person to do his bidding. The devil was considered the second most powerful force in all of creation and credited with fantastic powers of deception, especially over fallen believers. There was simply no way of knowing who was telling the truth—unless, of course, there were a valid test for witchcraft. And that brings us back to psychological procedures and issues of reliability and validity.

Salem's judicial magistrates were willing to doubt. Unfortunately, they did not know how to doubt. The most educated Puritan leaders did not know how to doubt. Even the Harvard graduates (the Reverends Increase Mather and his son Cotton Mather) did not know how to doubt. None of them had acquired the skills that every psychology major must demonstrate before she or he graduates: how to conduct experiments on humans.

Salem's Almost Scientific Touch Test

The touch test was how the Puritans tried to resolve their doubts. Follow the logic of the touch test as the people of Salem understood it. If a person being afflicted by a witch were touched by that witch, then the afflictions would stop because the evil power had been discharged back to its source.

However, the Puritans' understanding of the touch test was exactly opposite to how it had first been used. And that first touch test had used a blind procedure by taking a supposedly afflicted person and putting "an Apron before her Eyes" and then secretly substituting a random, innocent person for the witch. When the supposedly afflicted person responded as if she had been touched by the witch, they knew that the afflicted woman was faking it. By the time the Puritans got hold of the touch test, its logic had been reversed the same way a whispering game muddles a message as it is passed from one person to the next. More important, the experimentally gained evidence that the touch test was bogus was ignored.

And so, on April 22, 1692, such a large crowd of spectators came to the Salem Village meetinghouse that even the window light was shadowed by observers. That day's interrogations began with the accused witch named Deliverance Hobbs—a woman not from Salem Village but from nearby Topsfield. Hathorne and Corwin, the chief interrogators, recognized an opportunity to test whether Deliverance Hobbs was really a witch because the afflicted girls would not know Deliverance Hobbs by sight.

It was a blind experiment because Abigail and Mary, the teen girl "witnesses," would not know that Deliverance Hobbs had entered the room. At first, Abigail Williams and Mary Wolcott could not identify the witch who afflicted them— but they covered their error by claiming that the witch had struck them blind. They recovered their sight after they learned, possibly from a large room full of gossiping people, that Deliverance Hobbs had entered the meeting hall. In an empty courtroom, a single-blind experiment might have been good enough. But in a crowded courtroom full of eager, gossiping observers, justice required a double-blind experiment.

Deliverance Hobbs avoided hanging by confessing to what she had not done. Instead, she named others as witches—and they were hanged because they refused to make a false confession. In this case, procedures like random assignment and double-blind procedures were matters of life or death.

The Need for Psychological Science

We humans can be cagy, clever, and self-deceiving. We can justify just about anything if we scare ourselves enough. And then we are slow to take responsibility for our own behavior, sometimes blaming our ancestors. That's who we are. And that's why the development of psychological science is so important. If we are to save ourselves from ourselves, then we must develop the habit of applying principles of scientific reasoning to everyday decision making.

Psychological science is especially difficult. Gravity never says to a physicist, "I think I'll only pretend to be sorry about that tree branch falling on my annoying neighbor's car." Soap molecules never change their minds and decide that today, they just aren't in the mood to separate grease from water. Learning how to conduct experiments on humans is a challenge like no other type of science. So we should not be surprised that in 1692, none of the magistrates had the slightest idea of the bag of procedural techniques that experimenters can use to circumvent all the barriers that humans put up when scientists try to probe their secrets. Those insights only entered formal development some 200 years later (1875), when Wilhelm Wundt and William James opened psychological laboratories.

Certainly, no one had told the most forceful Puritan magistrate, John Hathorne, about experimental procedures such as double-blind **experiments** or random assignment to groups. He had no way of naming (much less controlling for) confirmation bias, memory distortions, or the effects of having other people in the room when conducting an experiment. Nathaniel Hawthorne, author of The Scarlet Letter, would one day change the spelling of his name to distinguish himself from his embarrassing relative.

But in 1692, even John Hathorne was trying to do the right thing. So he looked for ways to use preexisting tests and some original experiments to test for the presence of witchcraft. They just weren't very good (reliable or valid) psychological tests. But let's give even the most maligned Puritans, John Hathorne and his fellow magistrates, credit for at least trying. A few of those experiments came tantalizingly close to stopping the Salem witchcraft trials before anyone had to die.

DISCUSSION QUESTIONS

1. Procedures are rules that guide behavior. Following proper procedures is critical to success in surgery, law, experimentation, and even when assembling a bicycle. Identify three other activities or professions whose success depends on following the correct procedures. What happens when procedures are not followed?

2. Imagine that you are a judge in the historic Salem witch trials. Design a valid and reliable way to test for spectral witches.

3. Provide an example of how the word witchhunt is used by politicians or other public figures as a way to draw attention away from their own bad behavior. What are the connotations of this term today, and how are those connotations based on the Salem witch trials?

4. Discuss the psychology behind false confessions and naming other people as the "real" witches or guilty parties as techniques to avoid blame or responsibility.

KEY TERMS

Double-blind 19

Experiments 23

Single-blind 19

The Social Self

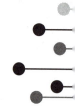

3.1 Who's Talking Now? Facilitated Communication and the Ouija Board Self

Ouija boards are spooky stuff, right? No one seems to be in charge, yet fingers on a sliding device are somehow directed to indicate one letter after another. The letters slowly form words; the words form sentences, name names, and answer questions that many people believe are coming from the dead. It can be fun and scary. What's really happening, however, is that the players have willingly opened themselves up to the power of suggestion, similar to stage hypnosis. So who's really doing the talking when we allow the Ouija board to take over?

Facilitated Communication

The case study of facilitated communication (FC) helps us understand how the self can disappear into a Ouija board–like device that seems to operate with a will other than our own. FC is nothing more than a respectable-looking version of the Ouija board—an alphabet board. The Ouija board was invented in the late 1800s as a way to communicate with the dead. It experienced a second wave of popularity during and after World War I when so many families desperately wanted to communicate with the sons, fathers, and brothers who had unexpectedly vanished. Their desperation to reach out was perhaps understandable—but their method was not scientific. FC became popular during the mid-1990s when so many families desperately wanted to communicate with their sons—and daughters—who had vanished into the mysterious disease called autism (and other developmental disabilities).

The case study of FC demonstrates (a) the hazards of relying *only* on case studies, (b) the social appetite for psychological fads, and (c) the clarifying power of the scientific method. But the most important effect of the FC story is about what it does to you and how wishful thinking can quickly escalate when people fail to use scientific thinking.

The website at Syracuse University's School of Education (2017) reports that an early appearance of FC (now called "supportive typing") occurred in Australia in the 1970s when Rosemary Crossley began using "physical support to help non-speaking individuals communicate." The FC method is a simple approach to what previously were considered to be mysterious neurological problems: A trained "facilitator" physically supports the hand, arm, sleeve—whatever seems to work—of a person previously thought to have a severe mental disability to the extent that she or he cannot verbally communicate.

As that person's hand hovers over an alphabet board, the facilitator guides his or her pointed finger to whatever letter on an alphabet board the facilitator thinks the individual intended to press—but couldn't without that person's help. You can probably see the superficial connection to a Ouija board. Those single letters became connected to words that formed sentences that, over time, were structured into paragraphs, exams, and essays that became college degrees—even for those previously thought to have profound developmental disabilities. It was an astonishing breakthrough!

The central question about FC has always been the Ouija board question: Who was *really* doing the communicating? The answer to that question was settled by what are called **crucial experiments**. They are called crucial experiments because they provide an unambiguous answer to a specific question. But to the believers (including many parents, social workers, guidance counselors, speech pathologists, and mental health workers), FC didn't need a crucial experiment. Who needed an experiment when they had seen FC work with their own eyes? They had felt its liberating power and rejoiced in the discovery and release of previously imprisoned creativity. Who wouldn't want to believe in something that gave so much meaning to their own lives as well as to the lives of those whom they had cared for? It took a few years for the revolutionary idea of FC to gain acceptance, but once it hit, it transformed the world of disabilities research and practice.

FC was evangelized with particular zeal by Syracuse University professor Douglas Biklen. According to the American Psychological Association (APA, 2003), FC soon "was spreading like wildfire all over the U.S. and Canada [because it] promised to transform the way people thought about people with autism and profound mental retardation." Now, with the help of FC, individuals once labeled as unintelligent and unteachable "scored well on standard IQ tests, wrote brilliant essays, and even composed poetry." FC was more than a revelation; it was a revolution in how we thought about and helped care for people with so-called disabilities.

People with what had been called developmental problems now were considered to have only motor difficulties, not mental disabilities (Biklen, 1990). FC worked by smoothing out their arm and hand movements enough to allow their previously frustrated inner intelligence to press letters on an alphabet board into words that blossomed in the light of normal society. The passion among advocates had been to treat people with disabilities with the same dignity and respect as "normal" people. Their motives were pure, even noble. Professor Biklen had been their champion and now FC had validated his beliefs. The remaining problems were merely matters of adjustment, getting better at the FC technique. And those problems were miniature compared to the joy of parents discovering that their precious child was no longer locked inside a world of profound retardation. Their child could now communicate.

Trouble in Paradise

Often, their children were typing messages that their parents had longed to hear. Sometimes it was a flood of previously frustrated words and ideas, but it might also be a heartfelt thank you to Mom and Dad for their steady love. Whose heart would not melt at such a moment? And it was all due to Biklen, FC, and the now hundreds of volunteers using FC to liberate the previously trapped personality, intelligence, humor, and gratitude of individuals. Many facilitators were so enthusiastic that they covered their own training expenses; they were the leading edge of a humanitarian revolution (APA, 2003)! The messages from people with autism and other disabilities were as deep and varied as the individuals themselves—and strangely familiar. FC seemed too good to be true. It was.

Messages of love and gratitude weren't the only messages being typed with the help of a facilitator. The Wendrow family in Bloomfield, Michigan, got a knock on the door. An FC facilitator with 1 hour of training had "facilitated" an important message from their daughter, Aislinn Wendrow. Aislinn had been diagnosed with autism at the age of 2. According to the FC facilitator, a recent message from Aislinn had been blunt, specific, and devastating. "My dad gets me up. . . . He puts his hand on my private parts," the adolescent Aislinn supposedly had typed. And just like that, Julian Wendrow became a sexual predator. The Wendrow family previously had been strong believers in FC, but now they *knew* that—at least in their case—it couldn't be true.

Two days later, Aislinn met with investigators at a county facility—but with the same facilitator at her side. Things got worse. Now Aislinn, through her facilitator, reported that the sexual abuse had been going on for years, involved photographs, and that her father had forced her 13-year-old brother Ian to participate in the abuse. Eight days after the initial charges, police arrested Julian, who was sent to the county jail for 80 days; he spent most of it in solitary confinement. Those isolated months gave Julian plenty of time to think about the 75-year sentence he was facing. Aislinn's mother, Tali, was released on bail but was required to wear a tracking device.

Ian was only 13 years old but was interviewed (without parental consent) by zealous police who were certain of his guilt and his father's guilt. They badgered him until he finally admitted that sometimes his father showered with Aislinn—something not uncommon for children with severe developmental difficulties.

The two children were shuffled around homes until Ian finally was placed in a juvenile facility. "I was moved in with kids who were like at the time 17, 18," Ian reported. People "who had actually been abused . . . it was scary" (Berman & Balthaser, 2012).

The Wendrow family could not know it, but they were not the only victims of false accusation of abuse delivered through FC. Other facilitators using "supportive typing" were also making reports of child sexual abuse. Could all those independent reports of child abuse be wrong? Probably not. So, either the reports were true or they were not truly independent. The FC practitioners were a passionate, engaged, enthusiastic group of diverse professionals. In their sincere enthusiasm, they wanted to learn more about FC. So they went to conferences, shared new FC techniques, worked out problems together, shared stories, and brought those stories—including stories about sexual abuse—back to the colleagues who had not gone to the conference.

It would be difficult, even irresponsible, for a facilitator not to consider a shocking possibility. Perhaps someone they had facilitated had been abused. After hearing just one story, it would be something that came easily to mind (**priming** and the **availability heuristic**). What appeared to be independent reports were probably not truly independent. The consequences were devastating.

Now parents who had dedicated their lives to caring for a difficult child were arrested and sent to jail. Since such parents could not be trusted, their children were sent to anonymous foster care families—all on the strength of testimony gathered through facilitated communication. Even though FC had never been tested with crucial experiments, their reports had been accepted by social workers, school systems, and many family courts.

It was a crucial situation for families who had been arrested, shunned by their neighbors, and become the subject of local news and community gossip. FC needed—and the people affected by it deserved—the kind of crucial experiment that should have been conducted *before* anyone accepted FC communications as coming from the person with disabilities. But what would a crucial experiment look like? It was also a crucial situation for the facilitators. What would it do to *your* sense of self if it turned out that your good intentions, hard work, and sincere enthusiasm had divided a family and sent parents to prison? Critical thinking probably had been taught in their college classes. But it might have been no more than an abstract idea, quickly forgotten when the class exam was done. Now critical thinking really mattered.

Testing Facilitated Communication

The "message-passing test" was a brilliant but straightforward way to answer two questions about FC: (1) Is FC real, and (2) is the communication coming from the individual or from the facilitator? These crucial experiments began with someone displaying an object such as a key and showing it to the individual with autism (or some other developmental disability) and then asking a simple question: "What is it?" In one condition, the facilitator has seen the key, and in the other condition, the facilitator has not seen the key. If the person with autism is able to type out the word *key* when the facilitator is there but is not able to type out the word *key* when the facilitator is not there, then the communication must be coming from the facilitator and not from the person with autism. And that means that FC is not real.

In one experiment led by a former believer in FC (Wheeler, Jacobson, Paglieri, & Schwartz, 1993), the researchers tested 12 individuals with disabilities. These particular individuals were considered to be "the 12 most competent producers of facilitated communication." In other words, the researchers arranged the experiment so that they loaded the dice in favor of FC being real. But when it had become a crucial experiment, they couldn't get FC to work. The only correct responses (such as typing the word *key*) occurred when the facilitator had seen the key.

Another crucial experiment by Montee, Miltenberger, and Wittrock (1995) asked seven clients with moderate to severe mental retardation to name pictures and describe activities they had just engaged in with a research assistant in a separate room. These seven particular clients had been communicating fluently using FC for 6 to 18 months, so once again, the experimenters were loading the dice in favor of FC—but they still couldn't get FC to work.

When both facilitator and client saw the same picture, FC seemed to work with a success rate of about 75%. But when the facilitator did not have access to the same information, the success rate was 0%. When both facilitator and client saw the same activity, FC seemed to work with an 87% success rate. But when the facilitator did not have access to the same information, the success rate was 0%. In 80% of the successful cases, the client typed exactly what the facilitator saw. FC failed to pass this (and many other) crucial experiments.

The American Psychological Association reviewed all the evidence regarding FC (or what is now called supportive typing) and concluded that "there was no scientifically demonstrated support for its efficacy" (see APA, 2003). The American Academy of Pediatrics (AAP, 1998), through a committee on children with disabilities, issued a similar statement:

> In the case of FC, there are good scientific data showing it to be ineffective. Moreover, as noted before, the potential for harm does exist, particularly if unsubstantiated allegations of abuse occur using FC. Many families incur substantial expense pursuing these treatments, and spend time and resources that could be used more productively. (p. 432)

Self-Justifying Excuses

Did crucial experiments, official medical authorities, and scientific societies convince the believers in FC that it was bogus? Would they have convinced you? Some accepted the science. Others, however, explained away such failures. One such excuse, for example, was that the experiments themselves had created a skeptical atmosphere of "intense critical scrutiny" that made it difficult for FC to work. That is a real possibility, but in this case, that explanation was probably embarrassed believers in FC grasping to hang on to their beliefs. The experimental procedures were simple and friendly. For example, an experimenter in the message-passing task would ask, "What is it?" or "Tell your Mom the word I just whispered in your ear." Those are surely less emotionally disturbing than asking children to report details of how they had been sexually abused. The experimenters weren't hostile, but they were skeptical. But their skepticism probably felt like hostility to believers in FC threatened by the clarity of crucial experiments.

But why would anyone want FC to fail if it really worked? And who would want FC to succeed if it were not real? If autistic children are being sexually abused, then we all need to know about it! But we also don't want to separate innocent, loving, dedicated parents from the children who desperately need them. FC failed one crucial experiment after another, and the more tightly controlled the experiment was, the worse that FC performed. The sloppier and less experimental studies were more likely to find slender bits of evidence that FC might sometimes work. And that pattern of sloppy research is why so many social psychologists are skeptical of case study research.

So, who is doing the talking? The facilitators. But just like a Ouija board, they didn't know it was coming from a **self** whose judgments had been compromised by good intentions.

DISCUSSION QUESTIONS

1. FC is enjoying a mild resurgence in popularity. Explain why, in the face of crucial experiments and formal objections from multiple professional societies, people continue to believe in FC.

2. Design a crucial experiment that could test who is doing the talking in a Ouija board. How could you test whether the spirits of dead people were really moving the pointing device on the Ouija board?

3. What do you imagine that the believers in FC thought about themselves at different stages of this case study: during their training, after experiencing its apparent effectiveness, and after learning that it was bogus? Even on an unconscious level, what would motivate an

FC facilitator to accuse a client's parents of sexual abuse?

4. Consider other "trendy" medical or psychological treatments, such as essential oils, crystals, and so on. Choose one example and design an experiment to test whether any positive effects (1) actually exist and (2) are caused by the treatment itself or by a **placebo effect**.

KEY TERMS

Availability heuristic 27	Placebo effect 30	Self 29
Crucial experiments 25	Priming 27	Self-justification 29

3.2 Personhood Versus Malignant Social Psychology

Who are you if you have lost your memory? You don't know if you like peas, cats, or basketball. You can't recall how old you are. You don't recognize your own family. All of these are real possibilities for people who have Alzheimer's disease (AD).

Such symptoms get worse as AD marches relentlessly through your brain, struggling through neural plaques and tangles that once effortlessly made such connections. People with advanced stages of AD look into a mirror and do not seem to know who is looking back at them (Biringer & Anderson, 1992). Self-concept and **self-insight** decline as the self slowly disappears.

The Disappearing Self Is Expensive

Caring for people with dementia is an emotionally difficult challenge for everyone involved with the disease: family members, part-time caregivers, hospitals, and long-term care institutions. In addition to the emotional costs, there are financial costs as well. Projections from the World Health Organization indicate that AD is turning out to be far more expensive than almost anyone had imagined. AD threatens to upend established social and economic structures. We have to take it seriously.

It is difficult to estimate financial costs because there are both formal/direct and informal/indirect costs associated with caring for people with AD. For example, a caregiver who takes off work or leaves a job to care for an elderly parent represents lost income to the national economy, yet often a savings compared to institutionalized care. There also are different expectations in different cultures, different economies in different regions, and different levels of infrastructure able to provide care.

However, it is safe to say that the costs associated with AD are (a) enormous and (b) escalating. There are intense efforts in the pharmaceutical industry to develop drugs that can, at the least, slow its progression. Nevertheless, AD already is soaking up significant amounts of money around the entire world. How much? Check out Table 3.1 and remember that the aggregated costs represent *billions* of dollars (see Wimo et al., 2013).

Table 3.1	Per Capita and Aggregated Costs of Dementia by WHO Global Burden of Disease Region and World Bank Income Classification							
			Aggregated Costs, Billions of U.S.$					
WHO Region	Per Capita Costs, U.S.$	People With Dementia	Total Costs	Total Costs as a % of GDP	Direct Costs as a % of GDP	Informal Care (All ADLs)	Direct Medical Costs	Direct Social Costs
Australasia	32,370	311,327	10.08	0.97	0.56	0	0.70	5.07
Asia Pacific high income	29,057	2,826,388	82.13	1.31	0.76	34.60	5.23	42.29
Oceania	6,059	16,553	0.10	0.46	0.12	0.07	0.02	0.01
Asia, central	2,862	330,125	0.94	0.36	0.20	0.43	0.28	0.24
Asia, east	4,078	5,494,387	22.41	0.40	0.13	15.24	4.33	2.84
Asia, south	903	4,475,324	4.04	0.25	0.11	2.31	1.16	0.57
Asia, southeast	1,601	2,482,076	3.97	0.28	0.15	1.77	1.48	0.73
Europe, western	30,122	6,975,540	210.12	1.29	0.75	87.05	30.19	92.88
Europe, central	12,891	1,100,759	14.19	1.10	0.44	8.59	2.67	2.94
Europe, eastern	7,667	1,869,242	14.33	0.90	0.40	7.96	3.42	2.94
North America high income	48,605	4,383,057	213.04	1.30	0.82	78.76	36.83	97.45
Caribbean	9,092	327,825	2.98	1.06	0.53	1.50	0.78	0.71

(Continued)

Table 3.1 (Continued)

WHO Region	Per Capita Costs, U.S.$	People With Dementia	Aggregated Costs, Billions of U.S.$					
			Total Costs	Total Costs as a % of GDP	Direct Costs as a % of GDP	Informal Care (All ADLs)	Direct Medical Costs	Direct Social Costs
Latin America, Andean	3,663	254,925	0.93	0.43	0.27	0.35	0.31	0.28
Latin America, central	5,536	1,185,559	6.56	0.37	0.28	1.58	2.61	2.37
Latin America, southern	8,243	614,523	5.07	1.02	0.54	2.36	1.42	1.29
Latin America, tropical	6,881	1,054,560	7.26	0.42	0.29	2.17	2.67	2.42
North Africa/ Middle East	3,926	1,145,633	4.50	0.16	0.09	1.90	2.05	0.54
Sub-Saharan Africa, central	1,081	67,775	0.07	0.06	0.02	0.04	0.02	0.01
Sub-Saharan Africa, east	1,122	360,602	0.40	0.17	0.05	0.28	0.08	0.04
Sub-Saharan Africa, southern	6,834	100,733	0.69	0.24	0.06	0.52	0.11	0.06
Sub-Saharan Africa, west	969	181,803	0.18	0.06	0.02	0.11	0.04	0.02
Low income	868	5,036,979	4.37	0.24	0.10	2.52	1.23	0.62
Lower middle income	3,109	9,395,204	29.21	0.35	0.12	18.90	6.74	3.57
Upper middle income	6,827	4,759,025	32.49	0.50	0.29	13.70	10.44	8.35
High income	32,865	16,367,508	537.91	1.24	0.74	216.77	78.00	243.14
Total	16,986	35,558,717	603.99	1.01	0.59	251.89	96.41	255.69

Abbreviations: GDP = gross domestic product; ADLs = activities of daily living; WHO = World Health Organization.

Source: Wimo, A., Reed, C. C., Dodel, R., Belger, M., Jones, R. W., Happich, M., . . . Haro, J. M. (2013). The GERAS study: A prospective observational study of costs and resource use in community dwellers with Alzheimer's disease in three European countries—Study design and baseline findings. *Journal of Alzheimer's Disease, 36*(2), 385–399.

Excess Disability in a
Malignant Social Psychological Milieu

What does social psychology have to do with this neurological disease?

The concept of a "malignant" social psychology does not mean that the discipline of social psychology is sick. Instead, it refers to the idea that any given social environment (or "milieu") can become sick—and social psychology can help understand and maybe improve that environment (see Kitwood, 1997). One specific idea in malignant social psychology, for example, is excess disability. A disease like AD will cause some functional incapacity—and if an individual's social psychological environment aggravates the symptoms, that's excess disability (Brody, Kleban, Lawton, & Silverman, 1971). The following account summarizes Steven Sabat's (1994) publication of a case study demonstrating how a malignant social psychological milieu led to excess disability. It is the case of Mrs. R.

The Case of Mrs. R. Mrs. R. was 64 years old when she was first diagnosed with probable Alzheimer's disease and was now 68. She and her husband had enjoyed a long marriage and continued to display affection and commitment to one another. Her medical records reported that she had severe problems with both short-term and long-term memory, needed assistance with personal grooming, and sometimes wandered aimlessly.

Her spouse reported that she needed help taking medication and that she no longer cooked, did housework, handled money, wrote, or used the telephone. She watched a great deal of television. Her husband also reported that he chose her clothing for her and sometimes fought with her over what to wear. One notable disagreement involved an outfit she had picked out for her birthday celebration at the adult daycare. When she wanted to wear it again the next day, he refused. He thought she had forgotten the previous day's celebration. He also put on her makeup for her because he thought she used too much.

Contrast the report from Mrs. R.'s husband to the report from the staff at her adult daycare: "Mrs. R. did not require any help whatsoever when eating. Her eye-hand coordination was coherent and she was able to cut her food and feed herself quite well." The summary of her personal grooming told a similar story. Mrs. R. was happy to pick out her own clothes and did not like her husband doing it for her. She was self-conscious about her facial appearance and used makeup to cover any blemishes. The aimless wandering at home was replaced by purposeful activities at the adult daycare. She would help move chairs as needed for new activities, helped others find the bathrooms, and navigated the rooms. She was able to comfort individuals in pain and developed a warm relationship with a woman who was losing her hair. Her only wandering did not seem aimless and only occurred when there was a break in the usual activities.

Was Mrs. R. dysfunctional or functional? Could she care for herself or was she dependent upon her husband?

Social Psychological Explanations for Mrs. R. Mrs. R. was experiencing what Kitwood (1990) called "disempowerment" because her husband was doing things for her that she was able to do for herself. She could feed herself, but he was doing it for her. This, in turn, produced a decreasing sense of "agency" in Mrs. R., especially as her husband gradually took over the various household chores that Mrs. R. had been completing by herself. So, she did nothing at home—and that cycled into him doing even more for her as he came to regard her as more disabled than she actually was.

The underlying process is familiar to social psychologists: the process by which assigning a label turns into a **self-fulfilling prophecy**. Mrs. R.'s husband embraced lower expectations until she was—at least at home—becoming more disabled than her disease actually dictated. Sabat (1994) pointed out another related social psychological feature: Stigmatization of Mrs. R. turned "going for a walk" into "wandering aimlessly." The term for this larger process is **confirmation bias**. In her husband's sincere, caring perception, everything Mrs. R. did confirmed that AD was stealing her sense of self, and he could not imagine evidence that contradicted what he "knew" must be true.

Malignant Social Psychology . . . and Its Antidote

Tom Kitwood (1997) identified the features that make up a toxic environment for someone with AD or another form of dementia. But he did so with an antidote in mind. Some of the characteristics that form a malignant social psychology are delivered with the best of intentions. A malignant social psychological milieu is not composed of malicious acts or deliberate cruelty. Instead, the resulting cruelty comes from good intentions to help someone with a dementia cope with a difficult life. The characteristics of a malignant social psychology include the following:

1. Treachery: using deception to gain compliance (e.g., to enter a nursing home)

2. Disempowerment: not allowing the person to exercise the skills he or she has

3. Infantilization: patronizing someone as if he or she were a child

4. Intimidation: inducing fear through threats and physical punishment

5. Labeling: using a category name as global descriptor (as in "lost his marbles")

6. Stigmatization: treating a person as an undesirable object

7. Invalidation: not recognizing how the other person is experiencing his or her world

8. Ignoring: behaving as if the person were not present

9. Mockery: pointing out and making fun of odd behaviors

10. Disparagement: sending verbal/psychological messages of incompetence

Kitwood (1997) summed up his antidote for a malignant social psychological environment with just one word: *personhood*. Personhood includes a sense of personal distinctiveness, personal continuity, and personal autonomy—what social psychologists think of as a sense of self. Personhood is pragmatically understood among gerontology nurses as "person-centered care" (see Dewing, 2007). It's not universally embraced, but it appears to resonate within the context of geriatric nursing. If you were experiencing some of the symptoms of AD, wouldn't you want the respect and empowerment of personhood?

The social costs of AD are enormous *and* escalating with an aging population. Let's not aggravate the situation by creating a malignant, social psychological environment. It may take more mental effort but be far kinder to others (and eventually to ourselves) if we respect and treasure the changing self.

DISCUSSION QUESTIONS

1. This case study used Alzheimer's disease as an example of a health issue for which a malignant social psychology milieu might make symptoms worse for someone. What other physical or mental diseases, disabilities, or conditions are good examples of contexts in which other people might make life more difficult for the person experiencing symptoms?

2. Mr. R. was likely unaware that he was conferring some of the malignant social psychological characteristics to his wife (see the list from Kitwood, 1997). First, identify which two or three items on this list that you think are the most emotionally or psychologically damaging for Mrs. R. and explain why. Then, discuss the psychological reasons why Mr. R. might—on an unconscious level—do this to a wife he loves. Why would Mr. R. perceive his wife to be in more need than she really was?

3. What are three specific ways that Mr. R. and/ or the staff at the adult daycare could increase the "personhood" Mrs. R. experiences on a daily basis?

3.3 Does My Bump Look Big in This? The Pregnant Self

Many women look forward to becoming mothers for their entire lives. Before it happens, the **self-concept** is focused on the individual self. But once pregnancy occurs, the "self" may quickly become all about someone else (the future baby). "Me" becomes "Mom."

How does a woman's sense of self change during pregnancy? Social identity theory anticipates many changes after the baby is born. For fathers as well as mothers, what worries you, brings you joy, or monopolizes your time will probably be different after an infant is involved. But what happens to a sense of self during pregnancy? Case studies and other qualitative research approaches seem like one appropriate way to get at such a complex experience.

Changes in the Body and Changes in the Self

The obvious changes for a pregnant woman are in her body and her sense of body **self-esteem**. Body dissatisfaction is common among both men and women. Contrary to the opinion that White women suffer the most from body dissatisfaction, a meta-analysis found that there is roughly equivalent body dissatisfaction among women across several ethnicities (Grabe & Hyde, 2006). The same is true for men, with slightly greater dissatisfaction among gay men and athletes (see Fawkner & McMurray, 2002).

The Role of Qualitative Research. Surveys and experiments can give us helpful clues about changes in body satisfaction during pregnancy. It is helpful, for example, to know an experience is common across individuals and cultures. But to capture the level of subtlety needed for this research question, Johnson, Burrows, and Williamson (2004) relied on an in-depth qualitative approach of semistructured interviews. Their study had a specific goal: to reconcile a strange contradiction in the scientific literature. Some studies found that women's attitudes toward their bodies became progressively more negative when pregnant. Other studies found opposite effects, including a shift to a more positive attitude toward their body among women who were overweight prior to pregnancy.

Their summary of the existing literature was that "no clear pattern emerges in reviewing the literature on variables that might influence body image or eating behavior during pregnancy" (Johnson et al., 2004, p. 363). Contradictory findings provoke new ideas. Their qualitative interviews, like a case study, collected rich data from a limited sample of six women who were 33 to 39 weeks into their pregnancy. Then they extracted themes from the verbal reports and conversations with the women. These interviews required careful listening and objective analysis because it is difficult to see past our own biases and assumptions.

Johnson et al. (2004) created a clever title for their article: "Does My Bump Look Big in This?" There's no mistaking that they were focusing on body satisfaction among pregnant women. Three themes emerged from interviews about changes in body satisfaction: (1) body satisfaction during pregnancy was dynamic—it might be positive at one stage, more negative at another, and so on; (2) the impact of pregnancy on perceptions of the body varied; and (3) the physical and social boundaries surrounding their body changed. Each of those themes helped explain the apparent discrepancies in the literature—and give us a subjective sense of what happens to the body satisfaction of first-time mothers-to-be. These critical subjective themes were less likely to emerge from a quantitative survey—but they arose spontaneously from qualitative research.

Theme 1: Body Satisfaction During Pregnancy Is Dynamic. One interviewee (called "Bea" in their report) demonstrated how her sense of self changed during pregnancy. She was initially excited, especially as she watched early changes in her belly. That changed:

> After [my] bump started to develop things really started to change about how I felt about me and it was quite distressing . . . I never contemplated that. . . . I was paranoid about becoming a really big, fat, pregnant person. (p. 365)

But Bea's body self-image changed once again "when it became more obvious that she was pregnant" (p. 365). Bea's dynamic (changeable) body self-esteem helps explain why some previous pregnancy studies found both positive and negative body satisfaction. The early literature was probably correct in this sense: *Something* was going on with women's body satisfaction while pregnant. What they did not capture was that it was changeable—and for reasons best explained by social psychology.

Bea's comments also demonstrate why the self is indeed a "social self." Her improved body self-esteem later in her pregnancy was influenced by having a socially sanctioned reason (being pregnant) for having a bigger belly. Her body self-esteem was influenced by what she believed others viewing her believed about her appearance—and that changed at different stages of her pregnancy.

Theme 2: Pregnancy Led to Varied Perceptions of the Body. One of the mothers-to-be followed her cultural tradition of not washing her hair at the start of her pregnancy—setting up an unflattering social comparison with other women. Her perception of her own body demonstrates again that the self is social and the importance of social comparisons on body satisfaction and self-esteem. Most of the women interviewed in their study spoke about being physically impaired, uncomfortable, and restricted. One mother-to-be, identified as Felice, admitted that

> I feel a bit robbed in some ways, just the fact that I've had to slow down and I can't do this and I can't do that . . . I'll do a few things and then sit down . . . so sometimes I feel frustrated because I can't do what I used to do, I can't do the sports I used to do as well. (p. 366)

However, there were also positive self-perceptions of their bodies during pregnancy. For example, the baby moving created an experience that was simultaneously weird, reassuring, and a stimulus for bonding with their baby. This kind of qualitative study captures the subtle variability of the pregnancy experience in ways that a conventional quantitative, self-report scale (such as ranging from 0 to 7) would not pick up.

Theme 3: The Boundaries Around Their Bodies Changed During Pregnancy. The social space around their bodies changed in two ways. First, even strangers would suddenly feel privileged to feel their tummy. One interviewee identified as Sum said, "You become public property and anyone can touch you." More than a few strangers had far too personal approaches to their apparent "rights" to touch their bodies. A second way that the space around their bodies was violated was through health exams. Most of the women had an understanding reaction to professional health exams. One interviewee, Denise, commented that "to some extent they burst the bubble that you are special because the care of pregnant women was a matter of routine to them." Sum, however, was not comfortable exposing her body to medical professionals. It forced her to merge her private self with her public self:

> And you could have loads of people in the room and to them, you know, if they've seen one woman's bits they've seen everybody

else's . . . but this is mine, this is me and it's private and it's between me and my husband and the baby as far as I'm concerned it's not for anyone else to see but, you kinda like feel you're open to, um, to public view. (p. 367)

The variability in the experience of this part of the pregnancy was because some of the women enjoyed the attention and others were offended. Some felt that the relatively impersonal health exams were reassuring because they suggested professionalism and competence; others were understanding but still found the experience deeply uncomfortable. Several women appeared to feel differently about the boundaries of their bodies at different stages of pregnancy.

A Second Study of Pregnant Women and the Self

It's not surprising that quantitative surveys missed these important, nuanced details of the pregnancy experience. Scales can be helpful, but it's only one of the knowledge-building tools in the social psychologist's toolbox. The contradiction in the literature about women being satisfied *and* dissatisfied with their bodies was reconciled by using a qualitative approach—something that could capture the complexity of what these pregnant women were experiencing.

Replicating Qualitative Research. We tend to trust studies that can be replicated. But how can you replicate a case study based on the unique circumstances faced by the six different women in the study by Johnson et al. (2004)? The answer is to ask the same or similar questions of another group of pregnant women and see if similar themes emerge from their interviews. About 6 years after publication of the study with the unusual title ("Does My Bump Look Big in This?"), another group of researchers also asked pregnant women about their body satisfaction.

The research team of Chang, Kenney, and Chao (2010) did not seem to be aware of the earlier study. However, the newer research team also decided that qualitative interviews (this time with 18 mothers) were the best way to capture the complexity of how the self changes during pregnancy. Assessing changes in body satisfaction and self-esteem during pregnancy was only one of the goals of the newer research. The other goal was to understand how "pregnant Taiwanese women in large cities" were expected to negotiate between longstanding traditions that were important to their families—even if they did not personally endorse the old, traditional beliefs. It was, in some ways, a study of the conflict within mothers-to-be between an **independent versus an interdependent self-construal**.

Cultural Conflict Changes the Self. The Chang et al. (2010) study extracted only two (rather than three) themes from their interviews with the 18 mothers-to-be, but they overlapped with the Johnson study. The first theme was about constructing a new self in the context of cultural values. The second theme was the women's need to build a new body image from the previous self. In keeping with the focus of their study, this change also was triggered by how the women reacted to the combination of modern medical practices, generational differences, public advice, and traditional beliefs.

This kind of cultural conflict among pregnant women in Taiwan also showed up in the Johnson study when one of the six mothers reluctantly followed a cultural tradition of not washing her hair during an early stage of pregnancy. The overlap between these two qualitative studies appears to be how pregnancy combines with cultural expectations to force changes in the self. It's not a perfect **replication**—but it may be more meaningful because it wasn't trying to be a replication. It was just another qualitative study about changes in the self-identity of pregnant women in two different cultures.

Social Psychological Theories in Action

In the first study, Bea reported that her body satisfaction improved "when it became more obvious" that she was pregnant. That comment is one of those small but telling observations that can emerge from qualitative research. Her simple observation is thick with social psychological theories.

The improvement in Bea's body satisfaction occurred when she knew that others could tell that she was pregnant. It demonstrates that Bea's self was social (**social identity theory**). Her private sense of self was influenced by what she believed that others believed about her (social mirror theory). The mechanism that triggered Bea's assessments of her body was comparing herself to other women (**social comparison theory**). The effect of those social comparisons depended on how she explained to herself (attribution theory) what she imagined other people were thinking of her when observing the size of her belly (self-concept theory). A big belly without the attribution of pregnancy decreased her body self-image (self-esteem theory). Without the pregnancy explanation, Bea was fighting against a social ideal she had internalized (self-discrepancy theory) of female thinness (social norm theory). Her general concern was how she presented herself in public (self-presentation theory).

That's a lot of social psychology in such a brief observation! But each of those theories has explanatory power because they apply to more people than Bea and to more situations than pregnancy. Each of those theories is useful but largely descriptive. Their strength is in describing *what* is happening at a more general level. However, they are weaker at explaining *why* Bea feels and thinks as she does, at *why* the self needs to be so flexible and responsive to cultural opportunities and threats.

A theory with a broader explanatory power is what Cosmides and Tooby (1989) describe as "**natural selection** and social exchange" theory. We humans evolved patterns of behavior, such as mutual cooperation, because they are mutually beneficial and increase our chances of reproductive success. On the other hand, some beliefs and behaviors entered our cultures because they once were useful adaptations. Their usefulness may have disappeared generations ago, but they persist as traditions. Here are just a few of what are often called old wives' tales about pregnancy:

Carrying high? It's a girl. Carrying low? It's got to be a boy.

If you have heartburn, then your baby will have lots of hair.

If the baby's heartrate is over 140 beats per minute, then it's going to be girl.

Craving ice cream means it is a girl but a taste for salty foods means it's a boy.

Taking a bath can drown your fetus.

Walking or eating spicy foods induces labor.

Cats have a natural urge to smother babies.

It's a reach, but there might be a grain of natural selection truth in some of these sayings. For example, cats are creatures of comfort so they seek out the warmest, coziest place to take a nap—and there is nothing so cozy as a new baby. However, it seems more likely that one mother may have feared the idea of their cat smothering their baby and told someone about it, that person passed it on . . . and pretty soon an untestable rumor was racing around the network of young mothers, becoming a superstition.

The woman in Johnson et al.'s qualitative study who did not wash her hair at the start of her pregnancy may have had a similar experience. In the Chang et al. (2010) study, some Taiwanese practices related to pregnancy were clashing with modern medicine and current advice. But the clash between traditional ways of doing things and modern cultures forced the mothers-to-be to reimagine a new, more modern self. And that makes sense in term of evolution. After all, there is nothing more crucial for the process of natural selection than a successful pregnancy.

DISCUSSION QUESTIONS

1. This case study discussed how a mother's sense of self changes through pregnancy and motherhood. But what about fathers? Discuss similarities and differences that mothers and fathers experience through pregnancy and after a child is born, in terms of how the experience of being a parent changes a mother's and a father's sense of self.

2. Discuss how women's experience of pregnancy, in terms of body self-esteem changes, is different from one woman to the next. Identify two or three personality traits that you think might be correlated to either satisfaction or dissatisfaction with experiences during pregnancy—or correlated to stability of experience. Explain your hypotheses.

3. Identify at least two stereotypes about pregnant women that your culture promotes or seems to endorse through things like media images. For each stereotype, do you agree or disagree with this stereotype? And for each, does cultural expectation for this stereotype help or hurt pregnant women in terms of both pragmatic matters (such as access to resources) and in terms of self-esteem?

4. Design scientific ways to test some of the "old wives' tales" about pregnancy. How can superstition either support or be refuted by the scientific method? Be sure to consider whether the procedures involved should be single- or double-blind, to avoid participant and experimenter bias.

KEY TERMS

Independent vs. interdependent self-construal 39

Natural selection 41
Replication 40
Self-concept 36

Self-esteem 36
Social comparison theory 40
Social identity theory 40

3.4 The Disappearing Self: Phineas Gage's Horse-Drawn Stagecoach

Phineas Gage's unusual story gave the world a small sample of what today is one of psychology's most exciting fields: **social neuroscience**, or the study of brain activity under different social conditions. The story started with a terrible accident. Then it became a dramatic symbol of the resiliency of the human brain. Today, neuroscientists Hannah and Antonio Damasio declare that the self created by the brain is more like a beautiful symphony, constantly composed, never rehearsed, and perfectly played.

The Accident

Phineas Gage's story began on September 13, 1848, when he was working as the foreman of a railroad crew (see Macmillan, 2000). Gage must have been an outstanding foreman. Many of the railroad construction workers near Cavendish, Vermont, were Irish immigrants who had carried their ancient regional feuds into America. These were tough men, and an unpopular foreman was subject to "violent attacks . . . some of which ended fatally" (Macmillan, 2000, p. 22). Imagine the human-relations skills Gage must have needed to keep the railroad projects moving forward. He had to be fair and be perceived as fair. He had to calm the impulses of violent men yet harness their energies into an effective team.

Dr. John Harlow (Gage's doctor) described the preaccident Gage as a man "who possessed a well-balanced mind," "a shrewd business man," and a man "of temperate habits and possessed of considerable energy of character." This description represents the baseline Gage. It was like the **personality** version of the "before" in a before-after advertisement for weight loss.

On the day of his famous accident, Gage was using a 43-inch, 13-pound iron rod to secure blasting powder into a hole drilled deeply into some rock. The crew's job was to explode the rock into small enough pieces so that the workers could cart it away and prepare the ground to lay track for the railroad. The rod was pointed at one end and flattened at the other to tamp sand on top of the blasting powder. The purpose of the sand was to direct the force of the blast deep into the rock rather than back out the hole toward the men.

It is unclear exactly what happened next. A likely scenario is that someone called to Gage that the sand had not yet been poured on top of the blasting powder. As Gage turned to his right, his head hovered over the hole just as the iron rod slipped from his fingers, sparked against rock, and ignited the blasting powder. The pointed end of the iron rod shot upward, entered Gage's head just below his left cheek, passed behind most of his left eye, continued through the front left portion of his brain, and shot out the top of his head, landing about 23 meters (about 75 feet) away. The men would retrieve his iron rod the next day and report that, even after rinsing it off in a nearby creek, it was still greasy with some of Gage's brain matter.

Gage was knocked over, of course, but he may never have lost consciousness, or only briefly. He then surprised everyone even further by getting up and walking, possibly without anyone's help, to an oxcart to be taken to a doctor. Some of the men ran ahead to alert the doctor while Gage, his back against the front of the oxcart, wrote a note in his foreman's log book. An iron rod almost 4 feet long had just passed through his brain and he was still writing notes about his day! His workers took him to the hotel where he was staying and Gage walked up the steps, again possibly without any help, and sat on the porch.

The first doctor to see him refused to believe Gage's story until Gage showed him the hole in his head. He even made a joke, something like, "Well, this should be work enough for you, doctor!" Another physician arrived, Dr. Harlow, and the two physicians cleaned the wound. Then they shoved pieces of Gage's skull back into place wherever they seemed to fit. Dr. Harlow started recording what would become one of the most famous stories in the history of brain science and psychology.

The Resilient Brain

Gage could still recognize his mother and uncle and, only a few days after his accident, made plans to return to work. But his physical and mental health cycled between recovery, infection, and delirium for several weeks. As his condition slowly stabilized, Dr. Harlow noticed some odd features about his patient. Gage's memory was "as perfect as ever" but Gage "would not take $1000 for a few pebbles." That was strange. Had Gage lost his ability to understand money?

About a month after the accident, Harlow wrote that Gage had become "exceedingly capricious and childish . . . will not yield to restraint when it conflicts with his desires." The change in personality was so great that Gage's friends described the postaccident Gage as "no longer Gage." Apparently, the damage to Gage's left frontal lobes was somehow linked to a profound change in his self—but not to all of his self.

It is easy to imagine Gage's acquaintances saying, "Why doesn't Phineas just get control of himself? Doesn't he know what he's doing?" The answer seems to be no. Gage seemed to have minimal **self-insight** (the ability to self-observe and evaluate our own behavior). In addition, the new Gage was probably less able to self-monitor (the ability to notice and adjust our own behavior across different social situations). Curiously, patients with similar brain damage (usually due to brain surgery) tell a similar story. When Beer, John, Scabini, and Knight (2006) allowed patients with similar brain damage to see themselves on a video recording, they discovered that they were disclosing personal and inappropriate information. What we call the "self" appears to be connected to particular regions and neural pathways within the brain.

That's where the story stops in most tellings about the life of Phineas Gage. But the most exciting parts of his life were still to come. Even though many social restraints had disappeared, Gage could still perform some very difficult tasks—even with a hole in his head! Gage got a job working in a horse stable—and appears to have held that job for about 18 months. He must have done good work because the owner of the stable offered Gage a job driving a four-horse (it may have been a six-horse) stagecoach through the mountain roads in Chile, South America.

Think about what Gage could still do. Managing all those horses is surely a complex skill, yet Gage—the man with a large hole in his head—held this difficult job for about 7 years. When he began to have seizures, he joined his mother and sister (now living in California) where, according to letters written by his mother to Dr. Harlow, Gage still worked well with animals and liked to tell his nieces and nephews hair-raising stories of his adventures in Chile.

Yes, Gage's personality was changed after the iron rod removed portions of the left frontal lobe of his brain—but he was not *entirely* changed. Gage still knew who he was and how to get home. He could still drive a stagecoach and tell a good story. Gage probably kept that long iron rod next to himself, even when driving the stagecoach; the iron rod was buried with him after he died, not long after moving to California. And then his mother generously agreed to send Gage's skull and the iron rod to Dr. Harlow so that one of the greatest stories in brain science could continue.

The Magnificent Self

We need both poets and scientists to describe how beautifully the brain pulls the scattered experiences of life into a coherent self. Fernando Pessoa (2002) wrote in *The Book of Disquiet* that "my soul is like a hidden orchestra; I do not know which instruments grind and play away inside of me, strings and harps, timbales and drums. I can only recognize myself as a symphony" (p. 310). The self simultaneously draws on each complex layer and region of the brain the same way that a symphony conductor simultaneously draws on multiple sections of an orchestra.

But Damasio (2010), who created a computer simulation of Phineas Gage's brain trauma, believes that the brain performs is something far more impressive than the music produced by the most beautiful symphony orchestra. "The marvel," Damasio wrote, "is that the score and conductor become reality only as life unfolds" (p. 24). The self is a symphony orchestra that plays magnificent music only once, without a score, and without any rehearsal—and then flows smoothly into its next performance. What a magnificent, creative self!

DISCUSSION QUESTIONS

1. People who are high in self-monitoring change how they present themselves to best fit into any given situation. People low in self-monitoring act more consistently, regardless of the situation. After his accident, Gage became extremely low in self-monitoring.

   What are advantages and disadvantages to being very low in **self-monitoring**?

2. It is possible that people who experience brain traumas lose at least some of their ability to consent to being studied by

scientists. Discuss the ethical considerations that should be in place regarding participants who may lose such abilities.

3. Gage appeared to have a changed personality and to have lost some types of abilities (such as financial reasoning). However, he retained many other important abilities, such as his memory. Which parts of the "self" are the most essential to our understanding of who we are? If you were to experience an accident causing brain damage, which function or ability would you be most concerned about losing, and why?

KEY TERMS

Personality 43

Self-insight 44

Self-monitor 45

Social neuroscience 42

CHAPTER 4

Social Cognition

4.1 Intuition in the NICU

The sun rises in the north. Growling dogs are friendly.

The weird thing about **intuition** is that you can't say how you know; you just know. You might have read the sentences at the beginning of this case study twice, furrowing your brow, a little confused. You might have thought, "Wait. . . ." Intuition kicks in without us doing it on purpose, alerting us that something is either right or wrong or about to happen. Intuition often arrives without warning and sometimes without us even realizing it's happening. We rely on intuition, and it often serves us well.

The certainty of intuition somehow survives in a world of profound uncertainty—and the business of living is full of uncertainties. For example, Gary Klein (2003) and his colleagues asked firefighters making life and death decisions how they used their intuition. A fire chief has to decide whether to send firefighters into a burning building based on uncertain information. Smoke, for example, has a color, produces a smell, has a particular density, and has an appearance that suggests a particular rate of burning. The fire might be in a residential, industrial, or mixed-use neighborhood. A rural fire in the barn of a small dairy farm might trigger different intuitive alarm bells than a fire on the 15th story of a downtown office building. For firefighters, several intuitive decisions must be made under conditions of profound, consequential uncertainty.

Another context in which life and death decisions are made every day is a neonatal intensive care unit (NICU). Note the diversity, or the generalizability, of what we're learning about intuition as it is used in so many different settings. A NICU is the section of a hospital whose mission is to save the lives of very sick newborn babies. It's a place where our heartstrings will be pulled and a place where we can see how human decision making often relies on the ideal balance between intuition and **logic**. Don't worry—this case study has a happy ending.

What Happened in the NICU?

Many NICU babies are born prematurely. The average gestation of a human birth is 40 weeks. Classification of a "preemie" is a birth before 37 weeks of gestation or at a birth weight less than 2,000 grams (about 5.5 pounds). Less than

1,500 grams is considered a very low birth weight, and the risks of infant mortality increase dramatically. The average birth weight of one sample of at-risk Canadian preemies (gestational age 23 to 25 weeks) was 715 grams (Fenton et al., 2013).

The survival rates of preemies are positively correlated with birth weight. A study in France found a .7% survival-to-discharge rate for preemies born before 24 weeks of gestation, 59.1% at 25 weeks, 75.3% at 26 weeks, and 98.9% at 32 through 34 weeks (Ancel et al., 2015). Those impressive statistics suggest that a lot of excellent care is being delivered in NICUs around the world. The case study you're about to read (Klein, 2003, pp. 13–20) takes us inside a NICU, where intuition in a world of uncertainty has profound meanings for both death and life, tragedy and hope.

Controlling the Environment. The preemie enters a world that its body is not equipped to survive. So the NICU creates its own tiny environment in an isolated bassinette, sometimes called an isolette. The temperature is controlled, the baby's vital signs are monitored through various leads, and its nourishment is delivered through an intravenous tube or a drip tube slipped down the esophagus and into the tiny stomach. The danger of infection, especially around these mechanical interventions, is carefully managed and always a threat (as it is with older patients). Anyone physically contacting the infant (the parents who want to hold and touch their infant) must scrub thoroughly; siblings, exposed at their schools and playgrounds to many childhood diseases, are generally not permitted to touch their younger sister or brother in the NICU.

The baby's health status is constantly monitored through visual inspection and through a variety of blood tests. Alarms sound whenever a monitoring device indicates that extra attention is required by a particular infant. The alarms often indicate nothing more urgent than a lead that has become separated or a fussy baby. Klein (2003) described a frequent situation that calls for an intuitive response from observant, experienced NICU nurses:

> With infants in these fragile conditions, many things can go wrong, and practically all of them can become life threatening. One of the greatest and most common dangers is sepsis, a systemic infection that spreads throughout the infant's circulatory system. . . . Sepsis can be detected by a blood culture, but this test takes twenty-four hours and by then the baby might be overwhelmingly infected and beyond help. (p. 14)

A Life Saved by Intuition. Consider the case of two nurses, identified as Darlene and Linda, and one premature infant referred to as Melissa. Both Darlene and Linda were experienced nurses, but Linda was new to the NICU and being mentored by Darlene. Linda's training was progressing well, and Darlene was monitoring her work less as Linda's skills increased.

It was near the end of the night shift. Baby Melissa's parents had gone home for a few hours of sleep after an uneventful day. Linda noticed that Melissa had been a bit lethargic at her feeding but not severe enough to seem concerning. After all, tiny Melissa had been welcomed into the world with a great deal of testing, poking, and sticking. Melissa's temperature also was in the normal range but slightly low. Blood from a heel stick from a fairly new medical technician had left slightly more bleeding than a skilled med tech would leave behind—but again, nothing terribly out of the ordinary.

Darlene glanced as she passed Melissa's isolette, and her intuition sent a warning. Something was not right or, as she later expressed it, something "just looked funny . . . didn't look good." She inspected Melissa more closely. The heel stick had not stopped bleeding. Her skin appeared "off color" and "mottled." Melissa's tummy might have been a little more rounded than expected. An exam indicated that Melissa was slightly bloated, and the pattern of her temperature, while within the normal range, was trending downward.

"We've got a baby in big trouble," Darlene quickly reported to the on-duty physician, who immediately ordered antibiotics. They also ordered a blood test that, 24 hours later, confirmed the presence of sepsis. But those 24 hours would have been too late for Melissa. Darlene's intuition, captured with a passing glance at an infant that she was no longer monitoring, had saved tiny Melissa's life.

How Intuition Works

Intuition is not magic. Calling intuition a "gift" is also misleading.

Folk wisdom from the world of medicine says, "Good judgment comes from experience. And experience comes from bad judgment." Making bad judgments about others' lives is a hard way to learn that we can't always trust our intuition. It describes why even the most senior physicians are still "practicing" the art of scientific medicine.

Darlene's intuition, in contrast to Linda's lack of intuition, was the product of deep experience. Darlene had many years' experience in the NICU; she had seen many cases; she had followed the arc of the stories of many infant illnesses. She had observed their small beginnings, participated in their climatic turning points, and observed their varied resolutions. She had participated in the life and death stories of many infants—yet she also was still "practicing."

What, specifically, had Darlene "seen" about Melissa that Linda had missed?

If we can discern it accurately, the details are trying to tell a story. Linda had noticed all the same details as Darlene, but she had not perceived the story of the struggle for life going on right in front of her. The details included Melissa's lethargy, the still-bleeding heel stick, the slightly rounded tummy, the mottled skin, and the lower temperature. But Linda's baseline observations were not as seasoned as those of Darlene. Linda noticed the lethargy but also knew that babies sleep a lot. She noticed the bleeding heel stick but had little experience about how long she could expect an infant's heel stick to keep bleeding. Linda had observed most of the other signs, but the details did not come together in her mind with the other observations. It was, Klein (2003) reported,

> not so much the individual symptoms that were key, but a particular constellation of symptoms. Linda could see all the signs but she was unable to piece them together into a story that revealed the larger pattern. . . . In our research we found that Darlene was typical of highly experienced NICU nurses who can detect sepsis in premature infants, even before the blood tests pick it up. (p. 18)

The Elements of Intuition

Research in **social cognition** has helped us understand that the "hunches" we call intuition are sometimes the result of whatever information we have most recently been exposed to: **mental accessibility**. A medical student made what seemed to be an uncanny diagnosis of a skull deformity, but it was really because she had happened across an article about that during her lunch break. Cultural influences also can guide us, through mental accessibility, toward interpretive intuitions that may be helpful, harmful, or simply benign. We see them, we feel them—but that doesn't make them true. The same is true for the schemas, scripts, and stereotypes that sometimes masquerade as intuitions that we believe without critically evaluating whether the evidence really supports them.

In addition to mental accessibility, the human brain indulges in all sorts of **heuristics** (mental shortcuts), often because we are just lazy-thinking "cognitive misers." We like to "satisfice" or settle for explanations that are "good enough" to get us through the day—even when we sort of know that they can't be right. But probably more often than we notice, those mental shortcuts are also a blessing in disguise because when they are right, they operate like Darlene's intuition and capture with merely a glance vital information that can save the life of a newborn infant. It's extraordinary, really, how beautifully the human brain automatically puts together the different pieces of information that, if we listen carefully, will tell us a story that is true—and sometimes even life-saving.

So, yes. We want to listen carefully for the evidence that our intuition is always trying to piece together into a story. Linda could have put together a story that baby Melissa was just a little tired and fussy—but Darlene looked for a story that was a "better fit" with her intuition and experience. In a similar way, you knew that the sun doesn't rise in the north and that you should stay away from growling dogs. Sometimes, intuition can even save a life.

DISCUSSION QUESTIONS

1. Identify two contexts from your life where you rely on using a balance of intuition and logic. Explain how both types of thinking processes are useful in that context and what the consequences would be if you had only one type of thinking instead of both.

2. Have you ever traveled to another region of the country, traveled to another country, or even attended an event that was unfamiliar to you? How did you use your intuition to learn how to act? Did your observations of how other people were acting surprise you—and did that surprise lead you to reflect on your own schemas or stereotypes in new ways?

3. Think of two times when your intuition turned out to be wrong. Can you identify why your intuition made a mistake in these two circumstances? What was it about the environment, your frame of mind, your emotional state, and so on that caused your intuition to fail you?

KEY TERMS

Heuristics 50

Intuition 47

Logic 47

Mental accessibility 50

Social cognition 50

4.2 Strange Symptoms and Dual Processing

You've got some strange symptoms.

You've been scratching your arm and neck. In addition to the little red bumps, some are turning into blisters that are taking over your left arm and the right side of your neck. You try some lotions in your house; no improvement. You pick up some over-the-counter medicines; again, no apparent effect after 2 days. You start thinking about where you've been and what might be causing it. Mostly, you hope that it just goes away. But more time goes by, blisters are forming, and it doesn't seem to be getting any better. So you go see your family doctor and describe your symptoms.

This case study is about the two types of thinking—**dual processing**—in your doctor's head when trying to diagnose your skin problem. It demonstrates how family physicians experience **cognitive load-shifting** as they use both their highly trained **logic** and three kinds of **intuition** to keep working their way toward an accurate diagnosis.

The Two Thinking Systems

We all have two thinking systems, summarized in Figure 4.1. One is slow and logical. The other is fast and intuitive. There are risks associated with each thinking system. With logic, you may be scratching and suffering while your physician slowly, rationally tries to think through all the possible diagnoses for your skin problem. With intuition, you might grab some topical cream in your medicine cabinet because it brought you relief from an itch 4 years ago—but the active ingredient may no longer be effective, or it might have an ingredient that bursts those little bubbles at the worst moment and spreads the infection. The point is . . . you don't know, but you sure hope that your doctor does.

Amanda Woolley and Olga Kostopoulou (2013) studied how family practice doctors combine rational logic and irrational intuition when making diagnoses. They started the published report of their case study with a specific warning: "The clinical literature advises physicians not to trust their intuition" (p. 60). But they also pointed out that the medical literature's understanding of intuition equates intuition with early impressions, the first diagnosis that comes to mind.

Woolley and Kostopoulou (2013) hypothesized that there is much more to how family physicians experience intuition than early impressions. Furthermore, doctors can't turn off their intuitions like a light switch. If something possibly useful is nagging at them, they can't help but listen. They probably will be skeptical. But even when a nagging intuition turns out to be harmful rather than helpful, it is still there for a reason—so it pays for us to discover the underlying mechanics of intuition.

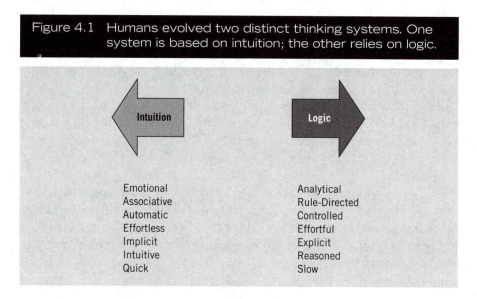

Figure 4.1   Humans evolved two distinct thinking systems. One system is based on intuition; the other relies on logic.

Intuition	Logic
Emotional	Analytical
Associative	Rule-Directed
Automatic	Controlled
Effortless	Effortful
Implicit	Explicit
Intuitive	Reasoned
Quick	Slow

Differential Diagnosis

Your doctor has been trained in a logical, rational process called "differential diagnosis." It's been an intense training. It may have started with medical volunteering in high school or even earlier. That was likely followed by 4 years of pre-med classes. If accepted into medical school, the doctor-to-be studies 4 more years in medical school and then spends another 3 to 5 years in a residency learning a medical specialty. That may be followed by a fellowship in a particular area of medicine and research. At every stage, physicians get more and more practice distinguishing between different types of diseases: differential diagnoses.

The Power of the Situation. Meanwhile, you've still got your itch and skin rash, and the ugly little blisters on your arm are popping. It's all pretty gross; you can't get a diagnosis and treatment fast enough. And when social psychologists consider the problem of fast *and* effective quality of care, they are aware that there will be more to your diagnosis than just the objective symptoms—the power of the situation matters, too.

For example, if the waiting room is empty and your doctor looks eager for a little mental stimulation, then you have a good chance of getting the benefit of all those years of logical training, residency practice, conference-going, and local experience. However, if the waiting room is crammed with frantic people, crying babies, and unhappy patients, then your doctor may be tempted as a practical matter to use the intuitive, first response that comes to mind and move you along and get to the next patient. Wait times are a big situational issue across health care because they influence both perceptions of patient satisfaction and actual care (see Jennings, Clifford, Fox, O'Connell, & Gardner, 2015; Waters, Edmonston, Yates, & Gucciardi, 2016).

The Logic of FID. Here's one way that many physicians and psychologists get started with a logical diagnosis: the rule of FID. If you listen carefully to the questions your physician asks, then you may notice that they focus on frequency (F), intensity (I), and duration (D). How frequently does this rash appear? (*I never had it before.*) How intense is the itching? (*Getting worse, fairly painful.*) How long have the rash and itching been on your body? (*About 10 days.*)

Psychologists and psychiatrists likewise use the logic of FID to help, for example, with differential diagnoses related to whether anxiety is due to a specific phobia or to a more generalized anxiety disorder (D'Avanzato, Joormann, Siemer, & Gotlib, 2013). How frequently do you experience anxiety? How intense is the anxiety? How long does the anxiety last? The rational, logical approach to medical diagnoses often begins with FID questions. FID is just a start, of course, but sometimes it's enough.

Diagnoses That Come Easily to Mind. Some diagnoses are pretty easy, especially if you are the fifth patient to come in that day with the same symptoms. The repetition of the same symptoms in many patients makes the diagnosis come easily to mind. The doctor glances at your arm and says, "Poison ivy; it's pretty bad this year." This fits fairly well with the definition of intuition adopted by Woolley and Kostopoulou (2013): making judgments without any awareness of reasoning. But there is an underlying reasoning going on. Your doctor thinks, "Just like the four previous patients." It's pretty close to an automatic, intuitive diagnosis. However, it still could be wrong—and that's always the danger with intuition: It's fast and intuitive, but it risks making errors that a slow, rational approach would have caught.

Diagnosing your skin rash more slowly probably won't take much more time. However, skin diseases can be tricky. At first glance, your rash is consistent with several possible diagnoses. In fact, when you look up all the symptoms online, you feel overwhelmed. It could be herpes simplex, herpes zoster, poison ivy, bed bugs, or several more possibilities—and they each may indicate slightly different treatment protocols. Do you want your doctor to use a slow but rational differential diagnostic process or take the risk that a fast, intuitive diagnosis doesn't make matters worse?

Three Sources of Intuition

Figure 4.2 tells us that there are (at least) three sources of intuition: **priming**, experience, and **heuristics**. The term *priming* means that after initially thinking about something, thinking about it again later will be easier and come faster. It's like priming a pump to get water flowing or priming a wall before you paint it. Priming speeds things up by providing the necessary mental preparation for what comes next. Experience, however, may be intuition's best teacher. If you have a lot of experience with something, you are already preprimed or prepared to go to the next step. Heuristics have the same effect. They are mental shortcuts that make it easier to solve difficult problems. Heuristics are the immediate way of thinking.

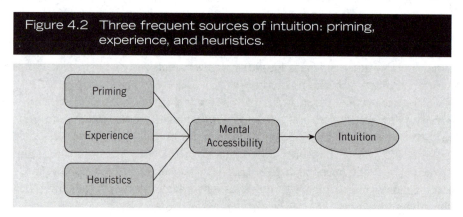

Figure 4.2 Three frequent sources of intuition: priming, experience, and heuristics.

Priming, experience, and heuristics all have one thing in common: **mental accessibility**. All three make it easier for certain ideas to come more easily to mind. Hopefully, the effect of all those years of medical training has made it easier for the right diagnosis to come more easily to mind.

Three Types of Intuition

The contribution that the case study by Woolley and Kosopoulou (2013) makes to the medical literature is based on interviews with 18 family physicians. The authors described their simple procedures:

> A week before the scheduled interview, participants were sent a standard e-mail asking them to think of 2 occasions when they felt they knew the diagnosis or prognosis of a patient but did not know how they knew: one case for which their feeling was correct and one for which it was incorrect. We requested 2 cases to overcome an anticipated bias to recall only positive instances. (p. 62)

Their analyses were more complicated than their procedures because they were dealing with qualitative data that could be interpreted in several ways. Fortunately, there are methods that help reduce the possibility of interpretive bias. Such methods typically involve blind, independent raters. In their case, they used an approach called the critical decision method (Hoffman, Crandall, & Shadbolt, 1998). Their analysis indicated that family physicians experienced three kinds of intuition when diagnosing patients.

Gut Feelings. This was the most common way to experience intuition (50% of the cases). First there was an initial impression based on the patient's medical chart or his or her expressed reason for being there. Early impressions are the kind of intuition that the medical literature says cannot be trusted. "Gut feelings," as these physicians used the term, were different. Their gut feeling intuitions signaled an alarm because "something didn't seem right," and it cast doubt over the first impression. The intensity of "gut feelings" was strong enough for these doctors to make an assessment that contradicted their rational training, even when they anticipated that their colleagues might disagree with their diagnosis.

Recognitions. They termed a second type of intuition "recognitions"; they selected the term because it represented a subtle but important difference compared to early impressions. With recognitions, "Physicians were aware of conflicting information and/or the absence of key symptoms and signs" (p. 63). They also were aware that colleagues might disagree with them. One physician reported that his rational guidance about one patient was to interpret the symptoms as an anxiety attack—but that he kept thinking about chest pain. The patient turned out to have heart disease; the intuition had been correct.

Insights. A third type of intuition was called "insights" because there was no apparent pattern of symptoms or clues that led to a diagnosis. Insight seemed to occur after several possibilities had been considered and then discarded through the process of a differential diagnosis. But then a clear interpretation occurred to the physician that made sense of all the symptoms and signs. One physician reported that "it suddenly flashed in my head. Something I'd read some-where . . . something about lupus connected with celiac disease. And so I got really excited" (p. 64).

The Emerging Science of Rational and Intuitive Diagnoses

What's going on in your doctor's head is often a combination of (a) trained logic and rationality that each lead to differential diagnoses and (b) the kind of intuition that results from priming, experience, and heuristics and then shows up as gut feelings, recognitions, and insights. Using both thinking systems through cognitive load-shifting is one of the remarkable things about the human brain. For physicians, it creates opportunities to use both ways of thinking to get to a diagnosis.

Differential diagnoses that combine logic and intuition are like learning to tell the difference between identical twins. If you know both twins well, then it's not much of a problem; they each have developed "tells," or little signals about their identities. Twin 1 tends to smile out of the side of her mouth, clears the hair away from her face with her left hand, and wears casual clothes. Twin 2 has a fully balanced smile, straightens up to clear the hair away from her face, and is a snappy dresser. You may not be able to list or articulate what it is about one twin that "tells" you who it is, but your brain conducts a rapid, intuitive differential diagnosis. You confidently declare, "Twin 1 is Anita."

Woolley and Kostopoulou (2013) were able to describe how family doctors applied one of the central insights of social cognition: We have two constantly interacting thinking systems. However, they were cautious about the implications of their study. (Scientists are, by training and experience, extremely conservative about how to interpret their scientific findings.)

In their conclusion, the two researchers noted the higher prevalence of "gut feeling" intuitions and compared it to a similar slowing down reported by surgeons "who realize that they need to be more deliberative at a certain moment during an operation but cannot always explain why" (p. 64; see also Moulton, Regehr, Lingard, Merritt, & MacRae, 2010). They compared recognition insights to what social psychologists call heuristics because they are seeing something that looks like a familiar pattern but don't know where the insight came from. They also compared insight-type intuitions to a literature about a type of intuition called "incubation." Incubation occurs after we have worked hard on a difficult problem but failed to find a solution. We turn away from the problem, perhaps for a rest, and that's when the solution pops into our heads. That's why intuitions that come from incubation are sometimes referred to as "Aha!" experiences.

Whatever we call them, dual processing that combines logic and intuition is just what you want as your physician diagnoses those annoying blisters on your arm and neck.

DISCUSSION QUESTIONS

1. This case study mentions that dual processing is useful for mental health diagnoses (such as anxiety) as well as medical diagnoses. Identify two additional mental health issues that would benefit from a doctor or therapist who uses both intuition and logic to help a client, and explain how each type of thinking could be used.

2. Identify a specific area or talent that you, personally, have in which you feel that intuition guides your thoughts and behaviors (e.g., athletics, music, studying). Explain how the three variables that contribute to mental accessibility (priming, experience, and heuristics) each contribute to your enhanced intuition in this particular context.

3. Which of the three types of intuition described by Woolley and Kostopoulou (2013) as present in physicians do you think is the most reliable? In other words, if your doctor were going to rely on one of these forms of intuition, which do you think would lead to the best treatment—and why?

4. Several of the doctors mentioned that they believed their intuition might lead to a diagnosis their colleagues would disagree with. When you have a "gut feeling" or intuitive inclination, and your friends or family seem to disagree with it, how do you react? Do you doubt your intuition, thinking that they might be right after all—or do you stick to your intuition, telling yourself that you have more information and experience than they do?

KEY TERMS

Cognitive load-shifting 51
Dual processing 51
Heuristics 54

Intuition 51
Logic 51

Mental accessibility 55
Priming 54

4.3 Schema Mode Therapy: The Case of Defenseless Jimmy

Psychology is a strange science.

As the behaviorists liked to point out, many of the variables we are most interested in are invisible: self-esteem, attitudes, prejudice, and so on. How can we talk about and test the things that we are so interested in if they don't really exist in the physical realm? Psychologists have created **constructs**, a hypothesized entity, process, or event that cannot be directly observed (see MacCorquodale & Meehl, 1948). Many sciences do this; have you ever seen an atom or a black hole? But still, working with constructs is a risky business—it requires a lot of science to make sure we're all testing the same idea as we search for whether it is as important as we think. Fortunately, we also have some easy evidence that these invisible "things"— whatever they come to be called—really do exist.

One of the most famous demonstrations that mental structures exist comes from the Stroop test. If the word *red* is printed in blue ink, you will be slower to identify the color of the ink. Some structure in your head is making it more difficult to say the word *blue*. In another example, take a mental walk through the home you grew up in or remember best. Now count how many windows there are. If you are like most people, your eyes will physically dart about during your mental walk-through. But what are you really looking at? You're looking at a memory. It's invisible, yet you're looking at it even though it's only a mental construction.

Schemas: Types of Memory Structures

Memory structures have been crucial to the success of the human species. For example, you don't have to relearn how to read every time you pick up a book. Why? Because you have memory structures that maintain your ability to read. You remember the shapes of letters, the sounds they correspond to, the meaning of the sounds, and their grammatical arrangements; you can even apply those rules to new reading situations. In fact, it would be impossible for you to look at a book and *not* read the words because your memory structures for reading are so firmly in place. (You really are rather brilliant in the most important ways, even if you have never been a great student as society has defined it.)

So let's learn a little more about your marvelous memory structures—and how they influenced "Defenseless Jimmy." Memory structures are also called **schemas**, and they operate like automatic email spam filters. They discard some information so that we can pay attention to the more important information (Bartlett, 1932; Johnston, 2001). There are two specific types of schemas: **scripts** and **stereotypes**.

Scripts. A script is a particular type of memory structure that tells us what happens next. We don't have to relearn how to behave every time we go to a sit-down restaurant, for example, because we have a mental script for the expected order of events: (a) waiting to be taken to a table, (b) being seated, (c) reviewing the menu, (d) ordering the meal, (e) eating the meal, (f) paying the bill, and (g) leaving the restaurant. The script is modified for a fast-food restaurant because you have a slightly different memory structure for how to behave in that setting (e.g., there, you are required to pay before you get the food). Scripts even govern romantic behaviors that we often think of as spontaneous. For example, there is a widely shared script about consensual sex that begins with kissing and then proceeds in a very predictable sequence to touching particular parts of the body, and in a particular order (see Gagnon & Simon, 1987; Laumann, Gagnon, Michael, & Michaels, 1994).

Stereotypes. A second type of schema is a stereotype that assumes that everyone in a certain group has the same characteristics. Stereotypes are an efficient way to think because they minimize individual differences or diversity within any given group. Whatever groups you belong to—fraternity, psychology major, garage band, or football team—trigger a stereotype that others use to make judgments about you. Like other mental shortcuts, stereotypes are efficient ways of making decisions but also can lead to errors in judgment—that sometimes lead to disastrous effects.

Schema Mode Therapy

Martin Bamber (2004) at the Adult Cognitive Behavioural Therapies Service in York, England, provided this case study as a way to report on a new therapy: schema mode therapy (SMT; see Young, 1994). SMT is a therapeutic approach reserved, at least for now, to the most resistant psychological problems. It attempts to identify "early maladaptive schemas" (EMSs) that Bamber also refers to as "life traps." These are memory structures developed during childhood or adolescence that are elaborated upon and strengthened with life experiences (see Harris & Curtin, 2002; Lee, Taylor, & Dunn, 1999; Schmidt, Joiner, Young, & Telch, 1995). Bamber (2004) asserts that, like other schemas, EMSs

> are triggered when the individual encounters environments reminiscent of the childhood environment that produced them, and when this happens there is an intense and often overwhelming negative affect elicited. (p. 425)

Something in your present reminds you of something terrible in your past—and you automatically start reacting. These memory structures, like other schemas, influence what you ignore, what you pay attention to, and how you interpret ongoing life events. The term *modes* in SMT refer to enduring parts of the self such as an assertive mode, a resentful mode, or a helping mode—something with enough persistent, meaningful life experiences to build a memory structure.

The problem comes in when the individual cannot integrate various modes and shift from one to the other as required by different situations. Commonly experienced modes include a child mode, a maladaptive parent mode, a maladaptive coping mode, and a healthy adult mode (see Young, Klosko, & Weishaar, 2003). A critical part of the therapeutic approach appears to be limiting the number of modes to four, so that their interactions do not overwhelm the therapist and client.

Defenseless Jimmy. "Jimmy" was a 47-year-old man who, for 30 years, had suffered from agoraphobia (see Bamber, 2004, pp. 427–430), the fear of having an anxiety attack or being embarrassed in a large, public setting. He perceived that the outside environment was unsafe, experienced extreme anxiety, and therefore went to great lengths to avoid those situations. Several theoretical interventions had been attempted without success, including psychoanalysis, hypnotism, traditional cognitive-behavioral therapy, and various drug therapies, including Ativan and Prozac.

When SMT began, Jimmy was unable to leave his home alone, was socially isolated and lonely, had not been in a relationship with a woman for 25 years, and was essentially unemployable. He only left home in the company of his elderly mother. However, he was completing a college degree by correspondence and was willing, but understandably skeptical, about trying yet another therapy. He had concluded that he was one of life's losers.

His personal history included material comforts, but his emotionally distant father openly acknowledged that he never wanted or even liked children. Jimmy endured physical punishments without knowing why he was being punished. Although Jimmy's father

> presented a respectable face to the world, Jimmy described him as a
> "weak, asocial, worrying, malicious man" who took his frustrations out
> on him and his brother, usually when his mother was out of the house.
> (p. 428)

Jimmy did not enjoy school. He described himself as a "fat kid" who was frequently bullied. Teachers would sometimes join in the bullying. On one occasion, a teacher initiated the teasing and led a chorus of "lazy bones" when he came late to school. Jimmy was able to recall when he began to avoid these many unpleasant situations that typically had negative consequences. In addition, his mother

> would collude with him in avoiding things that he did not want to do
> both at school and at home. She would write letters to enable him to
> stay off school and avoid games, and always used to emphasize the
> dangers in the world and the importance of not taking risks. (p. 428)

A positive turning point occurred when Jimmy was 16 years old; he beat his father in an arm wrestling contest. A cascade of confidence helped him confront rather than avoid threatening situations. He left school, got a girlfriend, started working, bought a motorcycle, and improved his appearance. He thought he was leaving his past behind him. But then two apparently minor incidents "reactivated all the old thoughts, feelings, and behaviors, which came flooding back with a vengeance" (p. 429).

The first triggering event was an anxiety attack at a party where others were smoking dope in a hot, stuffy room. Jimmy felt that he could not escape. The second triggering event was at a school disco when his girlfriend was paying more attention to her friends than to him—which he interpreted as no longer being interested in him. Jimmy had subsequent girlfriends and eventually married one, but it ended in divorce after 2 years when she got weary of playing the role of nurse. He had a series of several jobs that all ended poorly. Jimmy described his career as a failure.

Helping Jimmy. The course of Jimmy's schema mode therapy lasted about 26 weeks and proceeded across five phases of treatment. The goal was for Jimmy to experience a unified self, a self that allowed his healthy memory structures to battle against his harmful memory structures. The imagery techniques the therapist used to work through later treatment phases are more reminiscent of a creature-filled first-person shooter video game than a traditional therapy. For example, the modes were given names: The Vulnerable Child mode was named *Defenseless Jimmy*. The Protector mode was named the *Black Knight*. The Punitive Parent mode was named the *Hydra*. The Healthy Adult was named *Charles Darwin* and later *Sean Connery* (the actor who played 007 in some of the James Bond movies).

In Phase 1 (Sessions 1–5), Jimmy and the therapist redefined Jimmy's situation by identifying four schema modes, particular memory structures that were important to Jimmy: the Vulnerable Child mode, the Healthy Adult mode, the Punitive Parent mode, and the Detached Protector mode. Jimmy's history makes it easy to believe that these were authentic memory structures that influenced Jimmy's life.

In Phase 2 (Sessions 6–8), the therapist and Jimmy used vivid imagery to recall memories of upsetting events from his childhood and articulate how each mode was reacting to those events. He began naming his modes according to their roles in his life.

In Phase 3 (Sessions 9–11), the sessions were really an exercise in persuasion. Jimmy was reluctant to continue therapy. The imagery exercises seemed "silly." The therapist proposed that Jimmy's reluctance to continue was an expression of his protector mode. Jimmy persevered.

In Phase 4 (Sessions 12–18), the use of imagery described a battle between the various modes, or memory structures, that had been trying to help versus harm

Jimmy's life. The therapeutic approach had Jimmy voice the messages each mode was sending to the different parts of his self.

In Phase 5 (Sessions 19–24), Jimmy and the therapist continued to use imagery and having Jimmy voice what each of his modes was now saying. This phase involved the Healthy Adult mode reparenting the Vulnerable Child mode.

Jimmy continued in therapy, and the report has a happy ending:

> Jimmy reported that he had got engaged to be married! He had also got rid of all his old letters and his old wedding ring from his first marriage and had thrown them all in the river. He described himself as feeling calmer in himself and more in control of his emotions. He was having lots of successes with his behavioural desensitization programme and was doing many more things on his own. (p. 435)

DISCUSSION QUESTIONS

1. This therapeutic technique makes use of healthy and unhealthy schemas. What other explanations could account for the apparently successful outcome of this therapy?

2. Do you have reasons to believe that the success of this therapy will—or will not—endure over time? List the arguments for and against long-term success.

3. Are dramatic therapies such as this one, which incorporate creation of characters and labels, more appealing to therapists than mundane but effective "homework" therapies, more typical of traditional cognitive-behavioral approaches?

4. Do you have reasons to believe that EMSs (early maladaptive schemas) really exist? Try to identify schemas or modes that you, personally, have that seem to influence your thinking, decisions, relationships, and path of life.

KEY TERMS

Construct 58

Memory structure 58

Schema 58

Script 58

Stereotype 58

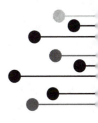

CHAPTER 5

Person Perception

5.1 Tell Me the Truth—Am I Too Pretty? Marilyn Monroe and the Halo Effect

The most famous studies in person perception (see Asch, 1946; Kelley, 1950) may be the elegant little experiments that used just two words to alter perceptions of another person. Two groups of students (created by random assignment) read identical descriptions of someone who was about to come speak to them—identical, that is, except for the words *cold* and *warm* lurking in the middle of the sentence:

> "People who know him consider him to be a rather cold person, industrious, critical, practical, and determined."

Or

> "People who know him consider him to be a rather warm person, industrious, critical, practical, and determined."

Halo Effects

The students formed starkly different impressions of the speaker based only on those two little words. The experimentally critical words produced what Kelley (1950, p. 435) called **halo effects** because they influenced their entire perception of the speaker as consistent with being a "warm" person or a "cold" person. We don't need words, however, to form halo-like impressions of one another.

The Beauty Bias. Physically beautiful people also enjoy a social halo that credits them with being not only smarter (Clifford & Walster, 1973) but also deserving of higher salaries and more raises (Frieze, Olson, & Russell, 1991)! It seems unfair, but the beauty bias doesn't end there. Beautiful people also are given lighter prison sentences if they should get caught committing a crime (Gunnell & Ceci, 2010). But why bother committing a crime when so many good things come to you by just standing around being beautiful?

The list goes on. Physically attractive people are more likely to be given scholarships (Agthe, Spörrle, & Maner, 2010), get more friend requests on Facebook from strangers (Wang, Moon, Kwon, Evans, & Stefanone, 2010), and get more opportunities to practice their social skills (Feingold, 1992). Those tangible opportunities to practice your skills set up a **self-fulfilling prophecy** so that beautiful people really do develop and then enjoy the benefits of having better social skills. Beautiful people didn't ask for these benefits and may be only dimly aware that they are receiving them. This particular type of halo effect—that being physically attractive leads to people assuming all sorts of other wonderful things about you—is called the **what-is-beautiful-is-good effect**.

However, beautiful people also have a few problems that don't plague the rest of us. First, physically attractive people may have difficulty diagnosing the sincerity of any compliments they receive about their skills or abilities (Carrington & Carnevale, 1984). Are these compliments cheap manipulation or authentic? Not knowing can create a lot of personal uncertainty. Second, highly attractive women do not always report having higher self-esteem (Fleming & Courtney, 1984; Marsh & Richards, 1988); perhaps on some level, they are aware of how fleeting or superficial judgments of others can be. Third, being "too pretty" might lead to jealousy and discrimination against the beautiful by others competing for scarce resources such as jobs (e.g., Agthe et al., 2010). Still, most of us probably would accept the trade-offs of being not just beautiful but *more* beautiful than the others around us.

The Effect of Being Beautiful on Others. Nancy Etcoff (1999) found that it was easier to describe the effects of experiencing beauty than defining whatever "it" is. Aaron Spelling produced a series of television shows and movies based on little more than placing beautiful people in almost any excuse for a story. Even current generations of college students may be familiar with *Melrose Place, Beverly Hills 90210, The Love Boat,* and *Charlie's Angels.* Spelling's simple formula was to use beautiful-looking people, especially women, to attract huge audiences. Spelling said about beauty that "I can't define it but I know it when it walks into the room." A modeling agent said, "It's when someone walks in the door and you almost can't breathe" (Etcoff, 1999, p. 8).

A YouTube (2013) video portraying the beautiful-looking women serving as newscasters for conservative television channel FOX News attracted a wide range of comments. Viewers emphasized the personal and social consequences of experiencing the physical beauty of newscasters:

> "A far cry from the hideous ugly women of the left . . . liberal women are always so butt ass ugly and generally look like men."

> "All smoking hot and intelligent. Love em."

> "Not hot at all, plus about as sharp as marshmellow [sic]."

"All the women on fox [sic] are beautiful and intelligent no matter their party views."

"Yea, it's amazing how they try to squeeze into a dress that's 3 sizes too small for them . . . they all do it."

Marilyn Monroe's Story

Marilyn Monroe was that kind of beautiful: distracting, alarming, and powerful—but also troubled. Marilyn Monroe (1926–1962) started life as Norma Jeane Mortenson but sometimes gave her last name as Baker. Her story (as well as her beauty) makes it easy to sympathize with her.

An Awkward Childhood. Norma Jeane's mother, Gladys Monroe, had married for the first time when she was just 15, to a man named Baker who later left her and took their two children to Kentucky—sisters whom Norma Jeane would not even know about until much later in her life. Gladys remarried a man named Mortenson in 1924, but the couple separated 10 months before Norma Jeane was born—making the identity of her biological father unclear. Her foster parents, Albert and Ida Bolender, were more stable but also strict evangelical Christians. They hoped to adopt Norma Jeane, and she spent 7 relatively tranquil years with the Bolenders.

Gladys most often worked as a Hollywood film cutter. She enjoyed a brief period of emotional stability—enough to reenter Norma Jeane's life and move them both to Hollywood. Gladys introduced her daughter to actors and others in the movie business. About a year later, Norma Jeane's mother was committed to a state mental hospital with a diagnosis of paranoid schizophrenia; she would be in and out of hospitals for the rest of her life. However, one of Monroe's biographers voiced skepticism about the validity of that diagnosis. Donald Spoto (1993) wrote that Gladys "did not suffer from hallucinations, paranoia or frank schizophrenia" (p. 106). There was, however, a "retreat from the ordinary business of living . . . she seemed to have suffered a loss of affect [or emotional expression]." Those symptoms sound more like depression than paranoid schizophrenia.

The legal consequences of an absent father, a revolving door of older men, and her mother's instability resulted in Norma Jeane eventually becoming a ward of the state and spending much of her later youth in foster homes. She entered adolescence as a shy young woman with a stutter. She was about to be placed in a Los Angeles orphans home, but she found another way out when she turned 16: marriage. She married their neighbor's son, Jim Dougherty. He spent much of his time on duty with the merchant marines in the Pacific, ferrying troops home from the war. That quickly turned Norma Jeane into a bored and lonely housewife.

A Career in Hollywood. Norma Jeane was working in a defense plant factory when an army photographer took her picture—images that were never published. But apparently that nudge was all that she needed to sign a contract with a modeling agency. She started dying and straightening her dark, curly hair, became the iconic-looking "blonde bombshell," and soon began getting work. She appeared first on magazine covers and then in small roles in movies. She typically played an attractive but empty addition to the film's plot. But her career in the entertainment business had begun. She began calling herself Marilyn Monroe in 1946, when she was 20 years old.

The glamorous industry of filmmaking and fantasy wasn't a bed of roses for this classic pin-up girl. During World War II, she had decorated many soldiers' barracks in poster form—so yes, she was perceived as extraordinarily beautiful with a deliberate sex appeal. And yes, she also enjoyed the many benefits of those person perceptions. However, as an actress, she was consigned to playing the stereotypical dumb blonde. That stereotype probably disarmed many people because, as a person who happened to be beautiful, Marilyn Monroe had the wit to recognize that her beauty gave her social power.

Monroe skillfully leveraged that power all the way to a business victory over the entrenched studio system in Hollywood and to a controversial personal relationship with the president of the United States. But the beauty bias, for Marilyn Monroe, was a two-edged sword. She had to fight within herself, with others, with the movie system, and with the general public to be taken seriously. Monroe used her beauty skillfully and with humor—and scriptwriters began to recognize and use the intelligence beneath the blonde bombshell with a gift for comic timing. In the film *Gentlemen Prefer Blondes* (1953), she is accused, by a wealthy father, of dating his son for his money.

Son: I love her. I've never had a feeling like this.

Father: Oh, shut up! [To MM] Young lady, you don't fool me one bit.

MM: I'm not trying to. But I bet I could, though.

Father: No, you might convince this jackass that you love him but you'll never convince me.

MM: [To the son] That's too bad, because I do love you.

Father: Certainly. For his money.

MM: No. Honestly.

Father: Have you got the nerve to stand there and expect me to believe that you don't want to marry my son for his money?

MM: It's true.

Father: Then what do you want to marry him for?

MM: I want to marry him for *your* money. [pause] Don't you know that a man being rich is like a girl being pretty? You wouldn't marry a girl just because she's pretty, but my goodness, doesn't it help?

An Early Ending to a Troubled Life. Marilyn Monroe died at the tender age of 36 from an overdose of barbiturates. Her death was officially described as a "probable suicide." But that conclusion is not shared by Spoto (1993), her most serious biographer. The only thing close to a suicide note was an unfinished, forward-looking love letter to former husband Joe DiMaggio. It included these now famous lines: "Dear Joe, If I can only succeed in making you happy, I will have succeeded in the biggest and most difficult thing there is—that is, to make one person completely happy."

The age of 36 is a significant point in how pretty women are perceived. Nancy Etcoff (1999) writes in the book, *Survival of the Prettiest,* that "physical beauty is like athletic skill: It peaks young" (p. 63). Hollywood was (and is) full of age discrimination that works against long careers for women. Etcoff points out that many award-winning movies pair older men with younger women—and even same-age pairings in which the woman plays the mother to a male actor who is actually about the same age. For example, in the classic film *The Graduate* (1967), Dustin Hoffman is seduced by an "older woman." The scandalous older woman was Anne Bancroft—who was only 6 years older than Dustin Hoffman.

Etcoff also explores how gender differences in the cosmetic and hair industries reinforce what Marilyn Monroe was experiencing at age 36. Fashion model Lauren Hutton used an evolutionary framework to explain women aging within the entertainment business: "As soon as they were out of eggs, women were out of business" (see Etcoff, 1999, p. 73; Gross, 2011, p. 222). When biographer Spoto (1993) looked into Monroe's family (on her mother's side), he found more than physical beauty. One grandparent had died of dementia at the age of 41. Was this a clue to the tragic ending of Marilyn Monroe's life?

Otis Monroe's behavior and health deteriorated with alarming rapidity. His memory was erratic, his responses often inappropriate, he suffered severe headaches and became uncharacteristically slovenly. His fits of rage . . . alternated with fits of weeping and the poor man soon developed violent tremors . . . followed by seizures that, at least once, sent six-year-old Gladys in a panic to stay with neighbors for two days. (p. 4)

But the biographer dug into the medical records in ways that Gladys was never able to do (or pass along to her daughter). Otis Monroe's diagnosis was syphilis of the brain but probably "not of the type contracted through sexual activity but through the dangerously unsanitary, virus-infested conditions in which he had worked in Mexico." The result was that the entire family, including Marilyn Monroe's mother, "wrongly believed their husband and father had died of insanity, when in fact he was killed by an infection that destroyed his brain tissue."

Marilyn Monroe grew up self-perceiving that serious mental health problems ran deep in the family's history. And perhaps they did. But the subtle work of a self-fulfilling prophecy (a belief that makes itself come true) also may have influenced the tragic course of Marilyn Monroe's life.

An Archival Approach to Person Perception

The "experts" in any age have perceived people with mental illness according to the dominant theory of their time (see Appignanesi, 2008). The "raving lunatic" of one era and culture might be locked away but credited as a genius in another time and place or sent for compassionate pharmaceutical treatment in a third setting. Marilyn Monroe lived from 1926 to 1962 when the dominant perspective was the Freudian psychodynamic approach combined with powerful drug therapies. While she was alive, Monroe communicated with Anna Freud, Sigmund Freud's famous psychologist daughter.

Consequently, one postmortem psychological diagnosis of Monroe described a "psychoanalytic pathography of a preoedipal" (Chessick, 1983)—a Freudian approach to understanding Monroe's life and death as a lost parental attachment. Those early life experiences probably did have some effect on the adult that Marilyn Monroe came to be. But a more recent approach to understanding Marilyn Monroe relies on data: personal notes, letters, and poems she wrote (see Fernández-Cabana, García-Caballero, Alves-Pérez, Garcia-García, & Mateos, 2013). These researchers used Monroe's own words to identify four distinct periods in her adult life.

A collection of the materials containing those words was published (many for the first time) in the book *Fragments* (Buchthal & Comment, 2010). This **archival data** approach to understanding her life used content analysis to organize those materials by time, across the four stages of Monroe's life shown in Table 5.1. The researchers then counted the number of words, entries, and words per entry for each period. Table 5.1 suggests that she was writing fewer but longer entries during the shortest period, just before she died.

The research team also analyzed Monroe's writing according to the use of words with more than six letters, personal pronouns, third-person plural pronouns, swear words, words related to negative emotions, and words related to religion. Figure 5.1, for example, tells us that Monroe's use of swear words, religious

Time Period	Words / # Entries = # Words per Entry	Life Events
Table 5.1 When Monroe's Writing Is Analyzed, Four Distinct Periods of Her Life Seem to Emerge		
1943–1951	2,341 / 8 = 292	From her first marriage to her first film success
1952–1955	2,838 / 15 = 189	Marriage to and divorce from Joe DiMaggio, founding her production company, classes at Actors Studio, first contact with psychoanalysis
1956–1959	2,786 / 21 = 133	Marriage to Arthur Miller
1960–1962	3,806 / 6 = 634	Psychoanalysis with Dr. Greenson, divorce from Arthur Miller, difficulties in meeting her work commitments, brief psychiatric admissions, and relationships with J. F. and R. F. Kennedy

Figure 5.1 Mean number and type of words in Marilyn Monroe's writing across four time periods.

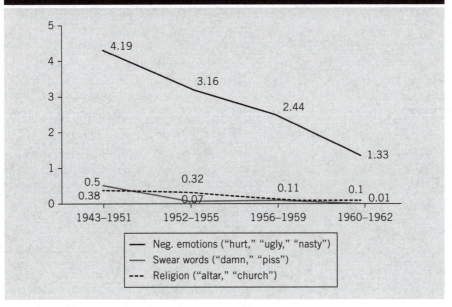

Source: Fernández-Cabana, M., García-Caballero, A., Alves-Pérez, M. T., García-García, M. J., & Mateos, R. (2013). Suicidal traits in Marilyn Monroe's fragments: An LIWC analysis. Crisis: *The Journal of Crisis Intervention and Suicide Prevention, 34*(2), 124–130.

references, and especially negative emotions declined across all four periods of her life. These downward trends all qualify as statistically significant, and they tell a data-driven story. But the most prominent pattern is that her use of negative emotion words steadily declined across the four life periods identified in this study.

Being beautiful created opportunities for Marilyn Monroe but also brought unwelcome attention and everyday annoyances. The psychodynamic theorists tried to understand Monroe through a particular theoretical lens; they voiced confident declarations based on a grand psychodynamic theory of hidden motivations and fears. By contrast, the linguistic researchers reached cautious, evidence-driven conclusions based on archival data. Both approaches have merit in the scientific process, if only to provoke better hypotheses.

DISCUSSION QUESTIONS

1. Which way of knowing about Marilyn Monroe do you think is most effective: the psychodynamic approach or the linguistic analysis using archival data such as poems and journals? What are the strengths and weaknesses of each?

2. What are the advantages of using a case study approach to understanding Marilyn Monroe, the life she lived, and the decisions that she made? How useful is the social history of that time period, for example?

3. Is the what-is-beautiful-is-good effect real? List some ways that you see the beauty bias operating in the people and events you are familiar with (in other words, think of real examples you've seen in your own life). Try to identify at least two specific ways that being physically attractive seems to be beneficial for people, as well as at least two specific ways that being attractive may be a *disadvantage*.

4. List some observable gender differences related to beauty and physical attraction. In other words, is the what-is-beautiful-is-good effect equally influential on what men/boys versus women/girls experience? In what contexts will gender influence how people are perceived based on their looks?

KEY TERMS

Archival data 68
Halo effect 63

Self-fulfilling
prophecy 64

What-is-beautiful-is-good
effect 64

5.2 From Street Kid to Magician to Scholar: The Self-Fulfilling Prophecy of Robert Merton

Robert Merton had a knack for naming things. His phrase **self-fulfilling prophecy** has become so common, even beyond formal psychology, that we have nearly lost its interesting origins in the life of its creator. The term *role model* is also attributed to Merton. "Unanticipated consequences," "Dysfunction," "the Matthew Effect," and the "Focused Interview" (focus groups) are other social psychological concepts that came from the wide-ranging thoughts of a scholar who started out as a street kid in South Philadelphia.

Most of the personal information in this case study of Robert Merton's life comes from a talk he gave in 1994 to the American Council of Learned Societies, the Charles Homer Haskins Lecture. Merton received many awards over his life, but he was the first sociologist to be honored by this group. The event took place at the Benjamin Franklin Hall of the American Philosophical Society in Philadelphia—and in walking distance from the home in which Merton was born 84 years earlier.

From Street Kid to Magician: A Structure for Geographical Opportunity

Robert Merton was born with the name Meyer R. Schkolnick and was the child of immigrant parents from Eastern Europe. He grew up as one of thousands of street kids in South Philadelphia. But Merton, with the sociologist's insistence on precise language, was not comfortable with calling it a slum. Their home was in rooms "above my father's newly acquired milk-butter-and-egg shop." It was uninsured, however, and after it was destroyed in a fire, they moved to a smaller, red-brick row house.

That small house had everything this young boy could want. It had a dining room where he built a crystal radio, a kitchen with a coal-burning stove, and an outhouse in the backyard. More important, his home was "fueled with the unquestioned premise that things would somehow get better, surely so for the children" (Merton, 1994, pp. 3–4). His mother in particular believed in and acted as if they were headed for a better life that did not yet exist; she was confident that it somehow would become a reality. She was the energy behind his first experience of a self-fulfilling prophecy.

As he looked back on those years, Merton realized that he actually had many geographical advantages in life, and the most important one taught him that "much consequential education takes place outside the walls of classrooms" (p. 4) He told his audience that

> I had a private library of some 10,000 volumes, located just a few
> blocks from our house, a library thoughtfully bestowed upon me
> by that ultimately beneficent robber baron, Andrew Carnegie. The
> neighborhood was secure enough for me to make my way alone to
> that library of mine from the tender age of five or six. (p. 4)

The library exposed the growing boy to alternative lives through literature. It allowed him to vicariously travel the world with the help of friendly librarians. He could even listen to the famed Philadelphia orchestra from the 25-cent cheap seats in the concert hall a few blocks away. He described the urban village of his upbringing as an "opportunity structure." It wasn't a slum to him; he had everything in South Philadelphia except financial capital. Merton observed that the

> seemingly deprived South Philadelphia slum was providing a youngster with every sort of capital—social capital, cultural capital, human capital, and above all, what we may call public capital. (p. 7)

Chance stepped into Merton's life once again with another geographical advantage (after another move when his father lost his job at the Navy Yard). Their new neighbor, Charles Hopkins or "Hop," stopped by with a strange question: Had they seen his pet mice and rabbits? It was not the most elegant introduction, but there seemed to be a plan behind the strange request. Hop was courting Merton's older sister and eventually would become her husband. Whatever his motivation at the time, Hop's animals really were related to his work as a magician, and he soon took Merton on as his apprentice. He was a quick learner and "became fairly adept by the time I was 14." His abilities as a prestidigitator were good enough to support him when he entered nearby Temple College 3 years later. He performed "at children's parties, at Sunday schools and, for part of one summer, in a small and quite unsuccessful traveling circus" (p. 8).

Merton is credited with coining a phrase that everyone from experimental social psychologists to worried parents now rely on: "role model." In this case, Merton's role model was the magician Harry Houdini. Houdini's original name was Ehrich Weiss, but he had renamed himself after the celebrated French magician Robert Houdin. So, the 14-year-old magician Meyer R. Schkolnick became Robert K. Merlin (after the wizard from King Arthur legends) and later changed again to Robert K. Merton. His college friends took to calling him "Bob Merton." By the time he was in college, Merton had renamed, relabeled, and re-created himself, and always with social support—especially from his mother.

> With the warm consent of my devoted Americanizing mother—she attended night school far more religiously than the synagogue—and the bland agreement of my rather uninterested father, this was followed by the legal transformation of my name some 65 years ago. (p. 9)

Merton was learning that in a world of self-fulfilling prophecies and with an **internal locus of control**, he could rename himself whatever he liked and forge a path of his own making.

From Magician to Scholar:
A Structure for Intellectual Opportunity

The specific direction of Robert Merton's life was influenced because he first had dared to apply to Temple College, a college not fully accredited at that time. He reported that he "had ventured into a class in sociology given by a young instructor, George E. Simpson, and there I found my subject" (p. 10). Simpson was working on his doctoral dissertation titled *The Negro in the Philadelphia Press,* and he recognized a promising student in the young magician-turned-college-student.

Simpson recruited Merton to help in a simple (but laborious) research project based on archival data. He was to summarize "all the references to Negroes over a span of decades in Philadelphia newspapers." In those precomputerized days, tracking down that information represented a great deal of work, but the story of people embedded in that topic fascinated Merton. That research project with Simpson brought him into contact with Ralph Bunche and Franklin Frazier and, some time later, with Kenneth Clark. That networking allowed him input on the social science brief about desegregation of the public schools that influenced the famous *Brown v. Board of Education of Topeka* (1954) legal case. Merton, of course, could not know the life-changing networking opportunities that were waiting for him when he first followed his curiosity into that sociology classroom.

Simpson did more than plug Merton into his research topic. He took the young magician-scholar to a professional meeting of sociologists—and made sure he attended particular presentations. That was where he met a remarkable scholar, Pitirim Alexandrovice Sorokin, the founding chairman of the Department of Sociology that still was being established at Harvard. Merton reported that

> I would surely not have dared apply for graduate study at Harvard
> had not Sorokin encouraged me to do so . . . he was the teacher I was
> looking for. Moreover, it was evident that Sorokin was not your ordinary
> academic sociologist. Imprisoned three times by czarists and then three
> times by the Bolsheviks, he had . . . a death sentence commuted into
> exile by the normally unsparing Lenin . . . I did nervously apply to
> Harvard, did receive a scholarship there, and soon found myself on a
> new phase in a life of learning. (p. 11)

Merton now had a mentor for graduate school. That meant, as many graduate students have learned, that he became Sorokin's research assistant, teaching assistant, "man-of-all-work," and an occasional stand-in for other responsibilities.

Summoning me to his office one day, he announced that he had stupidly
agreed to do a paper on recent French sociology for a learned society
and asked if I would be good enough to take it on in his stead. Clearly,
this was less a question than an unforgiving expectation. . . . This turned
out to be the first of several such unpredictable and fruitful occasions
provided by the expanding opportunity structure at Harvard. (p. 11)

That project led to another, and to another, and suddenly this second-year graduate student was a published scholar. He also developed some peculiar academic
habits, based on yet another role model named Talcott Parsons. As an instructor,
Parsons had developed the habit of what Merton called "'oral publication'—the
working out of ideas in lecture, seminars, and workshops" (p. 12). Originality was
the coin of the realm in the world that Merton had entered at Harvard, and he
believed and acted as if his ideas were as worthy as those who were teaching him.
Once again, the elements of a self-fulfilling prophecy were shaping the young student's life: By acting as if his ideas were important and interesting, others perceived
them to be so as well.

Merton plainly had developed impressive networking skills. However, he
described himself as an "inveterate loner working chiefly in libraries and in my
study at home." But as a lowly graduate student, Merton still was reluctant to
approach the well-known historian of science, George Sarton. Sarton was rumored
to be such "a remote and awesome presence, so dedicated to his scholarship as
to be wholly inaccessible." But looking back on those years in his 80s, Merton
commented,

Thus do plausible but ill-founded beliefs develop into social realities
through the mechanism of the self-fulfilling prophecy. Since this
forbidding scholar was unapproachable, there was no point in trying
to approach him. And his subsequently having very few students only
went to show how inaccessible he actually was. But when in the fall of
1933 I knocked on the door of Sarton's office in Widener Library, he did
not merely invite me in; he positively ushered me in. (p. 13)

Merton was then finishing his graduate work in the midst of the Great
Depression—when even Harvard was pulling back on staff. But when his dissertation was complete, the street kid who became a magician who became a graduate student was still fulfilling his mother's "unquestioned premise that things
would somehow get better, surely so for the children"—his mother's self-fulfilling
prophecy. Merton was already a well-published, recognized scholar when he
completed his dissertation. Fortunately, "Tulane University beckoned with a pro-
fessorship in that bleak economic time" and

for a provincial whose life had been confined to Philadelphia and Cambridge, the fanciful culture of New Orleans provided a distinct attraction. After a relaxing—and intellectually rewarding—two years at Tulane, I moved to Columbia and entered upon another, wholly unpredictable, phase of learning: what turned out to be 35 years of an improbable collaboration with the mathematician-psychologist turned sociologist, Paul F. Lazarsfeld. (p. 15)

The Collaborative Scholar: A Structure for Networking Opportunity

Although credited with naming the social psychological process called the self-fulfilling prophecy, Merton recognized that the concept was not new. He pointed first to W. I. Thomas (see Thomas & Thomas, 1928), who asserted that "if men define situations as real, they are real in their consequences" (see also Merton, 1994). But he also credited the concept to "observant and disciplined minds" in previous centuries: in the 17th century to Bishop Bossuet, in the 18th century to Mandeville in *The Fable of the Bees,* in the 19th century to Karl Marx, and in the 20th century to Freud.

Merton's wide-ranging reading habits, developed at the Carnegie Library in South Philadelphia, were paying intellectual dividends. But when Merton introduced this concept, he didn't use the customary empirical formula familiar to social psychologists. Instead, Merton used what he called a "sociological parable." He described how in 1932, bank manager Cartwright Millingville was feeling justly proud that his bank was flourishing in the midst of the Great Depression. One Wednesday morning, the men from the local steel plants were coming in too soon—payday wasn't until Saturday. But a nasty rumor had gotten started that the bank was insolvent. More and more customers starting withdrawing their money—and by the end of the day the bank *was* insolvent. Rumor had become reality: a self-fulfilling prophecy. It wouldn't have happened unless people already thought it was true.

The bank failed. But it failed because of a self-fulfilling prophecy. And the way Merton presented and named the concept made it possible for everyone to understand it. Geographic, intellectual, and personal networking opportunities—combined with hard work and an internal locus of control—were the basic ingredients of Robert Merton's career. The street kid from South Philadelphia was launched into what would become one of the most honored, diverse careers in academics.

A child of immigrant parents was raised on the rough streets of South Philadelphia. He was first named Meyer R. Schkolnick. Then he renamed himself after being inspired by magician Harry Houdini. He became an internationally famous scholar and named several of the concepts crucial to the development of social psychology—including the "self-fulfilling prophecy." He had lived the self-fulfilling prophecy that his mother had predicted.

DISCUSSION QUESTIONS

1. Merton described the tough streets of South Philadelphia and the refined atmosphere of Harvard as "opportunity structures." What are opportunity structures, and can you identify any opportunity structures in your own life? Have you been blessed by privilege and opportunity—or have you had to overcome challenges that were the lack of opportunity for most people in those environments?

2. Did Merton's ability to name social phenomena contribute to his fame and the many honors that he received? Do you find that the name for a phenomenon—such as self-fulfilling prophecy, halo effect, or mere exposure—can help or hurt understanding of the concept and whether it becomes popular?

3. What might Merton have learned as a magician that contributed to his life as a scholar?

4. Merton appears to have had a fairly strong internal locus of control. How might his life have turned out differently if he had an external locus of control?

KEY TERMS

Internal locus of control 72   Self-fulfilling prophecy 70

5.3 Pygmalion in the Classroom: The Slow Creation of a Classic Study

Perhaps there is some faster way to gain scientific knowledge. If there is, we don't know what it is.

The long arc of the research story about **self-fulfilling prophecies** is made up of many smaller research stories. The formal beginnings of this research story began with Robert Merton's anecdote about the sudden failure of a healthy bank (see Case 5.2). One morning a rumor got started that the local bank was going to fail; frantic depositors withdrew their money; by that afternoon, the bank had failed: a self-fulfilling prophecy. Merton (1948, 1987) stayed with this idea, blended it with many others, and passed it along to the next generation.

About 20 years after Merton got things started, Robert Rosenthal began to systematically test that same idea in a series of experiments. However, he was testing this idea under a different conceptual banner: expectations research. Those experiments accumulated into a classic case study conducted in a San Francisco elementary school. After the classroom study, skeptical researchers spent another 20 years questioning, qualifying, and refining all those previous studies. The research community slowly started to gain confidence that this was a trustworthy, fairly accurate description of how life unfolded for many people.

Expectancy Effects in Pharmaceutical Psychology

Self-fulfilling prophecies are now recognized as a general phenomenon and explored in almost every scientific discipline (Crum & Phillips, 2015). For example, medical and pharmaceutical researchers have to control for expectancy effects called placebo effects that frequently occur during drug trials. Participants in a drug trial for depression may experience an improvement in their symptoms when they take a pill that, even though it looks the same, does not contain any of the medication being tested. This may be a bigger deal than you imagine, and it usually leads to the need for highly controlled, double-blind research procedures. A **meta-analysis** by Kirsch and Sapirstein (1998) of depression-prescribed medications found (quoting from their abstract) that

> mean effect sizes for changes in depression were calculated for 2,318 patients who had been randomly assigned to either antidepressant medication or placebo in 19 double-blind clinical trials. As a proportion of the drug response, the placebo response was constant across different types of medication (75%), and the correlation between placebo effect and drug effect was .90. (p. 1)

However, the title of their article tells the meta-analytic story even more bluntly: "Listening to Prozac but Hearing Placebo." The take-home message is that placebos seem to work just about as well as drugs. The expectation effect that Prozac will reduce depression has become part of what Wampold and Imel (2015) refer to as "the great psychotherapy debate." The debate is about not only what works in terms of psychotherapy but also *why* it works. What if, for example, almost all therapeutic interventions work, somewhat, simply because they all are different ways of paying positive attention to a problem (Seligman, 2002)? These expectation-based placebo effects are self-fulfilling prophecies that could rearrange the foundations of talk therapy—and shake the foundation of pharmaceutical treatments for depression. The participant's expectation of an improvement creates a placebo effect (a.k.a. a self-fulfilling prophecy, sometimes called the Pygmalion effect).

Building a Classic Experiment

Robert Rosenthal was building toward what would become a classic experiment in social and educational psychology. But it started small (and almost by accident).

It required a number of intermediate experiments. Conducting the experiments would involve deceiving participants. It was a complicated endeavor—but it led to fascinating results.

Lab Rats Labeled "Maze Dull" or "Maze Bright." In his first experiment about self-fulfilling prophecies, Rosenthal told a lie. He was working with some student-experimenters in a rat lab. The students were training their lab rats to run a maze. But Rosenthal was really testing whether the students' expectations would influence how well the rats could run that maze. Half of the students were led to believe their rats were "maze bright" (genetically bred to be good at mazes), and the other half believed their rats were "maze dull." That was the lie.

It was a lie because the only real difference was in the students' expectations. In reality, the rats were all alike. They all had been randomly assigned to be labeled either as "maze dull" or "maze bright." Despite being labeled purely by chance, those labels started to matter. Maybe the students with "maze bright" rats worked a little harder, fed their lab rats more often, or petted them more frequently—we don't know. We only know that whatever those students did seemed to work. By the end of the study, the rats' maze-running abilities fulfilled whatever their student-experimenters believed (Rosenthal, 1994; Rosenthal & Fode, 1963). "Maze bright" rats really did run faster than the "maze dull" rats. What the students *expected* to happen did happen: a self-fulfilling prophecy.

Elementary School Children Labeled "Intellectual Bloomers." Our understanding of the power of expectations on humans accelerated when Rosenthal replicated what he did with his students—but this time with elementary school teachers. Instead of how fast lab rats could run a maze, they studied elementary school children's IQ tests. As you can imagine, such a replication would add to the generalizability of expectations research. But it does sound like a bit of leap, right? Will elementary school students respond to their teachers' expectations the same way that lab rats responded to their student-experimenters' expectations?

When Rosenthal began corresponding with Lenore Jacobsen, a school principal in San Francisco, the stage was set for *Pygmalion in the Classroom,* one of psychology's most famous—and still debated—experiments. Rosenthal and Jacobsen (1968) gave students in 18 different classrooms across six different grade levels a test with a fancy (but meaningless) name, the "Harvard Test of Inflected Acquisition."

Let's reflect with Shakespeare about the name of this test. In *Romeo and Juliet,* Juliet tried to cross the bridge between two families by asking, "What's in a name? That which we call a rose by any other name would smell as sweet." The name of this bogus test, however, gives off a distinctly different odor. The "Harvard Test of Inflected Acquisition" sounded authoritative. After all, it has the name "Harvard" at the front end followed by words that were difficult to understand together, even if you know what each word means by itself. This word combination seems designed to intimidate teachers and encourage them to turn off their critical thinking skills. (Its only reference in Google Scholar is its use in this experiment.) As part of a lie, it was an excellent lie. Teachers in the school administered the test to their students and believed it was important.

Previously, Rosenthal had lied to his students about whether their lab rats were "maze dull" or "maze bright." This time, Rosenthal and Principal Jacobsen lied to the teachers about a randomly selected 20% of the students. They told the teachers that, according to the Harvard Test of Inflected Acquisition, these 20% of students across six grade levels were *expected* to be "intellectual bloomers." They elaborated on what the label of "intellectual bloomer" would mean to the students.

The students identified as intellectual bloomers by the (bogus) Harvard Test of Inflected Acquisition would "show surprising gains in intellectual competence during the next eight months of school." What a welcome message: Expect to be surprised at how wonderful these students grow, academically. The results were more detailed than what is presented in Figure 5.1 but the graph tells the general story about what happened at the end of this 8-month experiment. Even though there were no real differences in the students at the beginning of the year, what the teachers expected to happen did happen—but only for the students in first and second grades (especially for boys' verbal ability and girls' reasoning ability).

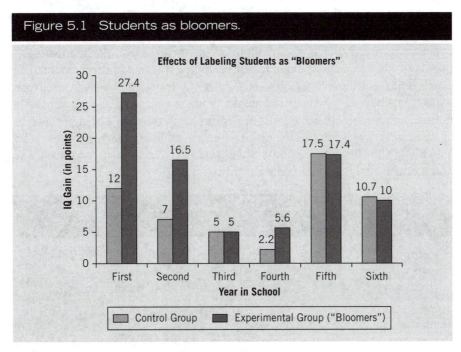

Figure 5.1 Students as bloomers.

Source: Rosenthal and Jacobson (1968)

Halo Effects From the Label of "Intellectual Bloomer." The positive label of "intellectual bloomer" created powerful **halo effects**. For example, teachers described the children in the experimental group as more likely to succeed, more interesting, and more curious. But that wasn't the end of it. They also described these positively labeled students as more appealing, better adjusted, less in need of social approval, and even happier. Remember that these students had been chosen completely at random! That's one bright halo—but that still wasn't the end of the subtle but powerful Pygmalion effect. The glow from this positive halo was so bright that it revealed some weird reactions in the teachers.

For example, some students who were not identified as intellectual bloomers also showed significant gains in IQ. What effect did their *unexpected* success have on their teachers? "The more children in the control group gained in IQ, the more *un*favorably they were judged by their teachers" (Rosenthal, 1994, p. 179). They were "blooming" when they were not expected to bloom—because the bogus Harvard Test of Inflected Acquisition had told them so. But apparently, the teachers did not blame the test for having poor predictive validity. These high-achieving students had violated their teachers' expectations—in a good way—but they still were judged unfavorably for their success. It makes you wonder what in the world a kid has to do to shake off a bad reputation. Figure 5.2 shows the steps that must have taken place for the teachers' expectations to have affected their students' outcomes.

Refining the Research. Rosenthal and Jacobsen's (1968) report triggered a controversy, partly because their findings finally gave people someone whom they could blame for all the ills of education: It's the teacher's fault! If those darn elementary school teachers would only believe in their students a little bit more, then all the other sociological, motivational, and family-related problems in education would magically melt away. For example, if girls aren't doing as well as boys in middle school math classes, it must be because math teachers are simply encouraging boys and ignoring or discouraging girls. In addition, whenever there is an attention-getting finding from the world of research, you can count on the press to exaggerate its findings to sell more advertising.

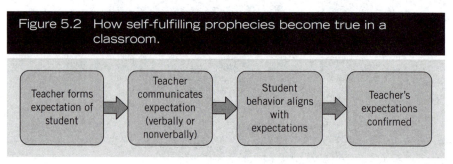

Figure 5.2   How self-fulfilling prophecies become true in a classroom.

Source: From Rosenthal and Jacobson (1968). Pygmalion in the Classroom. Irvington Publishers: New York, p. 75.

More important, chronically skeptical researchers scrutinized how the research was conducted and tried to replicate the findings—repeating an experiment is always a scientifically sound endeavor. Hundreds of studies testing the reality of self-fulfilling prophecies have been conducted since that first dramatic experiment. In 2005, Jussim and Harber published a review of what we have learned about self-fulfilling prophecies since 1968:

1. Self-fulfilling prophecies do occur in the classroom, but they are only one of many influences on student achievement.

2. The effect of a self-fulfilling prophecy declines over time.

3. Self-fulfilling prophecies can be especially influential on students who belong to groups that are already stigmatized (prelabeled in a negative way).

4. It is unclear whether self-fulfilling prophecies tend to do more harm than good. More research is needed.

5. Sometimes, what looks like a self-fulfilling prophecy is an accurate assessment made by a teacher.

In 2002, Rosenthal himself also reviewed the now sophisticated scientific literature that he had helped create almost 40 years earlier. By looking at the meta-analyses, Rosenthal confirmed that self-fulfilling prophecies can occur in classroom settings, but exactly how they play out is complicated. He identified four ways in which teachers unknowingly communicate their expectations to particular students:

1. *Emotional climate,* through nonverbal cues that create a warmer social-emotional environment

2. *Expectations of effort,* by teaching more material and more difficult material

3. *Increased opportunities,* by giving students more opportunities to respond, including more time to respond

4. *Differential feedback,* by giving certain students more individualized feedback that allows them to assess their own progress

Wouldn't it be nice to have a faster way to understanding? It has taken decades of research, professional experience, and reflection to arrive at our present understanding of how self-fulfilling prophecies work in the classroom (and beyond). And it all seems so obvious in hindsight. Self-fulfilling prophecies are only one of several powerful social psychological dynamics that skilled teachers are called upon to harness for the welfare of their students.

DISCUSSION QUESTIONS

1. Identify one teacher from your own life who had a positive prophecy about you and one who had a negative prophecy about you. Did each become a self-fulfilling prophecy? In other words, did you live up to those expectations or defy them? Explain your answer.

2. The research reviewed here provides evidence that teacher expectations can have at least some influence on student outcomes. However, the pattern in Figure 5.1 showed that the results were only significant for students in first and second grades. What are two variables that might explain why the pattern wasn't significant for older children? How could you design a study that tests your hypotheses?

3. Imagine that you are the parent of a 6-year-old child. Identify three specific expectations that you would try to have for your child that might become a positive self-fulfilling prophecy. Is this type of optimism setting your child up for success—or is it actually unethical manipulation of your child? Defend your answer, either way.

KEY TERMS

Halo effect 80   Meta-analysis 77   Self-fulfilling prophecy 76

5.4 The Rock in the Coffin: Managing Fear of Death

This case study introduces you to the diamond trade, attitude change, and terror management theory (TMT). We'll start with the last one first because you may not like it. We're not asking you to believe in TMT—it's controversial, even among social psychologists. But we are asking you to think about what you are really trying to buy when you purchase a lottery ticket, go into debt for a fancier car than you really need, donate money to a particular cause, or start drifting by the jewelry store to look at diamond rings.

Terror Management Theory

What if, after life, there is . . . nothing?

To people raised in a religious faith, the possibility that there is no heaven or hell can be disturbing, even threatening. Many people want to believe that after this life, it's not the end—we'll be reincarnated, survive as a ghost, enjoy a blissful eternity with other deceased loved ones . . . something. But even believers can't really, honestly, be *sure* of what will happen. And that's scary. Unfortunately, we also can't avoid thinking about our own mortality. Every time we attend a funeral, cry over a pet who has died, or even notice someone's gray hair, we are nudged by another reminder of our own eventual death.

What can we do about our inevitable demise? Nothing. That's the problem.

What can we do about our discomfort and fear? Lots of things. And that's where the fun begins, at least for those who look at the world through the lens of TMT (Becker, 1973; Solomon, Greenberg, & Pyszczynski, 1991).

This theory suggests that to distract ourselves from thoughts of death, we manage that existential terror by burying ourselves in work, going to Disney World, debating over politics, disappearing for hours into a video game, or dedicating our lives to a cause we decide is vital. We fill our lives with distracting minutiae that we convince ourselves are important. Occasionally, we're reminded of death by some circumstance—scientists call this **mortality salience**. When our mortality becomes salient, we have two common reactions: (1) we become more positive about our own culture, perspective, and **worldviews**, often by denigrating others, and (2) we enhance our own self-esteem by buying more luxury goods (Fransen, Fennis, Pruyn, & Das, 2008). TMT asserts that most of us, in one way or another, are searching for immortality—or at least reassuring symbols of immortality. And that's where the social psychology of advertising and attitude change come into the picture.

Secular Immortality

"Diamonds are forever."

The De Beers advertising campaign to sell diamonds promised an immortality that the company knew they could not deliver. But people want immortality in some form, so their advertising strategy worked. When Charles Moore (2011) studied the De Beers advertising campaign, he distinguished between the secular immortality promised by earthly symbols and the religious immortality promised by most religions. The De Beers advertising campaign constructed a mental bridge that allowed consumers to psychologically cross back and forth between secular and religious immortality. If you had one, then you felt connected to the other.

Enjoying wealth now is a not-very-subtle form of secular immortality, especially when it is supported by the promise of an eternal paradise in the future. Hirschman (1990) pointed out that some religions actually promote the idea "that material wealth reflects one's true worth or value as a person" (p. 31). It sounds like a belief that would be especially appealing if you financially had been "born on third base and thought you'd hit a triple." In other words, many wealthy people did nothing to earn their status—but it sure feels good to tell yourself that God intended you to be better off financially than other people. A more subtle version of secular immortality is "that one's affluence directly reflects contributions and productivity on behalf of society." Capitalism, of course, implies support for this belief. Hirschman asserts that displaying affluence has "long been identified as a central value in the American consumer culture" (p. 31).

A few select people and families, by their extreme wealth and generosity, have achieved secular immortality. Those great "cathedrals of learning" (your local library) in many towns and villages across the United States were the product of Andrew Carnegie's immense wealth and generosity. Those libraries have survived many generations and so has the Carnegie Foundation that continues to support several social causes. The Rockefeller Foundations, the Morgan Library, the Whitney Museum, and the Gates Foundation all have been designed to use their founders' immense wealth to extend individual influence well beyond their own mortality.

But where does that leave the rest of us who have not achieved fabulous wealth, fame, influence—or even infamy? Most of us will not be remembered with a national monument, a local statue, a plaque on a bench—we may be lucky to get a one-time mention in the local newspaper. How do the rest of us achieve immortality? The De Beers diamond advertising campaign gave the rest of us a way to buy immortality.

A Brief History of Diamonds

There is, writes James Twitchell (2000), a unique paradox about diamonds: They're worthless, but we treat them as valuable. "The very quality that makes [diamonds] so valuable," Twitchell wrote, "is precisely what must ultimately render them worthless."

> Not only do they last forever, but diamonds have almost no practical use. All you can do is grind them up and put them on drill bits. Unlike gold or silver, carbon allotropes aren't malleable or electrically conductive; diamonds just sit there and sparkle. If . . . laws of supply and demand were applied, every diamond dug out of the earth would diminish by so much the value of every still-existing diamond that preceded it. (pp. 90–91)

The first appearance of a diamond ring on the third finger of a beloved's left hand may have occurred in 1447. Archduke Maximilian of Austria was honoring an ancient Egyptian belief that a vein of love ran from the heart to the tip of that finger. So he placed a diamond ring on the finger of Mary of Burgundy to symbolize his love. The idea did not catch on with the common people, however, and the diamond trade remained an indulgence for royalty.

But then, in 1866, a 15-year-old boy named Erasmus Jacobs found a transparent rock on his father's farm in South Africa—and a huge deposit of diamonds. The De Beers Consolidated Mining Company was formed the next year and suddenly the world was flooded with diamonds. A rare, beautiful, and expensive rock once used to decorate royal crowns suddenly had become common—and cheap. It was a tough business proposition, and Twitchell (2000) indicates that the situation for diamond merchants did not improve after World War I.

> Other rocks, such as rubies, sapphires . . . were more romantic, more colorful, more exotic and erotic than diamonds. Worse still, vast new fields of diamonds were being discovered . . . diamonds were anything but rare, and hence lost much of the value they might have had. . . . Diamond suppliers were facing every producer's worst nightmare: increasing supply, decreasing demand. (p. 92)

The De Beers company needed a social psychological transformation that would turn pretty but useless rocks into something that people would be eager to buy but never to sell. So in 1938, they started a relationship with an advertising agency known for doing in-depth research before they created an advertising campaign: the N. W. Ayers agency. Twitchell (2000) describes how the N. W. Ayers agency dug into gender differences to manipulate the buying process of diamonds.

> Because men would be doing almost all the buying in America, a practical system had to be concocted that would calm them down and get them safely through the buy-hole. Hence the scientific-sounding voodoo about carat weight, color, cutting, clarity of the stones, *and* prices that invariably appeared in the bottom margin of the early ads. Women looked at the picture and read the body copy of the ad. Men were shown the small print over in the corner of the page. (p. 95)

But what should that ad copy say to the men looking at the fine print and the women leaning over their shoulders contemplating an engagement ring? One early ad simply read, "Is two months' salary too much for a diamond engagement ring?" Another ad shamelessly played on stereotypical emotions almost too drippy to be taken seriously:

> Each memory in turn is treasured in the lovely, lighted depths of her engagement diamond, to be an endless source of happy inspiration. For such a radiant role, her diamond need not be costly or of many carats, but it must be chosen with care.

But how could the ad agency transform a useless product into something that would be bought at a high price and never resold?

"Diamonds are forever."

With that famous slogan, the De Beers company had stopped selling diamonds. They were now selling immortality. Of course, there was a problem with all of this clever marketing: "Mortality cannot be revoked, even with great advertising" (Twitchell, 2000, p. 98). But if their advertising campaign worked, then some grieving spouse would tenderly place their diamond wedding ring in the coffin when a husband or wife passed away. It was one way to deal with the problem of oversupply—and it was surprisingly effective.

There was, and is, another problem far more important. De Beers has thrived despite bitter revelations about "blood diamonds," mined from the earth at the cost of amputated limbs—and murder of the most defiant. De Beers has tried to use its market dominance to limit the sale of these "blood diamonds" or "conflict diamonds" but is still widely criticized for its dominant role in the diamond industry for 150 years. Consumers in distant jewelry stores have no way of knowing whether a particular stone is a blood diamond (Global Witness, 2017).

Diamonds still have little intrinsic value—except for the value that consumers assign to it because their attitudes and behaviors have been changed through advertising to believe that "diamonds are forever."

DISCUSSION QUESTIONS

1. Terror management theory suggests that we distract ourselves from fears of death by becoming interested in relatively meaningless trifles, such as television shows or sports rivalries. Try to identify three things in your own life that might serve as evidence for their hypothesis. Does thinking about your interests from this perspective dampen your enthusiasm?

2. Watch a few short clips from the movie *Blood Diamond* and discuss whether it has changed your attitude toward buying diamonds for someone you love. On a broader level, do you support or not support companies that have politics or policies with which you agree or disagree? Do you boycott some companies and support others based on whether you agree with the way they do business?

3. Diamonds and other expensive, luxury items are one way for wealthy or privileged people to secure secular immortality or to feel that they have brought meaning to their lives. What can poor, struggling people with fewer consumer opportunities do instead? Which option seems like it might lead to greater, lasting happiness or a sense of satisfaction?

KEY TERMS

Mortality salience 83   Terror management theory 82   Worldview 83

Attitudes and Persuasion

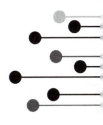

6.1 When Prophecy Fails: Prelude to the Theory of Cognitive Dissonance

This much seems clear: Jesus did not return in 1843 or in 1844.

The Millerites are a handy case study of **cognitive dissonance** because there is extensive documentation about William Miller, the Millerite movement, and the *increased* commitment of the believers after prophecy failed. However, the Millerites in the 1840s were not unique in miscalculating the return of Jesus. Jesus did not return as predicted by a prophet named Montanus in the second half of the second century. Jesus also failed to return in 1533 as predicted by the Anabaptists. In each case, most people in the movement left after the prophecies were proved wrong. What's psychologically intriguing is that after each nonevent, a significant number of followers became *more* committed to their beliefs after undeniable evidence that their belief system was wrong. Explaining increased commitment after prophecy *failed* was the puzzle of human reasoning that social psychologist Leon Festinger wanted to solve.

A Spiritual Quest

William Miller was born in 1782, a farm boy in upstate New York who was raised in a religious Christian home. An avid reader, Miller's trips to the local library slowly transformed his view of religion until he became the kind of deist described by F. D. Nichol (1944, see pp. 17–42) as "a halfway station on the way to atheism." Miller's newfound skepticism led him to mock his own previous beliefs. He "would caricature the tones of voice and the actions of the pious in the community, including among them his own clerical grandfather" (p. 7). When Miller converted to something, he went all the way.

Miller carried his deist skepticism into his service as an U.S. Army captain during the War of 1812. He happily substituted the joy of patriotism to the United States for the emotional comfort that religion previously had provided. But then the harsh realities of war dented his carefully constructed understanding of deism. As a soldier hardened by bitter realities in the Battle of Plattsburg, Miller could only credit a higher power for their victory: "The Supreme Being must have watched over the interests of this country in an especial manner" (Nichol, 1944, p. 8). His patriotism was merging with his religious beliefs.

At war's end, Miller appeared to settle down into a quiet life of raising his 10 children, farming, and being of service to his hometown in various positions. Yet Miller's "restless stirrings" and his spiritual questions remained unanswered. He could not stop himself from asking the big questions—and being frustrated by the lack of answers (Nichol, 1944):

> The heavens were as brass over my head, and the earth as iron under my feet. ETERNITY! *What was it? And death, why was it?* The more I reasoned, the further I was from demonstration. The more I thought, the more scattered were my conclusions. (p. 40)

Not long after that, Miller experienced a religious conversion. But he still asked himself, "How it can be proved that such a Being does exist?" He studied the Christian Bible intensely for over 2 years. He noticed specific days and times that promised to be the fulfillment of particular prophecies, especially in the Book of Daniel 8:14: "Unto two thousand and three hundred days; then shall the sanctuary be cleansed."

The Quest Becomes a Movement

The prophecy was clearly—to Miller and many others—about the second coming of Jesus, and Miller estimated that the prediction was first made around 457 B.C.E. The math worked out to estimate that the return of Jesus would probably occur sometime in 1843. The year of Miller's insight was 1818, and his calculations indicated that the world had only about 25 years to get ready. William Miller's revelation was a moment when reason and intuition appeared to join forces, and it was a thrilling experience (Nichol, 1944):

> Joy that filled my heart in view of the delightful prospect, nor of the ardent longings of my soul, for a participation in the joys of the redeemed. The Bible was to me a new book. It was indeed a feast of reason. (p. 12)

F. D. Nichol asserts that William Miller was never the money-seeking charlatan described in later newspaper reports. Instead of taking personal advantage of this revelation, Miller studied for another 5 years, carefully looking for flaws in his theory. Previously, he had not been able to find reasons to believe. Now he could not find reasons to doubt. Miller's inner contradictions between revelation and reason were resolving every time he opened his Bible and calculated the dates for the return of Jesus. It seemed inevitable; this devout soldier-farmer and untrained theologian began telling the world that Jesus was most likely to return sometime in 1843.

To Miller's surprise, this good news was not immediately received with corresponding joy. And so he waited and studied for another 6 years. One morning, he decided to bargain with God. He would not preach this good news unless, out of the blue, he received an invitation to preach. And that afternoon, there was a knock on his door asking him to deliver a sermon! That first sermon became a revival that lasted for a week; the revival became a movement that eventually turned into a branch of Protestantism called Seventh Day Adventists. The Millerites, as they had come to be called at the beginning, soon began publishing special newspapers announcing the advent of Christ.

Miller's studies had indicated a time interval of probabilities for Jesus' return that included dates from March 21, 1843, to March 21, 1844. But he also had calculated a few specific high-probability dates, one of which was April 23, 1843. When that day came—and went—the Millerites were of course disappointed. But they were not discouraged. Instead, like a child anticipating a gift, they became more excited after prophecy failed. There were major Millerite conferences in New York, Philadelphia, and Washington, DC. At its peak, there may have been as many as 200 "radiantly happy" ministers and another 500 lecturers preaching Miller's message about the Second Coming. The end really was near—and that holy event demanded that people get ready!

Joseph Bates, for example, had been a prisoner of war (the War of 1812) who became a sea captain. He had turned away from alcohol after witnessing the effects of rum on sailors, but he only converted to Christianity during a sea voyage after his wife placed a Bible in his trunk. Now he demanded that even his sailors never swear or drink. He also became an outspoken abolitionist against slavery. But when he embraced Millerism, his commitments to these other causes declined in the face of such profound urgency. To Bates, getting ready for the Second Coming meant settling all his debts, selling his home, and looking for new ways to be of service to the cause (see Nichol, 1944, pp. 193–218). His **attitude** toward the movement was positive, and his commitment was strong.

The Movement Demands Commitment

Joseph Bates was not alone in taking such drastic action. Some believers were so confident that the Second Coming would happen no later than the early months of 1844 "that they had not planted their crops" (Nichol, 1944, p. 90). And as specific dates came closer, it seemed hypocritical for believers to "go forward nonchalantly to all their routine labors." Believers unexpectedly found themselves in a mental dilemma that sorely tested their faith. If they did not sell their possessions and give to the poor, then they could be charged with hypocrisy—of not practicing what they preached. But if they did give up everything to prepare for Jesus, then they could be charged with fanaticism. It was probably a time of extreme **dual attitudes** for many of the Millerites.

Their dilemma was complicated by the word *if*. If Jesus did not come and they had given away all their possessions, then they would be impoverished, embarrassed, and labeled as gullible fanatics. For Millerites, there was trouble and mental dissonance in every direction except one: Jesus had to return within the time frame that William Miller had predicted (Nichol, 1944, pp. 250–253). There was, however, some confusion over whether the predictions were based on the Roman calendar or a Jewish calendar. So as the calendar unfolded and dates for the Second Coming came and went, there were always more reasons to believe, more ways to engage in **self-justification**. Days and weeks passed. But with no sign of Jesus having returned, the skeptics taunted the believers. "Wife didn't go up and leave you behind to burn, did she?"

But the believers kept right on believing, regardless of the growing evidence that their beliefs might be false. Among Millerites, with their admittedly uncertain dates, the excitement generated by disconfirming evidence only meant that the Second Coming was that much closer. The religious excitement became so intense that four states (Maine, New Hampshire, Vermont, and Massachusetts) began tracking the number of admissions to mental health asylums due to Religious Excitement (coded as RE in their reports) during the years 1842, 1843, and 1844. Across all four states, 6.5% of all admissions were coded exclusively as due to RE, and more than 22% involved RE (see Nichol, 1944, Appendix G, p. 513).

The unbelievers around them viewed Millerites as hopeless fanatics (see Nichol, 1944, pp. 240–263). The stereotypical Millerite was portrayed as emotionally disturbed or weak-minded. But a journalist from Philadelphia discovered that this was not accurate:

> There are to be found among the followers of Miller persons from almost every rank of society; from the educated professional man to the unlettered day laborer; and of women attached to the doctrines of the pretended prophet might be selected many whose presence would grace a fashionable drawing room. (p. 86)

Jesus, however, did not return on any of the high-probability dates in 1843. Nor did Jesus come back to Earth in the early months of 1844. There was, at last, only one last possible date remaining. Miller had continued his studies and on October 6, 1844, he wrote to a friend that

I see a glory. . . . Now, blessed be the name of the Lord, I see a beauty, a harmony, and an agreement in the scripture, for which I have long prayed, but did not see until today . . . I am almost home, Glory! Glory! Glory!!! (Nichol, 1944, p. 87)

The last possible date had to be October 22, 1844, about 6 months later than Miller had first calculated. By now the true believers were even more fervent in their faith. One shop window posted a sign declaring, "This shop is closed in honor of the King of kings, who will appear about the 20th of October. Get ready, friends, to crown Him Lord of all" (Nichol, 1944, p. 91). The editor of the Millerite newspaper *The Midnight Cry* wrote, "I intend, by the help of the Lord, to act as if there was no possibility of mistake . . . in less than one month the opening heavens would reveal my Saviour." The Millerites who gathered in their homes and churches on October 22 "were no longer believers in the 'advent near' but in the advent here." This was the day.

The Great Disappointment

To Leon Festinger and other social psychologists reviewing this peculiar case study many years later, the most interesting day was not October 22, 1844—it was October 23, 1844. How did the believers think, feel, and behave the day after prophecy failed? In a chapter titled "The Great Disappointment," Francis Nichol (1944) provided evidence of firsthand reactions (see pp. 94–99).

Joseph Bates (the sea captain): "The effect of this disappointment can be realized only by those who experienced it."

Hiram Edson: "Our fondest hopes and expectations were blasted and such a spirit of weeping came over us as I never experienced before . . . We wept and wept, till the day dawn. . . . Is there no God? Is all this but a cunningly devised fable?"

Luther Boutelle, a Millerite lecturer: "Everyone felt lonely . . . I found about 70 believers in a large house, living there and having meetings daily. They had put all their money in a milk pan, and when they paid for anything they took the money from the pan. All was common stock."

N. N. Whiting: "We were in some danger from the mob last Sabbath [October 20] at Franklin Hall [New York City]. The mayor, however, offered to put down the mob with strong hand if. . . ."

And from William Miller himself: "And the next day it seemed as though all the demons from the bottomless pit were let loose upon us." Nichol observed that

to suffer so keen a disappointment was exquisite pain in itself, but to that were added the jeers and ridicule of scoffers. . . . They know not how to answer the taunting question, "why didn't you go up?"

The leaders of the Millerite movement had to figure out how to support the believers who had sold all their possessions. They also had to respond to a long series of juicy rumors against the treasurer of the Millerite movement. Many left the faith. But many others still believed—they just didn't know exactly *what* they now believed. Gradually, a theology evolved that explained everything: The great disappointment had been "a test to discover those who really loved the Lord and His appearing . . . God overruled to make this disappointing experience serve a divine purpose" (Nichol, 1944, p. 277). Familiar scriptures came alive as examples of similar tests: Jonah preaching to Nineveh and Abraham offering his son on an altar. They soon began to see the wisdom of God in other ways.

When one prophecy after another had failed to come true, the effect on believers was to *increase* their enthusiasm, to *strengthen* their faith, and to become *more* devout in their private lives. Even after the Great Disappointment on October 22, 1844, there were agonizing efforts to justify what God had seemingly done—or not done—and to find some way to justify their own behavior and beliefs. This lasted until about 2 years later. Nichol (1944) concluded that there was a point beyond which even the strongest faith could not struggle against reality. "The scorching sun of disappointment beat down, and the burning winds of ridicule swept in from every side" (p. 290).

The Social Psychologists Take Note

A century later, social psychologist Leon Festinger and colleagues Henry Riecken and Stanley Schachter (1956/2008, pp. 13–25) reported the case study of the Millerites as just one of many examples of failed messianic movements that had the odd effect of increasing followers' faith. Their description of the Millerites in their book *When Prophecy Fails* is impressive historical scholarship in its own right and led to the following interpretation:

> Although there is a limit beyond which belief will not withstand
> disconfirmation, it is clear that the introduction of contrary evidence
> can serve to increase the conviction and enthusiasm of a believer.

The immediate effect of failed prophecy was that it strengthened the beliefs of the "true believers"—at least temporarily. For his part, William Miller acknowledged that he had made a mistake. (The world probably would have noticed if Jesus had returned.) But his admissions were not about a misplaced faith; they were about his own calculations. When Miller died in 1849, he was still not discouraged by disconfirmations. Despite poor eyesight, his last unfinished letter was in large and shaky handwriting: "We shall soon see Him for whom we have looked and waited."

DISCUSSION QUESTIONS

1. Leon Festinger and his colleagues used both historical case studies and controlled experiments to test for and explore the theory of cognitive dissonance. What are the strengths and weaknesses of case studies and experiments for the development of psychological theory? Which do you find more persuasive?

2. What current, modern-day examples can you identify of times when people cling to their beliefs, even when they are presented with evidence that they are wrong? Do these examples also seem to fit the theory of cognitive dissonance?

3. Can you identify any times in your own life when you have chosen to ignore evidence that was uncomfortable or went against what you preferred to believe? What eventually led you to see things from a more objective perspective?

4. Search online for people who claim or are claimed by others to be the Messiah. Try to estimate how many people have achieved notoriety for claiming to be or proclaimed as the Messiah. How could you organize the list to make more sense of it? How do we know these individuals are not the Messiah?

KEY TERMS

Attitude 89
Cognitive dissonance 87

Model of dual attitudes 90

Self-justification 90

6.2 When Prophecy Fails: Alien Apocalypse

The story of the flying saucer that never came is so strange that it creates a problem. We can tell ourselves, "I would never believe such nonsense."

The account of this case is outlined in the same book that references the Millerite movement (Case 6.1): *When Prophecy Fails* by Festinger et al. (1956/2008). The three researchers (and some paid observers) became **participant-observers** in an end-of-the-world group led by a suburban housewife identified in their narrative as Mrs. Marian Keech. Her real name, how she finished her life, and the original news articles described in *When Prophecy Fails* were reported by *Chicago Magazine* in 2011 and are of some minor interest. But the more important findings were based on this case study test of Festinger's new theory of **cognitive dissonance**— and for that, the real identities of the participants do not matter. The research team only wanted to observe and record how people behaved when their clearly stated public beliefs clashed with reality.

Mrs. Marian Keech Becomes a Prophet

Mrs. Marian Keech was a suburban housewife in the 1950s. Like many of us, she always was reaching out for something more while struggling to define what that something might be. "I have always wanted to be of service to mankind," she said (Festinger et al., 1956/2008, p. 35). For 15 years, Keech explored various psychic phenomena and searched her own consciousness for signs of a deeper life. And then early one morning,

> I had the feeling that someone was trying to get my attention. . . . My hand began to write in another handwriting . . . somebody else was using my hand, and I said: "Will you identify yourself?" And they did. (p. 33)

Her first "automatic writings" were messages from her dead father. They weren't especially interesting—he was concerned mostly with his garden. But communication had been established! Our 21st-century view obscures what it was like to live in the United States in the 1950s. The established meanings of life had been thoroughly shaken by a global war. The barriers to space exploration were being penetrated. The atomic bomb made it plausible to believe in the end of all human existence. There was relative openness to the idea of flying saucers from outer space and other mysterious phenomena. Keech's communications, full of authoritative but meaningless terms, were still crazy . . . but they were slightly more plausible then compared to today. And they might have been the **self-affirmation** that she needed to convince herself that she was interesting and important.

What Was Being Prophesied?

Keech's messages from "the other side" gradually became more frequent, descriptive, and "sciency" in their language. For example, her automatic handwriting revealed that

> the waves of ether have become tactable by the bombs your scientists have been exploding. This works like an accordion. . . . We have been trying to get through for many of your years, with alcetopes and the earling timer. (p. 37)

In Keech's strange spirit world, there were spirit beings, new planets, "sunspots," "magnetism," and "vibratory impulses." There were lots of made-up words and vaguely familiar concepts. "Avagada" meant spaceship, "the thermin" supposedly "records our thoughts, actions," in the "Losolo," a type of school. Her messages often sounded a note of hope for a world adjusting to the possibility of mass destruction. Keech had been reaching out for something more—and she had found something as large as her imagination could stretch.

The most thrilling yet disturbing news came from a spirit being named from Sananda. It was an implied promise to Keech and a select few of her followers that sounded strangely like a dinner reservation:

> We are trying to make arrangements for a party of six from Westinghouse to visit our territory. Is that a surprise to you? There is one in Syracuse, New York, one in Schenectady, New York, one in Rockford, Illinois, one in California. (p. 45)

They were coming in peace, of course, but there was also a coming judgment that had to be accepted. The messages started coming sometimes as many as 10 times a day. Who could keep up? Keech's own husband was not a believer. Instead, he "simply went about his ordinary duties . . . and did not allow the unusual events in his home to disturb in the slightest his daily routine" (p. 38). But it was pure excitement to the small group of believers who had been gathering around Keech. On the morning of July 23, Keech's busy pencil wrote,

> The cast of light you see in the southern sky is . . . a turning, spinning motion of the craft of the tola [spaceship] which is to land upon the planet . . . at Lyons field. (p. 47)

"They" were coming to their local airfield! But on the great day . . . the flying saucer did not arrive. Keech reported her own tortured self-assessment, "I am more or less responsible if I have misled anyone today." The messages from outer space now came at a furious pace. Keech sometimes wrote for 14 hours per day. The authors of *When Prophecy Fails* encouraged readers to not conclude that "Mrs. Keech's pencil is merely the unique raving of an isolated madwoman"; instead, her ideas were well adapted to "our contemporary, anxious age" (p. 54).

On August 2, she received a message warning of an impending disaster: A great flood was coming. Her most devoted follower was a physician, Dr. Armstrong. He produced 50 copies of a seven-page "Open Letter to American Editors and Publishers" that warned of the coming catastrophe. A copy released in October added in handwriting, "Date of evacuation Dec. 20." Armstrong had made a testable prediction—and that's what got the social psychologists excited.

Who Responded to the Prophecies?

The most important followers of Marian Keech were Thomas and Daisy Armstrong. They and their three children had been medical missionaries in Egypt but returned to the United States at the end of World War II. Their idealistic hopes for a life of service were shattered, in part by Daisy Armstrong's nervous breakdowns. They, too, were seeking something more. Dr. Thomas Armstrong worked at the local college's student health services. The total number of believers was about 12 people, but their mailing list included 150 to 250 names.

However, they were not very interested in converting others. The social psychologists sent a male sociology student who presented himself as a lost soul ripe for recruiting. Dr. Armstrong never tried and never even mentioned Keech by name. However, a second attempt by a female sociology student was more successful. She contacted Armstrong, who responded enthusiastically, interpreted a (fictitious) dream the student had prepared, and "showered her with information about flying saucers" (p. 72).

One believer, Bob, was an Army veteran and an older college student. He sold off some valuable property to settle his personal debts and then spent Thanksgiving saying goodbye to family and friends. Kitty O'Donnell, a female friend of Bob's, was far more skeptical, apparently more interested in Bob than flying saucers. A single mother, O'Donnell quit her job and moved to an apartment closer to the group (and to Bob). She soon became one of the most committed members. She was so worried that her 3-year-old son might be taken up in a flying saucer without her that she gave him his Christmas presents 3 weeks early. She said, "I have to believe that the flood is coming on the 21st because I've spent nearly all my money. I quit my job, I quit computer school, and my apartment costs me $100 a month. I have to believe" (p. 80).

The Armstrongs' college-aged daughter, Cleo, had endured teasing at school and was worried about the new problems she would face if the flood did not come: Her father would be humiliated and lose his job, and she would have to quit college. Yet she also began buying lots of expensive clothes "because she wanted to enjoy wearing pretty things while she could, before the flood came" (p. 76). Cleo was right to be worried. Dr. Armstrong was asked to resign from the college health service because he had upset so many students.

Don't stereotype the believers in Keech as weak-minded, poorly educated people with few alternatives. Included in her group (at various points in time) were a physician, a PhD in the natural sciences, and others with varying degrees of education. Many were in college while attending meetings with Keech and Dr. Armstrong. Neither education nor mental capability helps us understand the appeal of groups with such extreme beliefs.

What Do You Do Just Before the End of the World?

None of the 50 news outlets that received Armstrong's seven-page news release/warning saw fit to publish it or even mention it. Armstrong tried again with a single-page dramatic summary that led to some light publicity. But the news of impending destruction was mostly ignored.

The month before the end of the world was full of emotional ups and downs—including a strange spiritual power struggle between Keech and a new member. Bertha Blatsky was a former beautician and follower of scientology who also began to speak authoritatively from the spirit world. Her communications were not through automatic writing but by voice—and she claimed to be the voice of "the Creator." This effectively reduced Keech to a position of minor authority and there were tense power skirmishes.

Blatsky belittled the "thee" and "thou" pseudo-biblical speech used in Keech's writings. Blatsky determined what lights would be turned on, where Keech could sit, who could reject someone wanting to join them, and who could call for such meetings in the first place. For the faithful, their experience of life became more petty as they approached the end of the world.

Cleo Armstrong endured another emotional roller coaster when reporters besieged her with questions about why her father had been dismissed and what she believed. Cleo quickly discovered the politician's trick of "no comment" and survived an ordeal that was sure to make her social life more difficult. She would be fine as long as the world ended from a flood within the next few days. But if it didn't, then she had a lot of explaining to do even as she tried to defend her father's honor.

Yet the faithful endured even as life became more exhausting, confusing, petty, and awkward. The true believers persevered, but like the Millerites, some of the believers abandoned their faith at the first sign of inconsistency; other believers hung on "just in case." A few, pure believers would never give up. Perhaps they had reached the point of no return in terms of their self-justification and self-affirmation.

The Last Hours

A number of pranksters had started ringing the Keechs' doorbell, calling them, and generally harassing them. There had been headlines about Armstrong's dismissal—and the bad press increased. It was actually getting crowded in Keech's home, and a television truck was parked outside. There were also last-minute instructions from Sananda. They were to remove all metal from their clothing. The flying saucer was on its way! One of the observers reported to Festinger, Reicken, and Schacter that

> Edna took me aside and said, "How about your brassiere? It has metal
> clasps, doesn't it?" I went back in the house and took my brassiere
> off. The only metal on me was the fillings in my teeth and I was afraid
> someone would mention those. (p. 145)

Their reports of the last 14 hours until midnight sound like a group that had arrived at the airport early to leave for a long-postponed vacation. There were 15 people gathered in Keech's living room as the final hour approached. Calm, happy, excited people. There were many last-minute instructions and Keech (writing on behalf of Sananda) and Blatsky (speaking on behalf of the Creator) carefully checked one another's messages for independent verification. The participant-observers, the social psychologists, summarized the orders:

> Precisely at midnight a spaceman would come to the door and escort
> them to the place where the saucer [tola] was parked. Everyone was
> instructed to be perfectly silent while en route to the saucer. When their
> escort knocked on the door at midnight, Thomas Armstrong was to act
> as the sentry and ask the caller: "What is your question?" (p. 160)

The group carefully rehearsed an elaborate series of questions and answers, like coded communications and passwords in a spy novel. They were to leave all identifying information behind. The secret books of Keech's messages were carefully packed in a large shopping bag for transportation. It was important to preserve, for the future, the history of this momentous event. At 11:15 p.m., Keech received a message ordering everyone to put on their coats and be prepared. One believer remembered at the last moment that his shoes had metal toecaps; they agreed that he should step out of them at the last moment before entering the spaceship.

> At about 11:35, one of the authors reported that he had not removed
> the zipper from his trousers. This produced a near panic reaction. He
> was rushed into the bedroom where Dr. Armstrong, his hands trembling
> and his eyes darting to the clock every few seconds, slashed out the
> zipper with a razor blade and wrenched its clasp free with wire-cutters.
> By the time the operation was complete it was 11:50, too late to do
> more than sew up the rent with a few rough stitches. (p. 161)

And then they had nothing to do for 10 long minutes. Midnight finally came . . . and went. It was 12:05 and no knock on the door, no spaceman, and no flying saucer. But there were two clocks in Keech's living room and they did not tell the same time. The slower clock on the mantel must tell the right time. That clock began to chime midnight . . . and once again nothing happened.

And nothing continued to happen.

After 5 more minutes, the voice of the Creator (Blatsky) assured them that there had been a slight delay. The phone rang from time to time with reporters inquiring whether they were still there. "No comment," was the standard reply.

They remained sitting, and then, at 12:30, they were startled by a knock on the door. Armstrong rushed to the door as everyone reminded him of the proper questions and answers. But he returned disappointed. The callers were just some boys, he reported, just some ordinary boys, not the man they all were waiting for.

They all had some explaining to do . . . to one another, and most of all to themselves.

DISCUSSION QUESTIONS

1. What do you think the members of the group did next—over the next hour, week, and years? What does cognitive dissonance theory predict about how they will react to the continued disconfirmation of their previous beliefs?

2. What specific explanations would keep the group together and energize them to become even more committed to their beliefs? Later, after the case study timeline described here, Keech did receive another message from Sananda, and it brought them tremendous joy. What do you think it was?

3. Were the social psychologists behaving ethically when they became participant-observers without telling Keech and the others why they were there?

4. This case study claims that "neither education nor mental capability helps us understand the appeal of groups with such extreme beliefs." If this is true, what variable could be used to predict interest and commitment to groups such as the one described here? What kinds of people will be most likely to join cult-like fellowships?

KEY TERMS

Cognitive dissonance 93   Participant-observer 93   Self-affirmation 94

6.3 Where Have All the Addicts Gone? Three Predictors Are Better Than One

By 1969, the U.S. Army finally had become concerned about drug use among American soldiers in Vietnam. It was about time. It was an open secret that many U.S. soldiers in Vietnam were using what are now called "recreational" drugs. But even that is a relatively polite term for what was happening among these men and women overseas. This was a serious, widespread drug problem.

A Collection of Crises

So many returning veterans from the war in Vietnam had become heavy drug users that their adjustment back into civilian society was bound to be difficult. In addition, many soldiers' readjustment challenges were aggravated with a confusing psychological disorder that, at the time, was often viewed as a personal weakness: posttraumatic stress disorder (PTSD). Along with barely acknowledged PTSD, the soldiers were returning home to a public that was often unsympathetic, crudely accusing soldiers of being murderers rather than patriotic warriors. So it is not a surprise that drug use was heavy both overseas and when soldiers returned home.

But the Army's concerns shifted into anxiety following the release of a formal study conducted by the Department of Defense (see Robins, 1993). What it found was more disturbing than it had predicted. About 45% of the Army's enlisted men had tried narcotics, 34% had tried heroin, and 38% had tried opium (and some had tried both). Over 90% had used alcohol and almost 80% had used marijuana. Not every member of the Army was stoned at the same time. However, a significant proportion of the American Army in Vietnam was stoned much of the time.

The DoD's research also indicated that soldiers' drug use was much more than an occasional pot party to relieve stress. The DoD study found that one out of every five soldiers had felt strung out or addicted to narcotics. Their report asserted that they had "used narcotics heavily for a considerable time and suffered the classic symptoms of withdrawal for at least several days" (p. 1044). You can see why the polite term of "recreational" drug use doesn't fit the experience of these young, returning soldiers who had been risking their lives fighting an unpopular war.

The news got worse when the Army realized what kind of soldiers it was sending back home. One in 10 of the men returning to the United States were "so addicted they could not stop their use when warned that they would be screened" (Robins, 1993, p. 1044). When you know that you are going to be caught and still can't stop using . . . well, that's a serious problem. And for the waiting families, that meant that each month, approximately 1,400 soldiers were coming back to the challenge of readjusting to life in the United States.

Coming Home

It is no wonder so many soldiers were having adjustment problems when they returned home. Using narcotics had become a social norm among the soldiers serving in Vietnam. But it wasn't just the extent of drug use in Vietnam that surprised the DoD as it looked at the results of this now classic study (Blomqvist, 2007). There were three surprises in the data.

First, the DoD indicated that it was surprised that so many soldiers were addicted in the first place. It was surprised, perhaps, at the proportion of soldiers using narcotics but not at the general reality of drug use. Drug use was not hidden. Second, the DoD was surprised to discover that the so-called gateway drugs (alcohol and marijuana) were *not* steppingstones into harder drugs (opium and heroin). The soldiers didn't need to be seduced into addiction; they went directly to the hard stuff. Third, given those high numbers and the level of use, the DoD was surprised that relatively few returning veterans relapsed into narcotic use when they got home: 5% after 1 year and 12% after 3 years. Robins (1993) reported that their post-Vietnam "addiction had usually been very brief." In addition, "It was not treatment that explained this remarkable rate of recovery. Only a third of the men addicted in Vietnam received even simple detoxification . . . and only a tiny percentage . . . went into drug abuse treatment after return—less than 2%" (p. 1045).

Of course, a 12% addiction rate means that about 168 of the 1,400 addicted soldiers returning home *every month* (or about 2,000 soldiers per year) were still using hard narcotics 3 years after their planes touched down on American soil. That's definitely a serious problem. But the problem of addicted soldiers was far less severe than the DoD had feared. Had the soldiers' favorable **attitudes** toward narcotic use magically changed when they got on the airplane home?

The Theory of Planned Behavior

In the history of social psychology, there was a long period when one particular concept seemed to be the key to explain social behavior: attitudes. Attitudes were thought to predict behavior—and it made intuitive sense. Attitudes were the product of beliefs and emotions, and we expected that people would behave in ways that were consistent with their beliefs and emotions. That was the theory; the reality was something different.

When researchers compared what people said they believed with how they actually behaved, there was a persistent discrepancy. Beliefs did not correspond with behavior, so the real-world evidence did not support the importance of attitudes. Many addicted veterans, for example, returned home with the same positive attitude toward narcotics they had in Vietnam. Yet many more veterans than the DoD anticipated were able to shrug off their addiction. The Army was able to breathe a small, partial sigh of relief. Drug abuse was only one of the many problems confronting the Army at that time.

Attitudes turned out to be a poor predictor of behavior. It took a long time for social psychologists to figure out why, but eventually a better explanation emerged from the data. The **theory of planned behavior** (see Ajzen & Fishbein, 1977; Fishbein & Ajzen, 2010) clarified that there were three roughly equal predictors of how people intended to behave—and those intentions predicted how people actually behaved. Figure 6.1 portrays that attitudes were just one of three factors or major influences on their **behavioral intentions** and subsequent behavior.

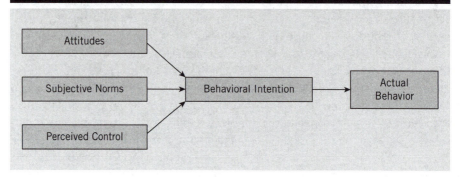

Figure 6.1 Three factors predict our intentions and, thus, our behaviors.

Attitudes

Subjective Norms → Behavioral Intention → Actual Behavior

Perceived Control

Perceived Control. In Vietnam, the cost of addiction to a pure version of opium or heroin was only about $6.00 per day. For the American soldiers serving there, getting stoned was easy, cheap, and convenient. They hardly had to do anything to access narcotics, and it was always within their budget; **perceived control** was high. After soldiers returned home, they could still find ways to buy their drugs— but now it was less convenient. Yes, it was a period of widespread drug use in the United States, but it still required more effort to get their drugs than it had in Vietnam. Perceived control went way down. The addicted veterans would have to work harder to find a ready supplier of what were now more expensive drugs.

Subjective Norms. The social norms in Vietnam during the war encouraged use of narcotics—the experience of soldiers was that "everyone was doing it." It is difficult to say no to any behavior when it has become a common, everyday practice. Moreover, it wasn't just the lower-ranking soldiers. A significant proportion of the Army leadership, from sergeants through captains, were also using narcotics. Getting high had become a pervasive social norm among U.S. soldiers. But that all changed when the soldiers got home—even during the infamous 1960s and early 1970s. The returning veterans were no longer surrounded by people using narcotics every day.

Attitudes. The soldiers' attitudes toward narcotic use probably didn't change very much when they came home. Opium still provided a welcome escape; heroin still felt good; the soldiers' bodies were accustomed to having the drugs. Attitudes probably played a minor role in the relatively low rate of drug abuse among returning Vietnam veterans. However, narcotics were no longer cheap, convenient, or as popular, so many addicted soldiers stopped using. Convenience—or perceived control—and subjective norms appeared to be far more powerful than attitudes when it came to predicting drug use.

The case study about the DoD's classic report of drug use demonstrated one of those hard-to-learn insights from psychology: what is obvious is not necessarily true—and what is true is not necessarily obvious (see LeDoux, 1998). It had seemed obvious that attitudes would predict behavior—but it wasn't true. What was true was that attitudes were just one of three predictors—and that wasn't obvious. The combination of attitudes, perceived control, and subjective norms was a much more precise predictor of what people intended to do—and those intentions were an even better predictor of how people actually behaved. Attitudes about race prejudice, politics, drug use, and everything else were only part of the answer to why people behaved in a particular way. Attitudes are still important. But they aren't quite as important to social psychology—or to human behavior—as was once believed.

DISCUSSION QUESTIONS

1. In this case study, there was some evidence that subjective norms and perceived control became more important behavioral predictors than attitudes were. Can you think of examples when attitudes would be the most important predictor? Why are attitudes more important in those cases?

2. One attitude that mattered in this case was soldiers' attitudes toward drug use. However, other attitudes might have been at play, such as the attitude of being a good family member once home, an attitude about being an "addict," and so on. Describe three additional attitudes not already identified

   that may have been involved in the soldiers' drug usage after returning home.

3. Identify a behavior in your own life that is particularly influenced by each of the three variables in the theory of planned behavior: perceived control, subjective norms, and attitudes. Has your behavior changed over time, as these three variables fluctuate?

4. How could an addictions counselor use the theory of planned behavior to help a client become less addicted to drugs over several sessions? What other therapeutic uses can you see for the theory of planned behavior?

KEY TERMS

Attitudes 101

Behavioral intention 101

Perceived control 102

Subjective norms 102

Theory of planned
    behavior 101

Social Influence

7.1 Mods and Rockers: A Moral Panic

"It's when people go crazy over something that never happened."

This informal definition of a **moral panic** was suggested by a student; it is only slightly less precise than the one based on Charles Krinsky's (2013) edited volume about moral panics: episodes of extreme anxiety about imagined morally reprehensible behavior by a specific group. Goode and Ben-Yehuda (2009) offered a similar definition: periods of exaggerated concern over a perceived threat that results in classifying (and targeting) a particular group as social deviants. Moral panics are one example of **social contagion**, when an idea spreads through a group of people—similar to a contagious disease. Such imaginings come easily to humans with our densely wired brains and dual thinking systems. It is easy to work ourselves up into a state of moral panic over something that never existed until we imagined it into existence.

In this case study, you will read about the kind of moral panic that was fueled by economic anxiety and maintained by fear. The end of that process was a prejudice that became a national embarrassment.

A Short History of Moral Panics

The concept of moral panic may have begun with the famous philosopher Friedrich Nietzsche's (1887/1996) notion of "ressentiment," a profound hostility displaced onto a scapegoat. But moral panics also include elements of Le Bon's (1896) general description of contagious crowd behavior. Moral panics are common across cultures and probably express some ancient tribal evolutionary impulse. Daniel Grey (2013) traced the course of one English moral panic that lasted from 1875 through 1914: the belief that infant life insurance policies had created an incentive that led many families to starve and neglect their children to collect the insurance money.

A mass media component seems to be necessary for a moral panic—it provides a communication network that allows a contagious idea to spread the emotional infection of fear. In this case, the fear that poor people were killing their children for insurance money was expressed repeatedly in newspapers and medical journals. The panic produced a new society called the Prevention of Cruelty to Children, made up of people who must have seen themselves playing a heroic role on behalf of innocent children. The society reported, contrary to the available data, that cases of lethal child abuse were endemic in the United Kingdom. The panic peaked in the 1880s but endured for almost 40 years. It was already in decline by 1914 when World War I suddenly gave the British public something far bigger—and more real—to fear.

Psychologists have referred to events like moral panics with slightly different terms: *mass hysteria, mass psychosis, mass panic,* and *social contagion.* The term *moral panic* comes from sociology; *mass hysteria* and *mass psychosis* come from psychodynamic psychology; *mass panic* and *social contagion* are closer to social psychology. The most precise term depends, in part, on which theoretical lens you happen to be looking through as you assess each situation. The idea doesn't seem to be going away and, as suggested by Figure 7.1, appears to be increasing.

Best (2013) reported that the term *moral panic* originated with British sociologists. The phrase and concept were slow to catch on until the second edition of Cohen's (1973/2002) case study, titled *Folk Devils and Moral Panics: The Creation of the Mods and Rockers*. Figure 7.1 indicates that, since the 1970s, many more researchers within psychology are referring to the construct of moral panic, roughly in parallel to the growth of the PsycINFO database. A partial list of specific topics

Figure 7.1 Numbers reflect the amount of entries in PsycINFO that include keywords and terms such as *mass hysteria* or *social contagion*.

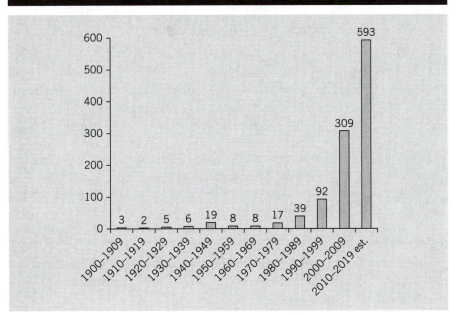

viewed through the lens of moral panics in the PsycINFO database includes (in alphabetical order) AIDS, ageism, asylum seekers, clergy sexual abuse, drugs in the workplace, enthusiasm for war, fetal alcohol syndrome, football hooliganism, gangs, horse maiming, Internet cyberporn, Muslim converts in prison, obesity, paint sniffing, plagiarism, police corruption, Ritalin use, runaway youth, Satanic rituals, and "wilding" (random youth violence).

Best (2013) also pointed out that the concept of moral panic became less precise as it gained popularity. Some researchers, for example, emphasize that a moral panic occurs when "the scale of response is disproportionately greater than the [perceived] scale of the problem" (Waddington, 1986, p. 245)—very close to the informal definition we offered at the beginning of this case: people going crazy over something that never happened. Others emphasize the panicky reaction to the perceived problem.

The term *moral panic* first entered the sociology community in 1971 when Jock Young described how a moral panic produced a self-fulfilling prophecy. In that moral panic, the public's fear of addictive drug use led to the creation of police drug squads. Those drug squads searched for and found more drug use and made more arrests. Those arrests became evidence that the original source of fear was justified and that all those arrests were justified (Young, 1971). Very little had changed in terms of overall drug use, but the moral panic helped produce a self-fulfilling prophecy. A self-fulfilling prophecy is easy to understand intellectually and after the fact. But it seems to be difficult to recognize when it is happening to you.

The First Case Study of a Moral Panic

The initiating description of a moral panic was Stanley Cohen's case study of a 1964 event in Clacton, an English resort town. Cohen's observations used this case study to suggest what other moral panics have in common (see Cohen, 1973/2002, pp. 16–25). That case study was instrumental at identifying features of a case study and arriving at a definition broad enough to apply to other events.

The Clacton moral panic probably began out of economic frustration. Clacton shopkeepers were annoyed that the coldest Easter in 80 years had provided them with little business on a major bank holiday. Some merchants refused to serve the bored youth who, when not annoying shopkeepers, were roaring up and down the street on their scooters (the Mods) and motorcycles (the Rockers). The two groups were then only loosely identified to the British public by their clothing and transportation preferences. However, in Clacton, a rock-throwing incident between the two groups broke a few windows and overwhelmed a modest police force.

There were 97 arrests, but the event was far less dramatic than was portrayed by the media. For example, property damage was estimated at only 513 British pounds, a modest amount even after accounting for inflation. But the *Daily Mirror* (Hughes, 1964) printed a large, bold print, provocative headline, "'WILD ONES' INVADE SEASIDE—97 ARRESTS." The first two sentences referring to the Wild Ones suggested that "wild ones" was the name of an identifiable group that posed a serious social threat: "The Wild Ones invaded a seaside town yesterday—1000 fighting, drinking, roaring, rampaging teenagers on scooters and motor-cycles. By last night, after a day of riots and battles with the police, ninety-seven of them had been arrested" (p. 1).

The role of the media is important to energizing a moral panic, and in Clacton, only 10 of those arrests were for violent offenses. What the news called "an orgy of destruction" included stealing a drink from a vending machine and fraudulently obtaining credit—to buy an ice cream. The news media also reported that, "all the dance halls near the seafront were smashed." That was technically true because Clacton had only one dance hall and some of its windows were broken (see Thompson, 1998, pp. 32–34). There were many other exaggerations that made for exciting, fear-promoting, but inaccurate news.

Probably as a result of this publicity and a bit of a **herd mentality**, there were three similar incidents at resorts over the next holiday, but they each produced fewer arrests and lower estimates of property damage. In other words, the actual problem was declining at the same time that the public panic was increasing, fed by a media frenzy. The rising panic eventually produced a resolution in the House of Commons that led to specific legislation. The resolution began with, "In light of the deplorable and continual increase in juvenile delinquency" and ended with pleas that young hooligans be subject to "such financial and physical punishment as will provide an effective deterrent" (Cohen, 1973/2002, p. 151).

Fear enables moral panics to take on a life of their own that is unrelated to reality. In the Clacton case, the British minister sponsoring the legislation acknowledged that "some of the reports of what happened at Clacton over the Easter weekend were greatly exaggerated" (Cohen, 1973/2002, p. 153). But by that time, the belief in what Cohen calls "folk devils" had settled in the public's imagination. At the beginning of the 1960s, Mods and Rockers were barely identifiable groups that distinguished themselves by their dress and lifestyle. Five years later, their actions were described in the press as without parallel in English history. Another 5 years later, the battles between the Mods and the Rockers were an all but forgotten footnote to England's cultural story.

Cohen's (1973/2002) case study identified four key elements of a moral panic: (1) The *mass media* prime the public for panic by defining social deviance and identifying specific individuals as "folk devils"; (2) *moral entrepreneurs* are individuals and groups that conduct an exaggerated but effective fear campaign to eradicate the moral threat; (3) the *control culture* calls on the institutions of government, such as the police and the court systems, to sensitize and, if necessary, prosecute the social deviants; and (4) *public opinion* shaped by vivid media imagery reduces the public's capacity for skepticism and critical thinking. A frequent outcome of a moral panic is a change in the law or how the law is enforced.

Critcher (2008; see Table 7.1) reviewed and summarized the many modifications to Cohen's initial description of a moral panic. That review makes it easier for both citizens and political leaders to ask critical questions *before* we start sending people to jail. For example, looking at events through the lens of moral panic encourages us to ask whether (a) stories (about youth violence, witchcraft, child sexual abuse, or parents killing their own children for insurance money) are being exaggerated or distorted, (b) the media have been instrumental in communicating a sense of moral panic, and (c) the panic is justified.

Table 7.1   Common Features of a Moral Panic
The mass media focus attention on a scapegoat.
Moral entrepreneurs posture as heroes resisting evil to protect the innocent.
A control culture creates ways to violate others' rights.
Public opinion turns against a particular group.
Those accused of evil can receive less punishment by "naming names."
People express unjustified certainty and overconfidence in their opinions.
Self-righteous statements exalt one group over another.
Panic leads to an official change in law or status.
A vulnerable group is targeted.
Exaggerated fears are publicized; contradicting evidence is ignored.
Actions are taken with a general disregard for evidence.
There is only superficial contact between the dominant and minority groups.
Legitimate anxieties are exaggerated.
A wide variety of social problems are blamed on a specific group (scapegoating).
Public opinion supports suppressing a targeted group to make problems go away.
The rule of law is weakened, changed, or reinterpreted to justify injustice.
Stereotyping of particular groups is accepted as fact.
Prejudice turns into overt discrimination against the targeted group.

Source: Critcher, C. (2008). Moral panic analysis: Past, present and future. *Sociology Compass, 2*(4), 1127–1144.

DISCUSSION QUESTIONS

1. Journalists are supposed to report accurate facts. However, newspapers and magazines are for-profit businesses, and more copies sell when facts are exaggerated. How do journalists and reporters deal with this conflict of interest, from a psychological perspective?

2. According to Cohen (1973/2002), one element of a moral panic is the public's loss of a capacity for skepticism and critical thinking. What psychological terms or theories you've learned about in earlier chapters of this book are relevant to this process? Explain your answer.

3. What are two examples of moral panics (in your opinion) in current events? What makes these examples of a moral panic? Why are moral panics more difficult to recognize when they are happening?

4. Consider Critcher's (2008) list of common elements in moral panics. Which three elements do you think are most central to this phenomenon, and why?

KEY TERMS

Herd mentality 107

Moral panic 104

Social contagion 104

7.2 More Than Obedience: Disturbing New Data From the Shock Experiments

You can count on nervous giggles whenever students watch Stanley Milgram's (1962) documentary film *Obedience*. Ordinary citizens think they are delivering powerful electric shocks to innocent people—and observers giggle with what appears to be self-recognition. If there were air bubbles of words floating above our students' heads, they would probably read, "Oh no! That could be me," or "Wait! Wait! I don't really want to harm this nice, innocent man!" or "I'm sure that I would never do something like that."

Milgram explained the findings from these experiments as examples of the evolutionary human impulse to obey authorities to strengthen the group. It was part of an earnest scientific effort by social psychologists to explain the **compliance** that produced the Holocaust. Hitler and Stalin did not have time to pull the trigger for each of the estimated 10 million deliberate murders committed in their names between 1939 and 1945. Those murders needed architects and engineers, bricklayers and plumbers, accountants and middle managers, transportation experts and building maintenance crews, and human resource specialists. Mass murder required many people turning valves, flipping switches, and digging trenches with heavy equipment.

It took a lot of getting-up-every-morning effort and extraordinary coordination between people and several complex organizations to murder so many people so quickly. **Obedience** to authority was how Milgram tried to explain such a profound level of human coordination in despicable behavior. Milgram died in 1984, so we do not know how he would have reacted to new interpretations of the data or to the many objections people have voiced to his experiments. But social psychologists are hearing the promising sounds of new data emerging from Yale University's archives of the Milgram experiments. The data seem to be saying, "Listen carefully. There's more to this story than obedience to authority."

The new data suggest that participants took on the role of eager followers toward a virtuous end. Perhaps it was the reign of a "righteous" Germany during the war and the cause of science in the Milgram studies (see Reichert, Haslam, & Smith, 2012) that motivated people in each case. Evaluate the evidence as you learn new details emerging from this famous set of experiments.

Milgram and the Art of Experimentation

Stanley Milgram was still an adolescent in the aftermath of World War II. He also wanted to know why people "who are in everyday life responsible and decent" (Milgram, 1974, p. 125) became knowing contributors to mass murder. Milgram's willingness to take risks as a scientist led to an experimental paradigm with procedures that simulated the phenomenon he was interested in—the psychology of ordinary people behaving in extraordinarily harmful ways. The paradigm may have been successful because Milgram had a background in theater. He knew how to stage a scene that could be replicated across many performances.

The Cover Story. Milgram placed an announcement in the New Haven, Connecticut, newspaper: "Persons Needed for a Study of Memory." It was a cover story that camouflaged the true nature of the experiment. When they arrived, the participants were assigned (through a rigged lottery) to play the role of a "Teacher" in the so-called memory study. So there were two deceptions before the experiment even got started.

The job of the Teacher was to read word pairs out loud (such as *fast/car* or *white/bird*) to the Learner. The Learner's job was to memorize the word pairs and take a memory test. The Teacher was to respond to any memory failures by delivering gradually increasing levels of electric shock—15 volts more with each failure, to a max of 450 volts. The electric shocks were not real; they were another deception that made it possible to simulate the psychology of ordinary people behaving in extraordinarily harmful ways. The dependent variable was simple: How far up the electric shock scale would they go?

How Did Milgram Vary His Experimental Paradigm?

Milgram conducted 18 variations using his basic experimental paradigm. In one set of experiments, he examined the effect of physical proximity on willingness to deliver electric shocks. Other experiments focused on exceptions to the rule of compliance, which, to his surprise, had been established at 65%.

Physical Proximity. In Milgram's first experiment, 26 of 40 Yale students (65%) shocked to the maximum. The Learner was behind a wall and said nothing. Those numbers were only slightly lower in Experiment 2 (62.5%) when Milgram added a scripted voice that the Teachers heard screaming in pain and complaining of a heart condition. They were lower again in Experiment 3, when the Teacher and Learner were in the same room: 40%. It continued to go lower in Experiment 4, when the Teacher forced the Learner's hand onto the electric plate to receive the shock: 30%. The pattern in the data suggests that physical proximity reduces the willingness to harm someone. The hesitation to harm others based on physical proximity between the Teacher and the Learner seemed to be important—and is something to consider in a world of remote, drone warfare.

Gender of the Teacher and a Role Reversal. In Milgram's one test with women, they behaved on average like men: Approximately 65% shocked to the maximum voltage. However, based on postexperiment interviews, Milgram believed that women's experience was different because they were caught between competing **social roles**: being warm, caring nurturers (do not shock) and being obedient and submissive to a male authority (do shock). In this case, social role expectations may have sent conflicting messages of what to do. The social role closest to their experience at that moment (obeying the male experimenter) demonstrated the most control over their behavior.

In Experiment 12, the experimenter stopped the study partway through, telling the Teacher that he was concerned about the Learner's heart condition. But surprisingly, the voice of the Learner then came over the microphone and stated that he *wanted* to go on with the experiment. So, the roles were reversed: The experimenter said to stop the experiment and the Learner wanted to continue. In this condition, every person playing the role of Teacher followed the experimenter's orders and stopped delivering shocks. Only the scientist's views mattered; the victim's opinion didn't seem to count. This is an important detail in light of the new interpretations of Milgram's data.

Insights From Qualitative Data

The participants in Milgram's experiments did not have to obey the experimenter. But, as Milgram (1974) described it, most of the participants appeared to be "bound into the authority system" (p. 95) by a "web of forces" (p. 31). For example, one participant, P. G., told his wife, "I think I did a good job." She responded, "Suppose the man was dead?" P. G. replied, "So he's dead, I did my job!"

Milgram's use of the term *web of forces* suggests that he recognized that the compliance achieved in his experiments was the product of much more than mere "obedience." Milgram may have eagerly endorsed the richer interpretations of his data that are now emerging. These kinds of **qualitative data**, harvested from follow-up observations and interviews with participants, enriched the experiment and gave it voices that continue to speak many decades after the experiment ended. Qualitative data improved Milgram's methods and our ability to understand the results. Multiple methods increase validity by mixing quantitative and qualitative methods that ask the same question in different ways.

Let's explore some more qualitative observations.

Looking the Other Way. In the initial pilot study, the Learner (who Milgram sometimes refers to as the "victim") could be seen vaguely through silvered glass. Milgram noticed that the students would shock the Learner (a pleasant-looking, middle-aged gentleman) but avert their eyes. This naturalistic observation suggested that the Yale students were willing to harm the Learner, but they did not want to see him as they were hurting him. It reminded Milgram of some odd social conventions, such as blindfolding a person about to be shot. Who benefits from that? Certainly not the person being shot.

Nervous Laughter. Milgram (1963) also reported that nervous laughter (similar to what our students display) was a "regular occurrence" that sometimes "developed into uncontrollable seizures" (p. 371). M. B. was a 39-year-old social worker whose laughter began as a "light snicker" but gradually became more disruptive, breaking into wheezing laughter triggered by the Learner's screams. The experimenter's notes report that M. B. was "rubbing his face to hide laughter," and later that he "cannot control laughter at this point no matter what he does." M. B. later described his behavior as "peculiar" and tried to explain.

"There was I. I'm a nice person, I think, hurting somebody and caught up in what seemed a mad situation . . . and in the interest of science, one goes through with it." He emphasized, "This isn't the way that I usually am." His laughter was "a sheer reaction to a totally impossible situation . . . I just couldn't deviate and I couldn't try to help. This is what got to me."

Family Reactions. When interviewed a year later, M. B. described his wife's blunt reaction: "You can call yourself Eichmann"—referring, of course, to the infamous Nazi bureaucrat who conscientiously helped murder millions of innocent people. Eichmann's dramatic trial began in August 1961, the same month that Milgram had begun testing subjects in the shock experiments (Benjamin & Simpson, 2009). M. B. said, "I hope I can deal more effectively with any future conflicts of values I encounter." M. B. (and his wife) believed that his participation had provided important insights into his own behavior.

Politeness. The people playing the role of Teacher tended to be courteous toward both the experimenter and their victims. Some participants called the experimenter "sir" or used other expressions of institutional respect. A few participants described the person they were shocking as a "gentleman" even when they were privately convinced that they were killing him. Their language may partly reflect the social norms of mid-20th-century America. But Milgram interpreted this consistent courtesy as a sign of excessive deference to authority. It also might indicate their high regard for a Yale scientist and the privilege of participating in an important experiment.

Taking Responsibility. F. B. was a 50-year-old man who asked, "Who's going to take responsibility if anything happens to that gentleman?" Assured that the experimenter would take responsibility, he reluctantly continued. At 195 volts, he once again tried to rebel. "Aw, no. I'm not going to kill that man. You mean I've got to keep going up with the scale? No sir." But he continued to 450 volts even though he asked, "What if he's dead in there? I mean, he told me that he can't stand the shock, sir. I don't mean to be rude, but I think you should look in on him." Perhaps by saying these things, F. B. felt like he was no longer responsible for what happened—even though he was the one flipping the switch.

Secretly Trying to Help. E. R. was a college-educated homemaker who volunteered for the Girl Scouts and the local Parent-Teachers Association. As shock levels increased, she began muttering to herself, yet administered the memory test with a show of officiousness and outward strength. Observing the many remaining shock levels, she asked, "Are we going all the way up there? Can't we stop? I'm shaking." At 270 volts, E. R. began giving the Learner hints by emphasizing the correct answer. At the postexperiment interview, she confided to the Learner, "I tried to push the switch down lightly."

Disgust for the Victim. B. B. was a 37-year-old welder who voiced respect for the experimenter but disgust for the Learner. At 330 volts, B. B. brutally informed the now silent Learner, "You better answer and get it over with. We can't stay here all night." After 450 volts, he respectfully asked the experimenter, "Where do we go from here, Professor?" He was always deferential to authority but reported that he felt "disgusted" when the victim—presumably now dead or at least unconscious—would no longer cooperate.

A Former Nazi Youth. By chance, one participant (G. B.) had been a young girl coming of age in Germany during Hitler's rise to power. She had been repeatedly exposed to Nazi propaganda during her childhood. G. B. was a 31-year-old medical technician when she participated in Milgram's so-called study of memory. When the Learner began to complain about his heart condition, G. B. calmly asked the experimenter, "Shall I continue?" After administering 210 volts, she stated, "Well, I'm sorry, I don't think we should continue."

Experimenter: It is absolutely essential that we continue. . . .

G. B.: I like you to ask him. We came here of our own free will. If he wants to continue, I'll go ahead. . . .

Experimenter: You have no other choice.

G. B.: I think we here are on our own free will. I don't want to be responsible if he has a heart condition if anything happens to him. Please understand that.

G. B. refused to continue, and the experiment ended. Milgram observed that her "straightforward, courteous behavior in the experiment, lack of tension, and total control of her own action seems to make disobedience a simple and rational deed . . . what I had initially envisioned would be true for almost all subjects" (Milgram, 1974, p. 88). G. B. had followed the path to *disobedience* by having inner doubts, expressing them, dissenting, threatening to end her participation, and then refusing to continue. When asked about how her experience as a youth might have influenced her, G. B. slowly replied, "Perhaps we have seen too much pain."

DISCUSSION QUESTIONS

1. Have you ever obeyed an authority figure or gone along with a crowd, even though you didn't agree with what you were doing? What motivated you to go against your own inner nature or better judgment? How do you reconcile your actions now, upon reflection?

2. Milgram's series of studies have been used as examples of highly unethical procedures, even though he claimed that his participants suffered from no long-term negative effects. Do you think these procedures were unethical, even if the participants reported being fine? When

studies from the past are unethical, should we continue to highlight them in books such as this—or does that only glorify them?

3. If they could be done in an ethical way (or if ethics weren't a concern), what other interesting variations could be done with the basic Milgram paradigm? For example, the Learner (or false shock victim) could be kind versus derogatory to the Teacher before the shocks begin, or the Learner could be a child versus an older person. Think of three variations that you think would be interesting, and explain what your hypotheses would be in each condition.

KEY TERMS

Compliance 109
Obedience 110

Qualitative data 112

Social roles 111

7.3 Big Fish Eat Small Fish: Social Coordination in a Violent World

Nancy and Rod sailed their 22-foot catamaran from their home in rural Wisconsin to New York City (yes, it can be done). For Rod, it was his first trip to New York, so imagine what it looked like from the lowest possible elevation on the Hudson River as he guided his small craft past New York's many skyscrapers. The Twin Towers were still there casting enormous shadows and somehow making 50-story buildings look small. After tying up at a dock on the New Jersey side, Rod looked up at the buildings, thought about the several millions of people living so closely together, and asked, "How does everyone get enough water?"

It was an excellent question with an even better answer. **Social coordination** is the organization of mutually productive behavior across individuals and groups (see Claidière & Whiten, 2012; Finkel et al., 2006; Oullier, de Guzman, Jantzen, Lagarde, & Kelso, 2008). Every day, a network of aqueducts and tunnels delivers approximately 1 billion gallons of the world's finest water from the Catskill Mountain rivers and reservoirs to homes and businesses throughout New York City.

It's wonderful drinking water, but delivering it requires regional sacrifices, coordinated planning, ongoing maintenance, and balanced public policies. Social coordination occurs between different departments of public works, ever-changing politicians, inattentive citizens, real estate developers, town planners, and public administrators. The most impressive element of this astonishing social coordination may be that the social coordination gets passed along from one generation of politicians to the next—an astounding example of **generational social influence**. And New York City is only one of many cities around the world that routinely accomplishes this impressive feat.

Social Coordination in Other Animals

Humans have an impressive talent for social coordination, but it's not a given. If you have ever been in a large city with poor social coordination, especially around the water supply and sewage needs, then you understand the importance of social coordination. Neither can you assume that humans are unique in accomplishing impressive feats of social coordination.

Social Coordination Among Sticklebacks. Sticklebacks are small fish (about 6 centimeters long; slightly more than 2 inches), and their main ambition in life appears to be avoiding getting eaten by bigger fish. They are very good at surviving. The world supply of sticklebacks is not likely to disappear unless threatened by pollution. Sticklebacks display impressive intelligence. When swimming in shallow waters, sticklebacks can assess the pros and cons of threatening situations. Then they explore their dangerous world with another stickleback to increase the chances of at least one of them surviving.

Two sticklebacks then employ a "tit-for-tat" strategy, a kind of test for a potential risk-sharing friendship. Their goal is to identify a stickleback willing to partner with them when checking the environment for potential predators (Dugatkin & Wilson, 1993; Milinski, Pfluger, Külling, & Kettler, 1990; Neill & Cullen, 1974). When two fish carefully swim together in a dangerous environment, the odds of being eaten by a bigger fish are cut approximately in half. Three fish lowers the odds even more, and so forth. In other words, evolution has devised a strategy of social coordination that is good for the group even though it won't be good for some individuals.

Sardines. Sardines, another small fish that you may recognize from small cans in the grocery store, use the same principle of social coordination. Their astonishing, coordinated, flashing movements appear to confuse big fish predators and minimize individual risk. Sardines are even selective about which of their own species they will school with. Sardines prefer "the company of individuals matching in body size" and age (Muiño, Carrera, & Iglesias, 2003, p. 1369; see Pitcher, 1993).

Herring. When sardines grow up, they become herring about 45 centimeters, or 18 inches, long. They continue to use the principle of social coordination by forming enormous balls of fish. They are using social coordination with what looks like a group mind that tells all the fish when to turn and in what direction. You've seen this when flocks of birds gather in enormous numbers and twist and turn in beautiful displays of social coordination. Herring are so committed to the principle of social coordination that even when attacked, most herring "continue feeding while retaining the risk-dilution advantages of schooling" (Pitcher, Misund, Fernö, Totland, & Melle, 1996, p. 449).

Humpback Whales. However, the safety advantages of social coordination, at least for herring, come with a cost. Think of it as "the large predator problem" that occurs when the fish-like mammals we call whales also have figured out the benefits of social coordination. So far, the strategy of social coordination has worked extremely well for sardines and herring—and for many generations. However, large predators require large food supplies; they also have learned the trick of social coordination to satisfy their needs (Connell, 2000).

Humpback whales demonstrate social coordination that places entire schools of herring at risk for mass destruction. Their social coordination is impressive. When they have discovered a large ball of herring, one submerged humpback circles below the ball while releasing a circular stream of bubbles that slowly rises to the surface. Then, another humpback emits a long, distinctive feeding call that appears to help drive the prey—hundreds of herring—into the corral of bubbles, like cattle being herded into a pen on their way to the slaughterhouse. That's when several humpback whales, parked below the ball of herring, open their gigantic mouths and rise to the surface in unison, swallowing great mouthfuls of herring. Search for "cooperative whale feeding" to see a brief, dramatic YouTube documentary demonstrating why social coordination—for herring—invites mass destruction.

The Dark Side of Social Coordination

Sometimes humans hunt humans. The human **herd mentality** develops when we are willing to believe almost anything to be a part of the group—and **normative social influence** can often lead us astray. A herd mentality encourages unlikely beliefs simply because so many others also believe; we're swimming in a dangerous ball of agreement.

It sounds ridiculous now, of course, but many Nazis talked themselves into believing that they were destined to reign for 1,000 years; 12 dark years later, that herd mentality was bombed back to its origins in its vile fantasyland. But that popular belief helped justify murdering millions of innocent people. We see the large predator problem when modern terrorists target large buildings with lots of people rather than small barns in unpopulated areas. We may *feel* safer by conforming even though we look more like a big juicy bull's eye to human predators with big ideas.

DISCUSSION QUESTIONS

1. New York City's water supply requires a vast amount of social coordination. Identify two examples of processes in your own town or campus community that require social coordination, and explain how their different elements cooperate.

2. This case study identified several examples of social coordination in nonhuman animals, especially fish and sea-based mammals. What other animals display social coordination to their evolutionary or group advantage?

3. This case study seemed to argue first that social coordination was an evolutionary advantage— but then it seemed to argue that social coordination can put a group at risk, which would certainly not be an advantage. Which side of the argument is correct? Can both be correct, under different circumstances?

KEY TERMS

Generational social
  influence 116

Herd mentality 117
Normative social influence 117

Social coordination 115

CHAPTER 8

Group Processes

8.1 More Than a Game: The Prisoner's Dilemma

Trust is a social glue that keeps groups together. Betrayal and the lack of trust drives groups—even groups of two—apart. The decision about whether to trust someone else is a constant. For example, you have to decide whether you can trust other people whenever you:

Activity	Can you trust that . . .
Drive a car	other drivers will stay in their lanes?
Order food	the restaurant follows health codes?
Let a child walk to school alone	others will not harm your child?
Go to work	the organization will pay you as promised?
Sign up for a class	the professor will be fair and the class have value?
Vote	the voting system is not rigged?

The negative outcomes are unlikely—but possible. If you decide *never* to trust anyone, then you will live a shriveled, fearful life because you never leave your home—and still have to trust that the person delivering your food hasn't accidentally poisoned you or ripped you off. On the other hand, if you implicitly trust every person in every situation, then the odds of being played for a sucker increase dramatically. Intelligent trust is essential for business transactions, for intimate relationships, and for almost any basic interaction between two or more people.

When you have to decide whether to trust someone else, the rules of a game called the **Prisoner's Dilemma** descend over your life. No individual or group can escape the rules of the Prisoner's Dilemma. You are taking an enormous leap of faith, for example, when you decide to go ziplining. You are trusting that the company and people strapping you into the harness know what they're doing, check the equipment for safety, and used quality equipment in the first place. Why do humans so often place themselves in situations where trust is an essential ingredient for success?

Welcome to the winning group strategy in the Prisoner's Dilemma.

The Rules of the Game

Table 8.1 displays a basic Prisoner's Dilemma, discussed in depth by Robert Axelrod (1984) in *The Evolution of Cooperation*. It is called the Prisoner's Dilemma because it is modeled on the idea of how two crime suspects will behave when interviewed separately and then asked by the police to snitch on the other suspect in exchange for a lower sentence. They have to decide whether they can trust the other suspect not to snitch as they also decide whether or not to snitch. The rules of the game imitate reality: The best possible overall outcome for both people is that they trust each other, keep quiet, and refuse to snitch. But trust opens you up to be played the fool if your partner sells you out.

As Axelrod (1984) pointed out, the rules of the Prisoner's Dilemma lie at the heart of the fundamental challenge of self-government. For example, what kind of government must we have if everybody decided to drive as if there were no rules of the road? Without trust and the cooperation it engenders, we must look to an authoritarian government. We would need a tyrant to force people to behave simply to avoid all those roadside fights and accidental traffic deaths. Nations often interact as trading partners based on trust. A trade war, for example, is a violation of that trust: If you put a tax on our goods going into your country, then fairness demands that we put a tax on your goods coming into our country.

The rules of the Prisoner's Dilemma permeate our lives. Axelrod (1984) noted that if you invite someone to dinner multiple times, and he or she never reciprocates by having you over, eventually you'll stop. An expectation of returned favors

Table 8.1	Each Prisoner in the Prisoner's Dilemma Is Faced With a Critical Decision Under Conditions of Uncertainty: To Trust or Not to Trust the Other Prisoner		
		Prisoner B	
		Confess	**Keep Quiet**
Prisoner A	Confess	Both go to jail for 5 years	Prisoner B goes to jail for 10 years, Prisoner A goes free
	Keep Quiet	Prisoner A goes to jail for 10 years, Prisoner B goes free	Both go to jail for 1 year

is common in many business and political contexts, and we see it in our own personal lives in things like dinner invitations. The **norm of reciprocity** is fundamental to **group cohesiveness**, and it explains how certain social exchanges produce positive or negative results. The Prisoner's Dilemma provides a quantitative way to measure those results.

The Computer Tournament

Winning in the Prisoner's Dilemma means that we have formed a cooperative group. It doesn't mean that we like each other or respect each other. But it does mean that we see the necessity of getting along with each other. That's why Axelrod wanted to learn if there was a reliable strategy for winning the game of Prisoner's Dilemma when it occurs over multiple interactions or rounds with the same partner.

He was not the first to recognize how important it would be to learn a strategy for success. Within the psychology literature recorded in PsycINFO, there have been hundreds of studies and thousands of references to the Prisoner's Dilemma. Google Scholar tabulates reports about the Prisoner's Dilemma in the hundreds of thousands. Axelrod (and everyone else who understood the importance of the Prisoner's Dilemma) wanted to discover the best strategy for winning at a game that we all have to play every time we make a decision involving trust. And that's where Axelrod's computer contest enters the picture.

Axelrod invited specialists in game theory to write computer programs that they believed had the best chance, in the long run, of winning the game of Prisoner's Dilemma. Each program would be required to play against every other program and accumulate points over multiple rounds. Axelrod also included a program called RANDOM that randomly chose to trust or to not trust within the game with equal probability. Don't think that computer programs made this a nonhuman decision. These were *people* writing the rules competing against other *people* who also thought that their views of human behavior were most likely to win.

We're going to take you to the finish line right away so you can understand the clever programs that the winner was up against. In the first round of competition, the winning computer program was named TIT FOR TAT. When competing against another computer program, this program always started with trust. However, starting with Round 2, it simply imitated whatever the opposing computer program did on its previous move. If the opposing program did not trust, that's what the TIT FOR TAT program did. Trust for trust, and no trust for no trust. TIT FOR TAT is a simple idea: Do unto others as they do unto you.

They measured the complexity of each program by counting how many lines of code were needed to write it. The program TIT FOR TAT required only 4 lines of code and came in first place—across multiple rounds with all the other programs, this strategy resulted in the best final outcome. In contrast, RANDOM required only 5 lines of code but came in last. The most elaborate decision-making strategy required 77 lines of code. There's something important that we can learn from this. Choosing a simple decision-making strategy does not necessarily make it a good strategy. The program TIT FOR TAT was not successful because it was so simple; TIT FOR TAT succeeded because it was real.

In the same way, a complex decision-making program does not necessarily make it a better decision-making strategy. One sophisticated competitor requiring 33 lines of code was a program called DOWNING that had been programmed "to understand the other player and then to make the choice that will yield the best long-term score" (Axelrod, 1984, p. 34). DOWNING will trust when its competitor trusts but will also try to get away with whatever it can when the opportunity arises. For example, DOWNING estimated the statistical probabilities of what its particular competitor was most likely to do and changed its short-term strategy accordingly. DOWNING came in 10th place in a field of 15 computer programs.

In the first round of competition, several computer programs were "nice"; that is, they were not the first to decide not to trust the other computer program. "Niceness" in one computer program reinforced "niceness" in the other program. Consequently, whenever the nice programs played each other, they each accumulated many points. Other programs had been set up to be "forgiving" of an occasional lack of trust. They all performed well—but not as well as TIT FOR TAT. There were also "sneaky" programs, such as a program named JOSS that would play tit for tat with an opponent for several rounds until it would, eventually, betray the other program. The TIT FOR TAT program outperformed the JOSS program because it always imitated whatever JOSS did. When JOSS started trusting again, so did TIT FOR TAT—but the moment JOSS stopped trusting, TIT FOR TAT imitated that strategy as well.

Theoretically, other programs could have won the first round but were not written by any of the contestants, even though Axelrod had used it as a sample in his call for programmers. One of the more forgiving programs was TIT FOR TWO TATS; it allowed its opponent to not trust twice in a row before imitating its opponent's "bad" behavior. A program called TESTER would have defeated TIT FOR TWO TATS but not TIT FOR TAT. TESTER started out by not trusting but responded in kind thereafter. A program called TRANQUILIZER tried to lull its opponent into letting down its guard by trusting repeatedly at the beginning and then trying to see what it could get away with toward the end. As Axelrod (1984) put it, the TRANQUILIZER program "tries to avoid pressing its luck too far" (p. 46).

In addition to multiple rounds of play between each program, there were also multiple rounds of the tournament overall. That meant that people could rewrite their programs with the knowledge that TIT FOR TAT had been the winner in the first round. But TIT FOR TAT also won the second tournament, then won five out of six variations on the tournament, coming in second place only once. So it is worth thinking through some of the characteristics that made TIT FOR TAT such a robustly winning strategy in the game of trust that we all must play. Several distinctive markers make TIT FOR TAT a winning strategy.

What Does the Computer Tournament Teach Us About Human Behavior?

TIT FOR TAT appears to be a strategy that effectively describes everyday decision making—especially whenever trust has become a concern. From the perspective of this particular case study, there appear to be several useful insights about how people and groups can most effectively relate to one another.

1. TIT FOR TAT is a "nice" strategy because it does not hold a grudge against those who fail to trust it.

2. "Niceness" reinforces niceness; the nicer the players are, the easier it is for everyone to perform well.

3. For the same reasons, TIT FOR TAT is also a "forgiving" strategy; the moment it sees trust reemerging, it trusts in return.

4. The strategy of TIT FOR TWO TATS is even more forgiving and will occasionally be more effective, but it also makes you more vulnerable to other kinds of stratagems.

5. TIT FOR TAT has a memory, but it is a very short memory. It is aware of what its opposition has done on the prior move but is unconcerned about anything other than its most recent past.

6. TIT FOR TAT is most effective under conditions of long-term uncertainty; its value declines when the future is known anyway.

7. TIT FOR TAT is assertive. It has no hesitation about returning lack of trust with lack of trust but also trust for trust.

The Shadow of the Future

Axelrod's computer tournament highlighted several ways we can strengthen cooperation between enemies or just people with different agendas. One of those influences is to "enlarge the shadow of the future" (Axelrod, 1984, p. 126). You may have heard of a particular principle of international diplomacy called MAD. It stands for Mutually Assured Destruction, and it may be the primary reason that nations armed to the teeth with nuclear weapons do not go to war with one another. MAD is a very long, dark shadow of a future that potentially ends the human race and much of life on Earth.

But that's too grim a way to end a case study. So, another example of the shadow of the future was reported by baseball umpire Ron Luciano and David Fisher (1982). Luciano would sometimes drink heavily the night before a baseball game and be in poor shape to call balls and strikes at home plate. But he learned that he could trust some catchers to call balls and strikes for him. The catcher would seem to be the worst possible person to turn the game over to. Luciano's explanation was about a trust that evolved out of the shadow of the future (see Axelrod, 1984):

> Over a period of time I learned to trust certain catchers so much that I actually let them umpire for me on the bad days. . . . If someone I trusted was catching . . . I'd tell them, "Look, it's a bad day. You'd better take it for me. If it's a strike, hold your glove in place for an extra second. If it's a ball, throw it right back. And please, don't yell." (p. 178)

The catchers never started making bad calls because they knew that Luciano would be umpiring again in the near future. Luciano could take his revenge later on. Consequently, Luciano reported that

> no one I worked with ever took advantage of the situation, and no hitter ever figured out what I was doing. And only once, when Ed Herrman was calling the pitches, did a pitcher ever complain about a call. I smiled; I laughed; but I didn't say a word. I was tempted, though, I was really tempted. (p. 178)

DISCUSSION QUESTIONS

1. The program TIT FOR TAT always started with trust as a first move. As a general rule, when it comes to other people, do you (1) assume you can trust them until they prove you wrong, or (2) assume you can't trust them until they prove you wrong? Which is your default assumption, and why?

2. Are there particular circumstances when you think it's ethically, morally, and/or socially

acceptable to "betray" the trust of someone else? Describe these situations and justify your answer.

3. It could be argued that the American legal and criminal justice system uses a "tit for tat" strategy. Explain how the system seems to trust people initially, punishes or sets up restrictions for bad behavior, but then rewards people for acting well again. Do you

think this is the best system for preventing and/or responding to criminal behavior? Why or why not?

4. The program TIT FOR TAT had a "memory" or response for what an opposing program did in the immediately previous round—but it didn't matter what had happened before that, long term. The program "forgave" past betrayals if trust was established a single time. What are the advantages and disadvantages for applying this strategy to human interactions with friends, relationship partners, or business associates?

KEY TERMS

Group cohesiveness 121   Norm of reciprocity 121   Prisoner's Dilemma 119

8.2 Social Rejection: A Case Study of 13 School Shootings

School shootings by students in the United States are a distressing but regular occurrence. Discovering the psychological causes behind school shootings creates an opportunity to devise potential ways to protect students from extreme violence by their peers. A frequently mentioned hypothesis in the news coverage is that social rejection or **ostracism** triggers vulnerable individuals to take the drastic step and start shooting their peers (see Leary, Kowalski, Smith, & Phillips, 2003).

The Benefits of Theory

School shootings, of course, cannot be investigated experimentally. We want to be cautious about the potential harm to participants of toying with input variables related to social rejection—and even more cautious about outcome variables related to harming others—even in an experimental simulation. Experiments can provide only limited realistic information about the psychological causes of school shootings. However, social psychologists have two approaches that can help understand this alarming phenomenon: a good theory and case studies.

A good theory can provide some practical help. According to evolutionary theory (for example), the impulse to form groups in the first place comes from our ancestors' needs for physical safety, emotional security, and—to put it bluntly— greater reproductive potential. It is much more difficult to find a sexual partner if you have only a small circle of introverted friends; joining groups increases the probability that you will meet, mate, and marry a suitable person. So, an evolutionary framework based on natural selection seems like a reasonable start. At a closer level, theories related to our need to belong, such as the **theory of optimal distinctiveness**, are a second source of guidance that helps explain our impulse to join groups (Baumeister & Leary, 1995; Williams & Nida, 2011). Theories give us a good place to start; we then need to apply hypotheses and look for data.

Applying Theory: Adolescence + Social Rejection + Narcissism = Aggression

Because belonging to a group is so important to us, we can expect negative consequences from social rejection. As theory suggests, the fear of being socially rejected awakens ancient terrors of being banished from our tribe. Our need to belong is frustrated. So, unable to receive or give social support, we fear for our very survival.

Social rejection is a difficult experience at any age. But it may be especially difficult during adolescence when it takes three forms: (1) teasing and bullying, (2) ostracism, and (3) romantic rejection. Teasing and bullying are public attacks intended to humiliate the individual in front of others. Ostracism (and ignoring) may reflect malice or simple disinterest. Romantic rejection is almost always distressing, is often hurtful, and provokes emotions of anger and resentment that are associated with violence. Leary et al. (2003) concluded that interpersonal rejection was a significant factor in aggression. By 2006, they were able to expand that conclusion beyond interpersonal rejection, reporting that "various forms of rejection cause anger and may lead to aggression" (Leary, Twenge, & Quinlivan, 2006, p. 123). These authors summarized the news coverage of 13 school shootings to look for further evidence of the role of social rejection in aggression.

They concluded that social rejection, by itself, does not predict aggression; most people find a way to cope with social rejection. However, when it is coupled with **narcissism**, social rejection becomes a stronger predictor of aggression (Twenge & Campbell, 2003). The dangerous combination of narcissism and social rejection brings us to a closer examination of case studies of school shootings (Leary et al., 2003).

The Case Study Approach

When Leary et al. (2003) decided to investigate school shootings, their primary interest was in documenting whether or not social rejection was part of the explanation. They also wanted to test for the presence of other predictors of school shootings. They recognized that "most students who experience rejection, even those who are bullied and ostracized, do not resort to lethal violence" (p. 204). There had to be more to the explanation than just social rejection.

They also recognized both the strengths and weaknesses of using an archival case study approach to testing their primary hypothesis about social rejection. Indicators that social rejection was part of the mix would support their hypothesis—and not finding indicators of social rejection would encourage them to look more closely at alternative explanations. They were, in effect, looking to the falsification principle as a way to rule out social rejection as a major explanation for school shootings. The weakness of the case study approach was that it was simply "the method of choice for a low-frequency phenomenon such as school violence for which experimental research is impossible" (p. 204).

To conduct this case study analysis, the researchers used three reviewers to examine descriptions of the school shootings represented in numerous media sources, including several news magazines, newspapers, news services, and respected Internet sources. They recognized that this approach raised the possibility of systematic bias. Reports may reflect the theories held by the reporters rather than the experience of the students who killed their classmates. Notice, however, that methodological flaws do not automatically cancel out the validity of the study. Instead, the shortcomings of this study suggest two pieces of practical advice, especially for new researchers:

1. You are never going to conduct a perfect study; there will always be flaws.

2. The important thing is to acknowledge those flaws, make reasonable judgment calls, and then report the decisions you made and why you made them.

Here is the list of school shootings included in their analysis and some of the words that suggested that social rejection was a relevant variable in the motivation behind school shootings. Try to analyze them for the presence of social rejection, to see whether the hypothesis by Leary et al. (2003) is supported by these data.

1. Moses Lake, Washington (February 2, 1996). Barry Lockaitis, 14, used a .30-caliber rifle to kill a teacher and two boys, as well as injure one girl: "severely depressed," "inferiority complex," "teased" by victim.

2. Bethel, Alaska (February 19, 1997). Evan Ramsey, 16, killed his principal and a student, as well as injured two other people: "teased by victim."

3. Pearl, Mississippi (October 1, 1997). Luke Woodham, 16, killed two students and his mother with a hunting rifle, as well as injured seven others: "often teased." Woodham reportedly said, "I killed because people like me are mistreated every day."

4. West Paducah, Kentucky (December 1, 1997). Michael Carneal, 14, killed three classmates with a semiautomatic pistol and injured five others at a prayer meeting before school: "teased as a 'dweeb' or 'faggot,'" "called 'gay' (in the school paper), and bullied," "unrequited love," and "infatuated with the first person he shot." Carneal said that he had grown tired of being teased and was quoted as saying "people respect me now."

5. Stamps, Arkansas (December 15, 1997). Jason "Colt" Todd, 14, wounded two students with a sniper's rifle: "tired of being picked on" and that "some of his schoolmates had extorted money from him."

6. Jonesboro, Arkansas (April 24, 1998). Andrew Golden, 11, and Mitchell Johnson, 13, opened fire with handguns and rifles on Westside Middle School, killing 5 people and injuring 11 others: "angry about being rejected by a girl," "repeatedly teased for being fat."

7. Fayetteville, Tennessee (May 19, 1998). Honor student Jacob Davis, 18, killed a male classmate who was dating his ex-girlfriend, who had recently broken up with Davis. The perpetrator and victim had recently had an argument about the girl.

8. Springfield, Oregon (May 21, 1998). Kipland Kinkel, 15, used a semiautomatic rifle and a pistol to kill 2 classmates and injure 22 others, in addition to killing his parents: "rejected by a girl," "embarrassed his parents," and "teasing from other students."

9. Littleton, Colorado (April 20, 1999). Eric Harris, 18, and Dylan Klebold, 17, used semiautomatic weapons, shotguns, and rifles, then committed suicide. At least 21 people were injured, and 13 people (12 students, 1 teacher) were killed: "taunted," "bullied, particularly by athletes," "rejected from the Marines," "turned down by a girl whom he asked to the prom," "episodes of teasing and ostracism," "I'm going to kill you all," Klebold said. "You've been giving us shit for years."

10. Conyers, Georgia (May 20, 1999). T. J. Solomon, 15, used a handgun and .22-caliber rifle stolen from his parents to injure six people: "depressed after a break-up," "picked on by a football player," and "feared becoming the school wuss."

11. Ft. Gibson, Oklahoma (December 6, 1999). Seth Trickey, 13, walked up to students at his middle school and started firing with a 9-mm handgun. He didn't seem to know the children he shot and said he did not know why he did it. Trickey was described as an honor

student whom others regarded as funny, nice, and good-natured. He was popular and well liked and clearly not a loner. Trickey has never provided a plausible reason for his actions.

12. Mount Morris Township, Michigan (February 29, 2000). A 6-year-old boy pointed a gun at a fellow first grader, said "I don't like you," and killed her. The victim had purportedly slapped the perpetrator, who wanted to get revenge by scaring her with the gun. The boy had been left in the care of an uncle, who lived in a suspected crack house, so that his mother could work two jobs.

13. Santee, California (March 5, 2001). Having boasted that he was going to cause trouble at his school, Andy Williams, 15, shot 2 students to death and wounded 13 others: "maliciously bullied" and "desired simply to 'fit in.'"

14. Williamsport, Pennsylvania (March 7, 2001). In the only school shooting reported here that was perpetrated by a girl, Catherine Bush, 14, shot the head cheerleader at her school: "teased and harassed at her previous school" and "felt betrayed by the victim, who ostensibly had revealed to other students the contents of e-mails Catherine had sent her."

DISCUSSION QUESTIONS

1. Describe at least one strength and one weakness of the case study approach applied to this particular analysis.

2. Discuss whether this summary of the case studies supports the hypothesis that social rejection is associated with school shootings. Recall that the researchers also wondered if other variables, such as narcissism, were involved. Based on this summary, can you identify any other variables that seem to be a factor in these cases? What variables, other than the combination of social rejection and narcissism, do you hypothesize as related to school shootings?

3. How might you devise an ethical experiment that would directly test whether certain personality types combine with social rejection to predict aggression? What would your independent and dependent variables be? In your hypothetical experiment, how could your procedural design allow you to test these three research questions:

   a. Does any particular personality type, by itself, explain school shootings?

   b. Does social rejection, by itself, explain school shootings?

c. Does the combination of a particular personality type and social rejection explain school shootings?

d. What situational variables, by themselves, would be most predictive of school shootings?

KEY TERMS

8.3 On the Shoulders of Giant Women: The First Computer Programmers

The main lesson to draw from the birth of computers is that innovation is usually a group effort, involving collaboration between visionaries and engineers, and that creativity comes from a drawing on many sources. Only in storybooks do inventions come like a thunderbolt or a lightbulb popping out of the head of a lone individual in a basement or garret or garage. (Isaacson, 2014, p. 85)

This case study focuses on the creative potential of groups—and it comes with a twist in space and time.

We normally think of a group as two or more people interacting with each other. But groups are also formed when two or more people are joined together by a common fate. Two random people in a town are not a group, but if they know each other and suffer from the same disease, then they become a group. Becoming a group, even with a small, short-term, or limited purpose, is laden with creative potential. The common fate of their disease may nourish a friendship, motivate them to form a support group, or inspire a fundraiser. Becoming a group generates previously unconsidered opportunities for creativity.

A Group That Ignores Space and Time

The forward movement of science is also a group process, but it is a slow process that routinely transcends space and time. Sir Isaac Newton famously wrote, "If I have seen further, it is by standing on the shoulders of giants." The history of computing demonstrates a scientifically creative group process that has transcended space and time *and* gender. Its story is beautifully summarized in Walter Isaacson's (2014) book about the history of computing, *The Innovators*.

The question embedded in every computer innovation is whether computers can now think for themselves. So far, the answer seems still to be just beyond our fingertips. The most famous test of whether computers can think is Alan Turing's imitation game, called the Turing Test: A human and a computer are questioned by someone who does not know which is answering the questions. If the questioner cannot tell which is responding, then the computer deserves to be credited with thinking. In the 1830s, Ada Lovelace peered into the future of an industry that did not yet exist. She believed that computers of the future would not be able to think independently (1843; see Krysa, 2012):

> The analytical engine [a computer] has no pretensions whatever to *originate* anything. It can do whatever we *know how to order it* to perform. It can follow analysis; but it has no power of *anticipating* any analytical relations or truths. Its province is to assist us in making *available* what we are already acquainted with.

Lovelace envisioned programmable computers (long before they actually existed) and believed that computers never would be able to think like humans. Instead, she imagined a different role for computers: a machine that could be programmed to partner with humans rather than compete against humans. And this case study is about the intergenerational group of creative women who crossed space and time to write the first computer program. The result of this group collaboration is the human-computer interactions that so many of us enjoy today.

The Six Women of ENIAC

At the start of World War II, "computers" were people—usually women. It was a job description, like "plumber" or "professor." You could be hired to be a "computer"—someone who applied a mathematical formula to a specific problem and then "computed" the solution. The U.S. Army was hiring lots of "computers" to solve a specific problem: producing artillery firing tables that would inform gunners about the proper trajectory needed to send shells to their intended targets. These complex sets of equations were being calculated by a room full of female "computers." Their calculations had to factor in many variables such as outside temperature and the amount of drag produced by the air around the shell.

The U.S. Army needed to speed up the calculating process. But they wanted to find a way to reprogram mechanical calculating machines so that another roomful of female "computers" would not have to start from scratch with each new set of variables. The solution was to build and program the ENIAC: the Electronic Numerical Integrator And Computer. All computers were physically huge at the start of the computer age. Jean Jennings (who later became Jean Jennings Bartik) described the 30-ton ENIAC as "the equivalent of about forty-five of the horses

I had ridden and driven as a teenager on the farm in Missouri." She added that now "a silicon chip smaller than the tip of a pencil can hold the same capability" (Bartik, Rickman, & Todd, 2013, p. 2).

Six women were pulled from the 100 female "computers" working on trajectories: Fran Bilas, Jean Jennings, Ruth Lichterman, Kay MacNulty, Betty Snyder, and Marilyn Wescoff. They gathered as a group for the first time on the railroad platform as they were preparing to travel from Philadelphia to the Aberdeen Proving Grounds in Maryland. They were uncertain why they were selected, but they represented, like many wartime groups, a clash of cultures that could have turned either creative or destructive. Group cohesion was needed for the Army to succeed.

Lichterman was from New York City, was Jewish, and had studied math at Hunter College but not graduated. Wescoff was also Jewish but from Philadelphia; she had earned a bachelor's degree in education and sociology. Snyder was a Quaker from Philadelphia; her father and grandfather were both astronomers and high school teachers. MacNulty was an Irish Catholic whose father had been jailed for his activities in the Irish Republican Army. Jennings described herself as

> a red-haired, freckled farm girl from Missouri. None of the other four in
> the group had ever been around anyone quite like me before. By that
> I mean someone from my rural, Church of Christ background who was
> so wide-eyed about the world and so excited about everything we did
> and everywhere we went. (Bartik et al., 2013, p. 71)

Bilas, who joined the group later, came from an Austrian/German immigrant family that was now living in South Philadelphia. Some of the women came from wealthier families; others had come from more modest homes. All of their families and the women themselves valued education. Valuing education was the necessary starting point for the common fate that made them a critical group in the history of computing. The group chemistry had to work, and Jennings remembered that

> we had a wonderful time . . . none of us had ever been in close contact
> with anyone from one of the others' religions. We had some great
> arguments . . . despite our differences, or perhaps because of them, we
> really liked one another. Of course, we had better like one another—we
> spent almost twenty-four hours a day together . . . then still wanted to be
> together in the evenings discussing everything about our lives. (p. 97)

They succeeded in programming the ENIAC by envisioning it as capable of doing much more than calculating artillery trajectories. They became so familiar with its inner workings that they could debug the machine down to a failure in one of its 18,000 vacuum tubes. They were a cooperative, hard-working group dedicated to a vision of achieving something greater than themselves. Social facilitation was high as they depended on each other, minimizing coordination loss. Their achievements as the world's first computer programmers were remarkable—and largely unrecognized. "In a perfect world," Jennings observed,

> The "Sensational Six" . . . would have ushered in an era of computer programming in which women led the way, or were at least on equal footing with men, and worked in equal numbers with them. . . . As for the ENIAC women, we were lost in the shuffle when World War II, which had ushered women into non-traditional roles, ended and the country reverted to its comfortable, male-dominated mode. (p. xix)

Before she died, Betty Snyder was awarded the Ada Lovelace Award, perhaps the highest recognition from the Association for Women in Computing. Grace Hopper knew her work and described Snyder as "the best programmer she had ever met" (Bartik et al., 2013, p. 123). "In a way," Jennings wrote,

> women became the first programmers by accident. If the ENIAC's administrators had known how crucial programming would be to the functioning of the electronic computer and how complex it would prove to be, they might have been more hesitant to give such an important role to women.

Group dynamics can be turned toward both destructive and creative purposes. The world's first computer program was the creative product of a scientific and cohesive group of women: Grace Hopper, Fran Bilas, Jean Jennings, Ruth Lichterman, Kay MacNulty, Betty Snyder, and Marilyn Wescoff. This group of visionaries and programmers within computer science knew each other in a way that exists beyond the constraints of space and time.

DISCUSSION QUESTIONS

1. Identify some other groups that transcend space and time. What holds them together as groups?

2. Jean Jennings believed that the credit for being the first computer programmers was stolen from the "Sensational Six," partly due to sexism. If the six women had been given credit, how might it have influenced the gender demographics among current computer programmers and other scientific fields?

3. Discuss how this particular group had to rely on social facilitation and what the potential consequences (short term and long term) might have been if any of the women in the group had been social loafers. What factors in this group promoted social facilitation and discouraged **social loafing** and/or diffusion of responsibility?

4. What kind of personality traits make for the "best" group members—and what kind of personality traits make for the "best" group leaders? Make sure to explain your definition of "best" and why you have chosen certain traits for members and leaders. Does the most effective or happiest group include people who are all similar or people who are all different?

KEY TERMS

Social facilitation 133

Social loafing 134

CHAPTER 9

Stereotypes, Prejudice, and Discrimination

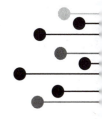

9.1 Economic Anxiety and the Forced Deportation of U.S. Citizens

Repatriation is the more polite term for deportation.

It sounded more polite in the 1930s because it implied that families now settled in the United States wanted to "go back home"—even though for most of them, the United States *was* their home, both legally and emotionally. From about 1930 to 1935, approximately 60% of the people forcibly rounded up and sent on trains and buses to the Mexican border were in fact U.S. citizens. Many had lived in the United States so long that, for their children, being "sent back" was being forcibly sent to a foreign country. The story of this moral panic was told by historians Francisco Balderrama and Raymond Rodriguez (2006) in their book *Decade of Betrayal: Mexican Repatriation in the 1930s*.

The Case of the 1930s Mexican "Repatriation"

A contagious fear grabbed hold of many Americans when the stock market crashed in October 1929. The sense of dread was aggravated by the contrast with the previous years of artificial prosperity in an unregulated stock market. Fear and anxiety grew as government and private industry proved themselves incapable of dealing with the crisis. The national mood became meaner as the unemployment rate moved toward 25% and politicians began looking for scapegoats. Just as **frustration-aggression theory** predicts, the rest of the country was also looking for someone to blame for their problems. Stereotyping, **prejudice**, and discrimination were spreading like a bad case of poison ivy into swelling blisters. Balderrama and Rodriguez (2006) described the social infection that was threatening the health of the American promise:

> For all Americans, the decade of the 1930s was one filled with frustration and disenchantment. The very tenets of our democratic/capitalistic system came under close scrutiny . . . some critics diagnosed the system's condition as terminal. . . . Americans, reeling from the economic disorientation of the depression, sought a convenient scapegoat. They found it in the Mexican community. (p. 1)

The result was mass deportation roundups, violence, and scare tactics. Those hated "Mexicans," including those who were in fact American citizens, were taking "American" jobs. It wasn't true or even logical, but many believed that

> getting rid of the Mexicans would create a host of new
> jobs . . . alleviating the unemployment situation would automatically
> end the depression. In a frenzy of anti-Mexican hysteria, wholesale
> punitive measures were proposed and undertaken by government
> officials at the federal, state, and local levels. Laws were passed depriving
> Mexicans of jobs in the public and private sector. (p. 2)

Despite pockets of resistance, the campaign to remove Mexican "aliens" was successful, but it did little to create jobs or strengthen the economy. Between 1930 and 1939, 46.3% of the people deported from the United States had some kind of historical connection to Mexico, even though Mexican immigrant families represented less than 1% of the total U.S. population at the time. The unofficial stamp of approval from the U.S. government was apparent by the open cooperation between citizen groups and government authorities. For example, C. P. Visel was a spokesman for the Los Angeles Citizens Committee for Coordination of Unemployment Relief. He sent the following telegram to Colonel Arthur M. Woods, the U.S. Government Coordinator of Unemployment Relief:

> Four hundred thousand deportable aliens U.S. Estimate 5 percent in this
> district. We can pick them all up through police and sheriff channels.
> Local U.S. Department of Immigration personnel not sufficient to
> handle. You advise please as to method of getting rid. We need their jobs
> for needy citizens. (p. 67)

This was a national moral panic, fed by the fears of economic disaster and the need for a scapegoat during the worst years of the Great Depression (see Balderrama & Rodriguez, 2006, pp. 67–71). The American Federation of Labor added to the problem by convincing its union members that getting rid of Mexicans would create more jobs. Mexicans were resented for two reasons. First, they would work for half the wages. Second, many employers believed that Mexican workers were loyal, worked harder, and often did better work. Whether this was simply a stereotype or based on a **kernel of truth**, it fed the fires of prejudice.

The Veterans of Foreign Wars and the American Legion also were outspoken against Mexicans. The Legion assisted the removal of some 3,000 people from East Chicago, Indiana, by supplying guards to ride the trains even though Mexican Americans "had served alongside them in the trenches in France during World War I" (p. 68). Congressman Sam Hobbs of Alabama offered a bill (H.R. 4768) that Balderrama and Rodriguez described as calling "for the establishment of concentration camps for all aliens ordered deported and who were not out of the country within sixty days" (p. 69). Fear was the foundation for this prejudice and economic anxiety the justification for gross discrimination.

Immigration officials made sure that Mexican American citizens were fearful of being deported. After immigration officials swept the streets of anyone who "looked Mexican," one radio announcer recalled seeing "women crying in the streets when not finding their husbands" (p. 70). Customs officials stopped Mrs. Angela Hernandez de Sanchez, an American citizen returning from visiting her relatives in Carrizal, Chihuahua. By law, she was not subject to deportation, and both of her children were born in the United States. However, customs officials demanded proof of citizenship and ordered tests of venereal diseases. The Department of Labor ordered both her and her children deported. Deportation itself was dangerous:

> *Excelsior*, one of Mexico City's leading newspapers, reported that on board one repatriation train twenty-five children and adults had died of illness and malnutrition during the trip to the border . . . a factor contributing to the sad plight of the repatriates was that vast numbers left the United States without ever contacting the Mexican consul in their respective districts . . . [and] arrived at the border without Certificates of Residency or any documentation needed to facilitate their processing. (Balderrama & Rodriguez, 2006, pp. 141–142)

Fear, feeding on fear, became a self-fulfilling prophecy that produced thousands of displaced citizens and tore apart families. Many states, and some federal policies, made use of **institutional discrimination**. But it was not how the well-meaning officials understood their own behavior:

> According to Mary Grace Wells, the Gary, Indiana repatriation program was a splendid success, for "all [repatriates] were happy enroute and were delighted to set foot again on their native soil." How Wells was able to surmise or arrive at that conclusion is a mystery, for she never made a trip to the border. . . . Only the younger children who did not fully comprehend what was happening to them viewed the trip with glee and good spirits. (p. 141)

The newspapers played an important role in encouraging this moral panic:

> Newspapers and journals had a field day in trumpeting the charges and accusation that were seldom verified but were accepted at face value. Mexican families were accused of harboring ignoble, un-American sentiments and characteristics. Slothfulness, shiftlessness, and lack of ambition. (p. 41)

Any individual act of defiance:

> produced dramatic press coverage. Newspapers underscored the fact
> that extended years spent contributing to the prosperity and economic
> development of the United States was not enough to gain Mexicans
> either permanent residence or acceptance . . . the Mexican worker and
> his family were ousted without any concern for citizenship status, length
> of residency, health conditions, or age factors. (p. 143)

There was significant resistance in several newspapers, but they mostly were
overwhelmed by the conventional press:

> Also fanning the flames . . . were influential newspapers and magazines.
> Among the most vociferous were the Hearst newspaper chain and the
> *Saturday Evening Post* magazine. In the Midwest, the *Chicago Tribune*
> repeatedly called for the elimination of the alien horde. The biased
> articles appealed to the public's base fears and added to the hue and cry
> to get rid of the Mexicans. (p. 68)

The year 1931, during the Hoover administration, was the peak year for repatriation. Officially, 123,247 Mexicans were shipped home in 1931 alone, and a total of 345,839 were deported between 1930 and 1935. But self-deportation, out of fear and confusion, may have accounted for about two million Mexicans being "repatriated," more or less involuntarily. The cycle of economic fear and official scapegoating when the rule of law was weakened was a powerful, effective psychological tool. However, "as economic conditions in the United States slowly improved, the tide of repatriation receded. In 1935, according to the official count, only 16,196 Nationals were repatriated [that year]" (p. 150).

The repatriation process continued into the administration of President Franklin Roosevelt, who was inaugurated in 1933. Roosevelt recognized that America's great economic depression had boiled into a moral panic and a lost faith in democracy, that American citizens had turned on one another, and that people had looked for and found scapegoats. So he opened his first presidential inaugural speech with words about the psychology of fear:

> So, first of all, let me assert my firm belief that the only thing we have
> to fear is fear itself—nameless, unreasoning, unjustified terror which
> paralyzes needed efforts to convert retreat into advance. (Roosevelt, 1933)

Roosevelt has been criticized for many decisions that sacrificed innocent lives, especially as Germany's murder of the Jews became more apparent. And by the time America went to war with Germany, the target of ethnic hostilities refocused from

Mexicans to Germans and the Japanese. But at this inaugural turning point in the American story, Roosevelt appealed to the opposite of fear: the "joy of achievement." Even though Roosevelt's inaugural address was advocating for specific economic actions, he didn't appeal to materialism or greed or try to give the nation a pep talk about working harder:

> Happiness lies not in the mere possession of money; it lies in the joy of achievement, in the thrill of creative effort. The joy and moral stimulation of work no longer must be forgotten in the mad chase of evanescent profits. (Roosevelt, 1933)

Roosevelt was echoing what Abraham Lincoln also had proposed during his inaugural speech, during another time of severe national testing: an appeal to the "better angels of our nature." This, plus plain social exhaustion, seemed to be instrumental at ending the cycle of fear, prejudice, and discrimination. "We are not enemies," Abraham Lincoln insisted, "but friends."

DISCUSSION QUESTIONS

1. Prejudice toward immigrants is still a problem in the United States and in many other countries. Can you find any evidence that this form of prejudice is correlated with either the perception of economic hardship or prosperity overall in a country or region? Explain how this correlation (if found) would be evidence supporting frustration-aggression theory.

2. This case study discussed how President Roosevelt was involved in changing people's views of "repatriation" efforts and prejudice toward other Americans. How much influence does any given U.S. president have on everyday citizens' views of each other, other countries, the future, and so on? Can you see evidence of your opinion in the current world in which you live?

3. Frustration-aggression theory is usually applied on a large group level, such as how an entire nation responds to economic hardship. Can the theory be applied on an individual level? Do people's prejudices and aggressive behaviors increase when they are personally frustrated or when their lives are not going as planned? As a rule, are poor people more prejudiced or aggressive than rich people—or does the form of prejudice and aggression simply change?

KEY TERMS

Frustration-aggression theory (scapegoat theory) 135

Institutional discrimination 137

Kernel of truth 136

Prejudice 135

9.2 Institutional Discrimination: The Accidental Conspiracy at Erasmus High

Institutional discrimination occurs when an organization formally or informally sanctions treating people differently based on their membership in a group.

Discrimination is not, by strict definition, a bad thing—it means treating people differently based on their characteristics. For example, we discriminate by rewarding higher-achieving salespeople, students, and athletes. Honors organizations such as Psi Chi—the national honors society for psychology majors and minors—discriminates because it only accepts people with a certain cumulative GPA. But when discrimination is based on anything unrelated to actual performance, then it is both prejudiced and—at least in the United States and many other countries—probably illegal.

Some forms of institutional discrimination would qualify as **old-fashioned prejudice**. Private country clubs that don't allow people of color to become members is a clear (and unfortunately very real) example. For many years, several prestigious colleges and universities wouldn't allow women to earn graduate degrees, assuming either that they weren't as intelligent or that educating them was a waste of time and resources because they would quit their jobs as soon as they became pregnant. That's blatant sexism. But, as times change and old-fashioned prejudice and discrimination become less socially acceptable, forms of discrimination can become more subtle.

Institutional Racism: Permission to Be Prejudiced

When people in authority give permission for others to behave badly, it is like releasing a flu virus into a community or organization. Some individuals just do not see the value of keeping their hands clean of stereotyping and prejudice. They are more likely to catch and spread the contagion of discriminatory practices. The particular danger of institutional discrimination is that it produces chronic, self-perpetuating institutionalized pathology, the kind of discrimination that leads to a sickness that harms both the victims and the perpetrators of the injustice.

For example, Bradbury and Williams (2006) report that dark-skinned European football ("soccer" in the United States) players have been repeated targets of behind-the-scenes institutional racism. When fans shouted racist taunts, the complaints of Black players were ignored and those who did complain were labeled "trouble-makers." These players may have been singled out for more penalties, too, but they will never know for sure. Institutional discrimination and **attributional ambiguity** make it almost impossible to discover what motivated any particular decision. But by failing to object to racism, the institution sanctioned racism. Institutional racism may be subtle to those who are responsible for it, but it will sometimes feel like a sledgehammer to those on the receiving end.

There are other ways to allow subtle discrimination to continue—one option is simple neglect. Jonathan Kozol's (1991) book *Savage Inequalities* examined the physical spaces in which children learn: the actual classrooms and the buildings in which they are housed. Dilapidated buildings and the absence of basic supplies such as books send a message: "It's not worth the effort trying to educate people like you." According to Dickar (2006, p. 26), reassigning budgetary resources away from needy students is a form of "institutionalized indifference." That appears to be what happened at what may be the most famous public high school in the United States: Erasmus Hall High School (originally named Erasmus Hall Academy) in Brooklyn, New York.

Erasmus Hall

Erasmus Hall High School is the second oldest school in the entire United States. It was founded in 1786 in Brooklyn, New York, as a private institution of learning but later became a public high school. It was built before the 20th-century immigration boom multiplied the population in the Borough of Brooklyn in New York City. Consequently, as these young immigrants started their families, educational opportunities at Erasmus High were waiting for their children. The plan worked—and far better than anyone could have anticipated.

The list of national and internationally recognized alumni from this public high school includes many notable names—and they represent the highest achievers across every discipline *and* over several decades and even generations. It is more than one or two occasional names such as you might recognize from your own high school reunion. The Wikipedia entry lists more than 100 notable individuals, and that does not include many others who made valuable social contributions but with less notoriety.

Pulitzer Prize winner Bernard Malamud is on the list of Erasmus alumni. Barbara McClintock and Eric Kandel are Nobel Prize winners. Notice the diversity: Erasmus graduates include chess champion Bobby Fischer, Hall of Fame basketball player Billy Cunningham, detective novelist Micky Spillane, New Jersey Governor Jim Florio, publisher of *Black Enterprise* Earl Graves, painter Elaine de Kooning, pop singers Neil Diamond and Barbara Streisand, opera singer Beverly Sills, Chicago Bears quarterback Sid Luckman, NFL coach Sam Rutigliano, art historian Arthur Sackler, rapper Special Ed . . . and more. Go ahead; look at the list on Wikipedia and be astonished that they *all* came from the same public high school. Oh, that we could bottle whatever was happening at Erasmus High!

Erasmus alumni offer a few clues as to the recipe for success. One 1937 graduate wrote, "I felt privileged attending Erasmus. The buildings themselves with their Gothic architecture, arches, the lawns and pathways, the statue of Erasmus, and the Old Building made me feel as though I was attending a college of lasting renown" (Kozol, 1991, p. 26). New York City had placed an early bet on education for the masses of immigrants from around the world pouring into Brooklyn, New York—and it paid off in social dividends far greater than Microsoft, Apple, or Facebook ever realized. The philanthropic activities of the super-wealthy are trying to match the achievements of this public high school set near the geographic center of Brooklyn. The "magic" of Erasmus endured across many social changes, decades, and generations—but it didn't last. Understanding the decline of Erasmus can help us plan for a more intelligent, productive future.

Diffusion of Responsibility

New York City suffered a long financial crisis. Banks began "redlining" the neighborhood around Erasmus. The now-illegal practice of redlining refers to lending institutions that identify (with red lines on maps) certain neighborhoods as poor risks. They refuse to lend money to people who live within those areas. Redlining made it difficult for the people moving into the neighborhood around Erasmus to buy homes. So, landlords subdivided their buildings into many smaller apartments, and the neighborhood and the schools became overcrowded.

At the same time, New York City's financial crisis meant that the physical campus was neglected for almost 20 years as lack of funding, overcrowding, and co-occurring events conspired to destroy what newspapers had once called the jewel of the city's public education system. Erasmus High School closed in 1994, after more than two centuries of service to the residents of Brooklyn. New York City made the difficult decision to not continue investing in Erasmus and the new immigrants coming to Brooklyn. The buildings were broken up to serve several other, smaller schools. The generations-long flood of diversity and creativity had slowed to a trickle.

No one bank, city administrator, or borough council ever consciously decided to destroy Erasmus. But during the same time period, "predominantly White schools were well maintained" (Kozol, 1991, p. 31). The effect of this institutional indifference meant that the once-beautiful physical space of what the newspapers now called "Rotting Erasmus" was physically fenced off from the public. Instead of noble arches, students entered the grounds by a side door and passed through metal detectors. By the early 1990s, the dropout rate from the most famous high school in America was close to 50%, and its test scores were close to the bottom.

No one person is to blame for the decline of Erasmus High School; the problem was deeply embedded within self-sustaining economic and social structures. We may not want to be racist, feel particularly racist, or wish anyone else to suffer. But when our income or jobs depend upon continuing a policy that might have a racist edge, we can usually find some way to justify our indifference to others' educational needs. The end effect is institutional discrimination, and it helped deconstruct the most famous high school in America: Erasmus High.

DISCUSSION QUESTIONS

1. Can you identify examples of institutional discrimination in any institutions, organizations, or groups in your own life? Think about, for example, your town, high school, college or university, teams or clubs, and so on.

2. Attributional ambiguity occurs when you're not sure why someone else acted in the way they did toward you. If you didn't get a job, is it because you interviewed badly or because the interviewer was prejudiced against you? If you were complimented by someone, is it because you deserved the compliment or because he or she was trying to manipulate you? Identify at least two specific examples of attributional ambiguity from your own life experiences. How does not being sure of other people's motives make you feel?

3. People in socially privileged groups within a given society often benefit from historical or cultural prejudice, even if they personally don't endorse or participate in the prejudice (e.g., male privilege, White privilege). Is it the responsibility of privileged groups to actively work against their own privilege and toward equality? Or, is it equally the responsibility of every citizen? Alternatively, is it unrealistic to believe that any society could ever truly be free of all forms of prejudice?

KEY TERMS

Attributional ambiguity 140   Institutional discrimination 140   Old-fashioned prejudice 140
Diffusion of responsibility 142

9.3 Footnote 11: After the Doll Studies

On May 17, 1954, the U.S. Supreme Court made one of the most consequential constitutional decisions of the 20th century—and social psychological findings were at the heart of that decision (Benjamin & Crouse, 2002).

The case was *Brown v. Board of Education of Topeka,* which ended "separate but equal" segregated public schools. Children of all different races now would go to school together, in the same building. It was a monumental change and a crucial moment for the civil rights movement. Chief Justice Earl Warren read the Court's unanimous opinion on May 17, 1954. The Court had concluded that "to separate [African American children] from others of similar age and qualifications . . . may affect their hearts and minds in a way unlikely ever to be undone." The Court came to this historic conclusion because of scientific evidence referenced in court documents as Footnote 11.

The story behind Footnote 11 involves the husband-wife team of Kenneth and Mamie Phipps Clark, the first two African Americans to earn doctorates at

Columbia University. The methodology that produced their famous "doll studies" grew out of Mamie Phipps's master's thesis at Howard University (see Johnson & Pettigrew, 2005). The Clarks provided African American children with identical dolls except that one was white-skinned with yellow hair, and the other was brown-skinned with black hair (Whitman, 1993).

Then they asked the children a series of questions about which doll they preferred: "Give me the doll you like to play with," " . . . you like best," " . . . is a nice doll," " . . . looks bad," " . . . is a nice color"—and finally, "which doll is most like you?" Some 90% of these 3- to 7-year-olds accurately indicated they were like the brown-skinned doll—but about two-thirds preferred the white doll! In examining their results, the researchers compared the responses of children attending segregated schools in Washington, DC, and those of children attending racially integrated schools in New York. The preference for the white doll—indicating a negative prejudice toward their own race—was much more pronounced in the children from segregated schools. Culture and segregation had taught them self-hatred, and they transferred those feelings to the dolls.

Some of the children's reactions were disturbing. One girl who had described the brown doll as "ugly" and "dirty" burst into tears; others refused to continue the experiment; some giggled self-consciously; one little boy tried to escape his dilemma by insisting that he had a suntan. The fact that this **internalized racism** was greater for children from segregated schools was a pivotal piece of information in the Court's decision that segregation led to negative outcomes. The Clarks' findings could be used as evidence to support both **social role theory** (that **stereotypes** become self-fulfilling prophecies because we train our children to live up to them) and **social learning theory** (that each generation passes stereotypes to the next through media images, toys, language, and so on).

But it's a complicated history. The Clarks discovered that changing people's stereotypes and attitudes was far more difficult than changing the legal environment, even after the historic *Brown v. Board of Education of Topeka* legal decision (Nyman, 2010). Riots broke out when some African American children, sometimes with armed guards, bravely walked into formerly segregated schools. When one child in Little Rock, Arkansas, was "summarily expelled from school," the Clarks took her into their own home (Jones & Pettigrew, 2005, p. 650).

The American Psychological Association was disturbingly quiet in the aftermath of *Brown v. Board of Education of Topeka* (see Benjamin & Crouse, 2002). In 1970, Kenneth Clark was elected president of the American Psychological Association and in 1994 honored for his lifetime contributions to psychology. But in his acceptance speech, he admitted, "Thirty years after *Brown*, I must accept the fact that my wife left this earth despondent at seeing that damage to children is being knowingly and silently accepted by a nation that claims to be democratic" (from Benjamin & Crouse, 2002, p. 48).

DISCUSSION QUESTIONS

1. Do you think that social psychological research should be used as evidence to persuade jurors, judges, or justices in court cases? Why or why not?

2. Discuss at least two strengths and two limitations of the Clarks' procedure as a way to test internalized racism or the effects of school segregation with very young children. For each of the limitations you have identified, how would you design a study that would overcome these limitations or challenges?

3. Kenneth Clark's speech in 1994 expressed disappointment that the United States had not progressed further in eliminating prejudice and discrimination. Do you agree with his conclusion? Do you see progress between 1994 and now—or do you agree with some social psychologists that forms of discrimination have simply become more subtle or concealed?

4. Explain how the Clark doll studies can be used as evidence to support both social role theory and social learning theory.

KEY TERMS

Internalized racism 144
Social learning theory 144

Social role theory 144

Stereotype 144

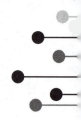

CHAPTER 10

Helping and Prosocial Behavior

10.1 Insects, Vampire Bats, Prairie Dogs, and Fish: Altruism in Animals

We humans are not alone when it comes to trading altruistic-like favors. Many other social animals also appear to have evolved **reciprocal altruism** (Van Vugt & Van Lange, 2006). This case study takes you on a quick tour of prosocial behavior among nonhuman animals—especially among those animals that humans deem unlikely to exhibit any so-called altruism, such as insects and vampire bats. Many social psychologists are not comfortable with the term *altruism* applied to both human and nonhuman animals—and with good reason: They are skeptical that "pure" altruism even exists.

Is Pure Altruism Possible?

Pure altruism is the idea that cooperative or self-sacrificing behaviors are performed with no selfish benefits. In contrast, **egoistic altruism** is the idea that there is almost always—if not always—some benefit from being a "good" person (or animal). Pure altruism can be tainted in many ways. Here are just a few subtly self-serving ways to be "altruistic":

(a) self-sacrificing so you can boost your self-esteem,

(b) donating your time in ways that strengthen your relationships with a group you want to be part of,

(c) increasing the positive thoughts that you think others will have about you as they learn about your volunteerism,

(d) reinforcing the comforting belief that "what goes around comes around,"

(e) trying to increase your reward in an afterlife,

(f) reducing your sense of guilt if you don't help someone in need, and

(g) building a reputation as a "good person" so that you have social capital you can spend at a later date.

All these (and many more) reasons demonstrate why many social psychologists don't believe in pure altruism. For many, the preferred term is *prosocial behavior*. It is a more general description that can include both pure and egoistic altruism. The phrase "prosocial behavior" is a little clunky, in our opinion, and doesn't quite challenge humans to think more critically about their own motivations. So, like some others, we will use the terms *altruism* and *prosocial behavior* almost interchangeably and leave it to you to weigh the evidence of each case about pure versus egoistic altruism in humans and other animals.

The motives listed above make sense for humans—but what about other animals? It's difficult for many humans to perceive that animals such as fish or insects might feel "guilt" about not helping each other or might help each other to boost their social reputation. So why do nonhuman animals seem to engage in selfless, prosocial behaviors that include making sacrifices to their own well-being to help others? Our altruism tour will include creatures on land, water, and air. We begin with insects because they tell us why it is smart for us, the reasoning human animal, to pay attention to altruism where it seems to be most *un*likely to appear.

Insects

We don't like 'em. And Marlene Zuk (2011) believes that our dislike of insects is precisely why they are so informative to humans. The usual problem in animal research is anthropomorphism. We humans easily project human characteristics onto creatures that can walk with two legs: cuddly bear cubs or misunderstood gorillas climbing tall buildings. It's a little more difficult to compare ourselves with four-legged creatures—but easier if they will at least stand up straight from time to time. Panda bears are cuddly, squirrels can be cute, and mice in children's literature are dressed in clothes and have elaborate social interactions. Four-legged creatures such as cats, dogs, horses, and even skunks are often treated like or compared to humans.

But six legs?! We resist reacting to six-legged creatures as if they were human. However, there are some easy cases of what looks like self-sacrificing insect altruism. One class of honeybees defends their hive by stinging intruders—and dying in the process. Ants will form impressive bridges that allow other ants to literally "walk all over them" because it is good for the larger community of ants. But on the whole, it seems more difficult to sympathize with the plight of cockroaches, uncomfortable to worry about the survival of earwigs, and downright weird to compare humans to the jewel wasp that turns cockroaches into walking zombies.

Marlene Zuk (2011) explains one reason that the jewel wasp inspires her to look for human insight from insects:

> Many wasps provision their young by paralyzing other insects or
> spiders and carrying them back to the wasp's nest. [Paralyzing] helps

the prey stay fresh while the young wasp larva feasts on the flesh. Of course, paralyzed insects can't put themselves into the nest, so the wasp usually has to do all the heavy lifting, staggering under the weight of her groceries as she flies back to her young. Except, that is, in the case of the jewel wasp. . . . The female wasp . . . makes it into a zombie via a judicious sting inside the roach's head, so that its nervous system, and legs, still function well enough to allow it to walk on its own. (pp. 3–5)

The jewel wasp then grabs the zombie cockroach's antenna and leads it like a dog on a leash to its doom: fresh food for the rising generation of jewel wasps—whose females will also possess zombie-making powers. There are several deep philosophical questions here. Is the jewel wasp committing a biochemical hijacking of the cockroach's free will? Do cockroaches and wasps even have a free will? Zuk declares, "Insects are even teaching us about mind control, and maybe even about consciousness itself" (p. 3).

The world of insects, Zuk (2011) concluded, teaches us that "it is possible to be unselfish without a moral code, sophisticated without an education, and beautiful wearing a skeleton on the outside" (p. 7). These mama jewel wasps are working to feed their children—one kind of altruism. But many would argue that the act of feeding your own children isn't exactly selfless; you're certainly interested in keeping them alive so that your genes are passed into the next generation. This kind of prosocial behavior is probably most easily argued as egoistic or self-serving instead of pure altruism. Notice, however, that the helping behavior benefits near relatives in the next generation (called kinship selection) rather than the individual jewel wasp. What other prosocial behaviors can we see in unlikely nonhuman animals?

Vampire Bats

Vampire bats famously feast on blood, usually from large mammals such as wild pigs, cows, and horses (but rarely from humans). They need a lot of blood. Vampire bats will drink about half their body weight during an uninterrupted feeding—so much that they sometimes have difficulty taking flight. Lisa DeNault and Don McFarlane (1995) discovered why vampire bats are so bloodthirsty. A vampire bat will die if it goes more than 48 to 72 hours without a blood meal. But they also found that both male and female vampire bats will, in an apparent act of altruism, regurgitate some of their blood meal and share it with starving neighbors. This act of charity and self-sacrifice surprises many, especially given stereotypes and fears about this particular species. And the story of vampire bat altruism is even more sophisticated—perhaps in ways that indicate egoistic altruism at a group level.

Vampire bats are selective in their sharing of blood. When Gerald Wilkinson (1984) studied vampire bats in Costa Rica, he discovered that they were more likely to donate blood to those bats with the greatest need for a meal. Furthermore, their altruistic food sharing was not limited to their immediate kin, which would have been predicted by the theory of inclusive fitness. Instead, frequent roost-mates were more likely to be the beneficiaries. Perhaps most interestingly, the evidence suggests that vampire bats are able to identify, remember, and *not* help those vampire bats that had *not* previously donated blood to other starving bats. In short, being selfish was punished. There was an expectation of helping each other in times of need—and if you left me high and dry (both metaphorically and literally in the case of thirsty vampire bats), I won't help you when you are in need. Among vampire bats, reciprocal altruism has evolved into a sophisticated social norm, complete with altruistic punishment for those vampire bats that are less altruistic.

There are at least two critical insights embedded in these observations about altruism among vampire bats. First, to assess the blood needs of its own and of its neighbors, the vampire bat has to be aware of itself as distinct from other bats—and that suggests self-awareness. Second, mutual sharing suggests reciprocal altruism, which implies an ability to track favors given and favors received and make a discerning judgment about a neighbor based on that information. This suggests that bats have a long-term memory, a sense of their social world, and the ability to make judgments about the relative worth of friends and neighbors.

Prairie Dogs

When they were left undisturbed by human development on the Nebraska grasslands, prairie dogs created huge, elaborately tunneled prairie dog towns. Their populations were estimated in the millions. As you can imagine, such a large collection of prairie dogs looks pretty appetizing to predators such as hawks. So "dog towns" developed elaborate, highly cooperative defense networks. For example, prairie dogs created numerous elevated lookout posts, posted sentries, and developed rapid emergency communication networks. The sentries' job was to warn the other inhabitants of dog town about perceived threats from approaching predators (Johnsgard, 2005). It was a risky job being the lookout for all the other prairie dogs. You have to stand there, vigilant, out in the open. If you let your guard down just for a moment, a fox could pounce, a hawk could dive, or a snake could strike—and you will be the first to die.

Do the prairie dogs doing lookout duty have more altruistic personalities than the other prairie dogs? They may not have been more altruistic—but some evidence suggests they were highly prejudiced—at least while on lookout duty. Why?

Evolution rewarded those prairie dogs that were prejudiced against all flying creatures, for example. A shadow passing over a sentry prairie dog's head might be
nothing more than a small cloud, a wandering crow, or a red-winged blackbird.
But it also might be a predator hawk or a cunning owl.

When a sentry prairie dog senses a shadow, it issues an alarm that triggers
automatic antihawk prejudices that ripple through the entire dog town community. All the other prairie dogs dive back down into their burrows. It might have
been a false alarm, but in the struggle for life, prairie dogs preferred prejudice
over death. They dive back into their burrows first and ask questions later. Like
prairie dogs, individual humans must also be vigilant about the welfare of their
group—and for the same reasons. Anything that threatens our particular group
also threatens us as individuals, which motivates the sentries to continue their
prejudiced, prosocial, and potentially self-sacrificing behavior.

Fish

Finally, cooperation among fishes has been studied by biologist Dugatkin
and mathematician Mesterton-Gibbons (Dugatkin & Mesterton-Gibbons, 1996).
They note that some species of fish form groups or schools to help in foraging.
When wrasse fish were in groups of fewer than 30 individuals, they almost never
gained access to resources, whereas groups of 200 or more were successful in
chasing away predators and even eating predator fishes' embryos as a tasty snack.
Cooperating and working as part of a group led to better chances of survival.
But joining a group isn't much of a sacrifice. These authors also note that several species of fish (e.g., minnows, bluegill, and guppies) sometimes designate an
"inspector" whose job is to swim slightly away from the group almost like a scout,
looking for potential predators. These inspector fish are less likely to get food and
are more likely to be eaten by the predators. This job seems a lot closer to the type
of altruism we think of in human examples.

In one final and interesting example of prosocial behavior in fish, Dugatkin
and Mesterton-Gibbons (1996) discuss the rare potential of deep-water seabass to
act as either "mothers" (producing eggs) or "fathers" (producing sperm)—in other
words, the *same individual fish* can produce both. When these hermaphroditic seabass mate, they alternate between releasing eggs and sperm over several alternating rounds. The selfish or tempting act would be to only release sperm, because
there is an infinite or unlimited supply of sperm, whereas there are only so many
eggs available over a lifetime. But the seabass don't appear to "cheat;" they seem to
cooperate and trust each other in this Prisoner's Dilemma type of sexual exchange
of reciprocal altruism.

DISCUSSION QUESTIONS

1. When a parent sacrifices time, money, or other resources to feed his or her children, does that count as altruism? Why or why not?

2. What is your opinion regarding the debate between "pure" altruism versus "egoistic" altruism? Do you think that pure altruism

exists? Provide evidence to defend your answer.

3. Find evidence for at least one other nonhuman animal species that appears to display altruism and summarize those patterns of behavior. Make sure to properly cite any sources you use.

KEY TERMS

Altruism 146
Egoistic altruism 146

Pure altruism 146

Reciprocal altruism 146

10.2 The Bacon Truce: Zig-Zags and the Development of Cooperation

Situations matter—especially on the frontlines of war.

That insight burrowed deep into Kurt Lewin's awareness as he fulfilled the duties that earned him the Iron Cross as a wounded foot soldier during World War I. The founder of social psychology had entered the German army as a private and exited as a lieutenant. But at heart, he was always a scholar carefully observing the world around him. Lewin noticed, for example, that under normal circumstances, a soldier would never deliberately burn someone else's fine furniture. But in a situation with freezing soldiers struggling to survive a bitter night, burning that same furniture made sense. The situation mattered, and so did your perception of the situation. The brutal battlefield of dead horses, overlapping shell holes, scattered limbs, and lines of gas-blinded boys and men clinging to the shoulder of the soldier in front of him—well, that just looked like a gentle pastoral scene when viewed from a distant hill. The same situation could hold different meanings depending on your perspective.

Sociologist and historian Tony Ashworth (1980) helped discover something almost hopeful about the human condition in the extraordinary misery of those brutal trenches: the evolution of cooperation. Ashworth concluded that cooperation between sworn enemies evolved not because some great healer, commanding general, or visionary politician brought it to pass. It evolved, in part, because the trenches of World War I were dug in a zig-zag pattern. This case study has to start with an explanation for why the situations created by those zig-zagging trenches existed in the first place.

Unintended Consequences of Zig-Zagging Trenches

The zig-zagging trenches that Lewin and millions of other soldiers lived in during World War I were not part of the original plan of any of the nations involved in this global conflict. Both sides presumed that this would be a short, glorious war that would be won by the army that could move the fastest. The infamous western front (in Europe) evolved because each army kept trying to speedily outflank the other until they both bumped into the North Sea and had to settle down into what Ashworth (1980) called a "long, narrow zone of violence" (p. 3). It was so narrow that towns and villages not far from the western front barely knew the war existed. During the early years, only the occasional sounds of explosions and the disappearance of so many young men from farms and villages signaled that their country was at war. The two armies settled into trench warfare because there was nowhere else for them to go. Ashworth (1980) explained that

> the western front emerged as the infantries of each deadlocked army huddled in countless hastily dug and unconnected rifle pits, then joined these together into two continuous but parallel and opposing trench lines. (p. 4)

From this simple beginning, a line of complex trenches stretched almost 500 miles from the North Sea to Switzerland, across different countries, and through varied terrain. Between the two armies was no man's land that each side gradually filled with barbed wire. The trenches themselves were purposefully dug not as straight lines but as small zig-zags. The purpose of the zig-zag was to prevent the enemy from aiming down a long, straight line of soldiers. The zig-zag pattern also provided more protection against shell blasts. While intended for military purposes, the zig-zags inadvertently created many small groups of soldiers. Over time, those groups became small, coherent, independent, decision-making groups.

These social groups lived within the bays created by the zig-zags. This was where soldiers brewed tea, fried bacon, and "chatted" while delousing themselves by picking lice off one another. The groups acted with relative independence because they were somewhat isolated from their neighbors and much more isolated from high command. However, they also were living very close to their enemy. And the same thing was happening on both sides of no man's land. Small groups of soldiers could make independent decisions about whether or not to fight, how to fight, and when to fight.

The zig-zag pattern had created 500 miles of small, relatively independent situations. Their living quarters created opportunities for deep **social exchanges** as young men on both sides struggled together through many life and death situations. Their proximity to the enemy across no man's land also created situations that gave cooperation with their enemy a chance to develop. The frontline soldiers on both sides were physically, emotionally, and—in terms of the supplies necessary for survival—much closer to their sworn enemy than to their own commanding officers. There were social exchanges both within groups and between groups, and the opportunity for **prosocial moral reasoning** presented itself.

Organizational Structures and Sampling Techniques

The organizational structure of the army contributed to the unplanned development of cooperation between enemies. A battalion in the British army included about 1,000 soldiers and 35 officers. The battalion was the administrative grouping that organized soldiers for battle, supplied food, paid salaries, delivered mail, and administered medical care. It included 64 sections with about 14 men each. That smallest grouping was approximately the number of soldiers who could fit into one, two, or three bays created by the zig-zagging trenches.

Four battalions made a brigade; three brigades made a division. The level of the division was how top military planners tried to strategically conduct the war. Ashworth's case study of cooperation between enemies during war focused on two levels: His sampling technique focused on divisions that were responsible for about 5,000 yards of the western front. But the actual cases that described how soldiers thought, felt, and behaved came from the section level. Ashworth sampled written materials that came from 57 divisions that had experienced direct combat for at least 3 months. He discovered data about informal truces from 56 (98%) of those 57 divisions and collected an average of three documents from each division. The most famous truce was the Christmas Truce of 1914, when opposing soldiers exchanged gifts and souvenirs and played football. But Ashworth has discovered something very important—and hopeful: Truces in the trenches were (a) fairly common, and (b) spontaneous.

The sample of documents testifying to informal truces included diaries, letters, and accounts written both at the time and afterward. It is important to note what is not included in Ashworth's sample. He did not use official histories or official war diaries because the behavior of interest, informal peacemaking, was not officially allowed. He also did not include his many interviews with surviving soldiers unless they could provide some form of written confirmation. This conservative research approach suggests that Ashworth's estimates of the frequency of spontaneous peacemaking are an underestimate.

"Live and Let Live" Versus "Kill and Be Killed"

Evidence for peacemaking is hidden behind crude statistics. For example, the official war history estimates that during May to September 1915, the British army suffered an average of 300 casualties per day. But that doesn't mean that on a typical day, there were 300 casualties. On July 1, 1916, the first day of the Battle of the Somme, the British army suffered an estimated 57,470 casualties. So the other face of trench warfare included many peaceful days such as those suggested by a report that "for twenty-one days we held 'E' sector . . . so peaceful was the outlook we might have been cloistered in a monastery" (Ashworth, 1980, p. 17). Soldiers asked to not be rotated out of their frontline positions to preserve the friendly lack of combat.

Not surprisingly, higher command did not approve of informal peacemaking between frontline soldiers. "Fraternization with the enemy" was not just frowned upon; some soldiers were executed because of their own commands for getting too friendly with the enemy. Nevertheless, the peacemaking persisted informally behind the backs of superior officers. Peacemaking between enemies was fueled by a simple philosophy that was more powerful than orders from a distant general: "Live and let live." The alternative, of course, was to "kill and be killed," and when faced with that choice, some number of soldiers in at least 56 of 57 British divisions chose to live.

The smallest, shortest truces could be between two soldiers on night patrol in no man's land such as that recorded in the diary of an officer in the 24th division who discovered a German and a British soldier chatting deep within a shell hole:

> I found Pte Bates . . . fraternizing with a German . . . Bates: "What rank are you in your army?" "I am a corporal," indicating stripes on his collar. "What rank are you?" "Oh," replied Bates, "I am Company Sergt Major." (Ashworth, 1980, p. 20)

Communications and Negotiations

How did Bates and the German soldier end up chatting amiably in a shell hole? Did they surprise one another on patrol, yet not fire their weapons? Before enlisting, most soldiers on both sides had been fed a constant diet of information that demonized the enemy. They had been enthusiastic volunteers for a grand cause that they believed in but could not articulate. They had been sent off to war with songs, pride, parades, cheering women, and in the company of thousands of other young men who were equally enthusiastic. It had been a powerful, patriotic social norm.

Now they found themselves in a muddy trench, often walking through soiled water, suffering from trench foot, plagued by rats feeding on the corpses of their comrades, and fearful of lifting their heads above the rim of the trench and into the scopes of snipers. The social norms of live and let live needed to be communicated to new recruits immediately before their enthusiasm for war set off new rounds of killing. **Reciprocal altruism** became very real. In one case, Ashworth (1980) described how a new recruit, Raleigh, was taken on a tour of the trenches and taught the informal rules of wartime sportsmanship by seasoned soldiers, one of them named Trotter:

Trotter: That's the Bosche front line. Bosche looking over this way now, maybe, just as we are—do you play cricket?

Raleigh: A bit.

Trotter: Could you chuck a cricket ball that distance?

Raleigh: I think so.

Trotter: Then you could do the same with a Mills bomb. . . . But you won't. Come on . . . let sleeping dogs lie. If we was to throw a bomb you can bet your boots the old Bosche would chuck one back, and Mr. Digby and Mr. 'Arris are both married men. Wouldn't be cricket would it? (p. 30)

Triggers for Truces

The most famous trigger for truce was the Christmas Truce of 1914, widely celebrated for the singing of carols, a soccer game in no man's land, exchanging of items, and taking photographs of one another before returning to the war. It involved nine divisions along 30 miles of the western front. It was verbally arranged, but trust was probably built slowly from many previous, smaller truces and both explicit and implicit social exchanges.

The first truce probably was triggered by food. They couldn't drive teams of horses and food wagons in the trenches, so it would have been easy for each side to shell the others' food trucks. Both sides delivered their rations to the frontlines at about the same time. One of the noncommissioned officers observed that

I suppose the enemy were occupied in the same way; so things were quiet at that hour for a couple of nights, and the ration parties became careless because of it, and laughed and talked on their way back to their companies. (Ashworth, 1980, p. 24)

Ian Hay of the ninth division wrote that

it would be child's play to shell the road behind the enemy's trenches, crowded as it must be with ration wagons and water carts, into a bloodstained wilderness . . . but on the whole there is silence. After all, if you prevent your enemy from drawing his rations, his remedy is simple: He will prevent you from drawing yours. (p. 26)

Breakfast seemed most likely to trigger a truce:

On December 1, 1914, a Private Hawkings from the 5th Division poked his head above the parapet of the trench when a sergeant suggested that the reason his "earnest curiosity had not been greeted with a shower of bullets was probably due to . . . Fritz enjoying his breakfast." (p. 25)

The soldier-historian Lidell Hart believed that breakfast truces were common, in part because

unforgettable, too, is the homely smell of breakfast bacon that gained its conquest over the war reek of chloride of lime, and in so doing not only brought a tacit truce to the battlefront, but helped in preserving sanity. (p. 25)

A bacon truce! The diaries indicated many other triggers for truces. There were rain truces that allowed each side to repair their trench walls and straw truces that allowed both sides to fetch some hay in no man's land for warmth. There were informal truces for a German violinist, a British trumpeter, and even a drunken Scot who wandered, bottle in hand, into no man's land yet made it safely back to his trench.

Conclusions

The historical case study that Tony Ashworth created from the written reports of trench soldiers brought attention to a hopeful element from a tragic war: the evolution of cooperation during war. Cooperation between enemies was the result of a live and let live philosophy that made more sense to the frontline soldiers than following the kill and be killed orders of their "superiors." The impulse to survive even in such distressing circumstances was able to take root because small, situational forces, such as the zig-zag pattern of the trenches, encouraged social exchanges between sworn enemies.

DISCUSSION QUESTIONS

1. Many soldiers' lives may have been saved, at least for a few months, due to informal truces between enemies on the frontlines who wanted to preserve their own lives. However, this may have delayed the war and affected lives of private citizens back home. What are the ethical responsibilities of "everyday" soldiers when it comes to following orders from their superiors in cases such as this?

2. Have you ever experienced the slow development of trust with someone whom you originally considered an "enemy," or at least with someone whom you did not trust originally? What situational circumstances led to that development—and did it end with positive or negative results?

3. Ashworth's study of informal truces couldn't come from official war archives because this type of truce wasn't allowed. What does this teach us about sources of data for research purposes? Can archival data be trusted—why or why not?

KEY TERMS

Prosocial moral reasoning 153   Reciprocal altruism 155   Social exchange 153

10.3 The Subway Samaritan: The Mathematics of Relative Altruism

Kinship selection and inclusive fitness combine to drive the evolutionary urge to favor those with closer genetic relatedness. It appears to explain a great deal of what we think of as altruism—but not all of it. This account was pieced together from reports from several sources: the Associated Press, the *New York Times*, television reports and interviews, and by a CBS News interview in 2012, 5 years after the incident occurred. The quotations vary slightly between sources but do not suggest any material difference in reporting—the facts are consistent across sources.

The 1 Train at Broadway and 137th Street

Many subway routes in New York City are identified by letters such as the "A train," the "C train," or the "E train." Others are identified by numbers and called the "1 train" and so on. This case study is about something that happened on the 1 train as it was headed downtown and coming in to the stop at Broadway and 137th Street.

"I'm still saying I'm not a hero," Mr. Wesley Autrey insisted, "'cause I believe all New Yorkers should get into that type of mode. You should do the right thing." In 2007, Autrey was trying to deflect the unexpected rush of praise he was experiencing. "And if I had to do it again, I probably would," Autrey also told the hosts of CBS's *Early Show*. "I was like, 'Wow, I got to get this guy' . . . somebody's gotta save this guy but I was the closest one." Perhaps Autrey wasn't affected by **urban overload**.

It was a Tuesday, 12:45 p.m. Autrey was a 51-year-old Navy veteran and construction worker. He was waiting with his two daughters (4 and 6 years old) for the downtown 1 train. Cameron Hollopeter, from Littleton, Massachusetts, was a 20-year-old film student at the New York Film Academy. Hollopeter also was waiting for the train when he experienced a seizure and fell onto the tracks. He got up and stumbled to the edge of the platform as two women rushed to help him. But he stumbled again and fell back between the tracks as the headlights of the downtown 1 train appeared approaching the station. The train screeched its brakes but could not stop in time.

Autrey left his girls with two strangers and jumped down onto the tracks to try to save another stranger. "The driver hit the horn so I knew from that sound he wasn't going to make it," Autrey told *CBS News* 5 years later. He tackled Hollopeter and held him down in what *CBS News* called "the murky, filthy water." He remained on top of him with a clearance of approximately 1 inch between his head and the five-car train that rumbled over his head. Autrey described what happened next (CBS, 2012):

> Everybody started to freak so I yelled from underneath the train saying "excuse me everybody, be quiet, I am the father. Please let my girls know that I am OK."

It took about 40 minutes for rescuers to get them out. During that time:

> Well, the kid, he was getting a little tight and I said, "We are underneath a train." He said, "Are we dead? Are we in heaven?" I said no. He kept asking . . . so many times, that I give him a pinch and said, "Dude, you're very much alive!"

Hollopeter was taken to St. Luke's Roosevelt Hospital. Autrey reported that nothing was wrong with him, so he continued his day and went to work. "I don't feel like I did something spectacular; I just saw someone who needed help. I did what I felt was right." But when he went to work the next day, his boss bought him lunch (a ham-and-cheese sandwich) and told him that he could "take yesterday off." While walking to his mother's apartment, a stranger put $10 in his hand. The media had tracked him down, dubbing him "the Subway Samaritan" and "Subway Superman."

The mayor congratulated him, Chrysler offered him a new car, and he gave guest appearances on *Oprah, Ellen,* and late-night talk shows. He admitted to being nervous before he appeared on the *Late Show With David Letterman.* When he met with President Bush, the president asked him, "You were scared of the audience but you weren't of a 32-ton train?!" Hollopeter's emotional father tried to read to the press from notes. "Mr. Autrey's instinctive and unselfish act . . . there are no words."

Empathy for his worried daughters was the first thing on Autrey's mind—a concern predicted by kinship selection. But it doesn't explain why Autrey jumped in front of the train in the first place. Hollopeter was 20 years old and came from a small Massachusetts town, about 25 miles north of Boston, with a population in 2007 of just less than 9,000. Autrey was 51 years old, had been raised in Alabama, but had lived in Harlem for three decades. They didn't appear to have much in common—except their shared humanity.

DISCUSSION QUESTIONS

1. Do you believe that humans are good, evil, or something else entirely? State what you believe and why you believe it.

2. Describe three small acts of kindness or helpfulness and any psychological rewards that the individual might receive.

3. On the surface, this case study might be used as evidence against strict evolutionary theories or explanations of altruism: Someone helped someone else who shared zero genetics. What defense could evolutionary theories use in the face of this case study?

KEY TERMS

Inclusive fitness 157   Kinship selection 157   Urban overload hypothesis 158

Aggression

11.1 Doloreisa's Story: Aggression, Prostitution, and Sex Trafficking

A Central American woman, Doloreisa (not her real name), needed money.

Doloreisa took the advice of an acquaintance who turned out to be a recruiter for sex traffickers. She left her daughter with her mother and joined a group of women expecting to earn $200 per month working in a restaurant in the north. Instead, they were imprisoned in an apartment, repeatedly raped, and then sold and resold as prostitutes and slaves several times across Central and North America.

The forced use of humans for commercial sex is a dark and violent business. Although some prostitutes have not been coerced into the business, Farr (2005) believes that arguing about the degree of personal choice misses the central point. Sex workers are the targets of **aggression** from recruiters, traffickers, clients, and governments (Gil & Anderson, 1998). According to the website EqualityNow.Org (2017), sex trafficking is the fastest-growing crime in the world, and over 20 million people are currently living as kidnapped workers. They also state that 60% of people who survive trafficking were first taken for sexual purposes.

The victims who are also the products in this global, tax-free, multi-billion-dollar business are usually poor women and children. Farr (2005) identified several forms of violence against women and children in sex trafficking. Violence and aggression can be direct—such as physically harming someone else—but it can also be indirect forms of abuse and exploitation. Aggression and violence can also be broken down in other **typologies**, such as physical versus emotional, or **instrumental** versus **hostile**. Consider the myriad forms of abuse that trafficked victims experience and how many different types of aggression these individuals are forced to endure.

Types of Violence

"Breaking-In" Violence. Breaking-in violence is a kind of "welcome to the industry" ritual used to suppress women and children who are initially resistant to becoming sexual slaves. Various forms of rape, starvation, and beatings are common.

Deterrent Violence. Beatings are most often administered as punishment for attempts to escape. Women forced into sexual slavery are reluctant to report violence, partly because they usually do not speak the local language, are unfamiliar with the local geography, and have no social support.

Routine Control Violence. Based on sampled reports from rescued women, violence against sex workers by their controllers appears to be routine: 89% in a study of approximately 1,000 women from Tajikistan, 73% of 37 women trafficked into the United States, 56% among a sample of 200 women from Kosovar, and 33% of 125 women returned to their native Albania (Doole, 2001; Farr, 2005; Kane, 1998; Raymond, Hughes, & Gomez, 2001).

The economics of prostitution and sex trafficking make it difficult to combat. Luise White's (1990) oral histories provided a glimpse into the personal economics of prostitution in colonial Nairobi. In that paternalistic culture, women used prostitution to generate personal income that they typically sent home to their rural families. Ironically, the risk of aggression was the price they paid to preserve their family structures (see Gilfoyle, 1999).

The Debt-Bondage System. The economic benefits of trafficking do not trickle down to the sex worker. Since the breakup of the Soviet Union, about 500,000 women from that region have been sold into prostitution every year. However, the sex trafficking debt-bondage system requires that women sold into prostitution repay the sex trafficker for inflated expenses (see Farr, 2005, p. 21). For example, a trafficker might tell a woman he's kidnapped that she actually owes him the money it cost to deliver her to another country—and that if she doesn't pay, she'll go to jail.

The recruiters make a significant profit at the back end in addition to even greater profits in the middle when squalid conditions keep overhead costs for slaveowners extremely low. As slaves, the women's work and income potential are not limited to paid-for sexual services. They may be a thank you gift to a corrupt politician, are expected to increase alcohol sales while soliciting customers, and work in the garden and kitchens when the brothel is not busy. The price of poor production is a beating and sometimes death.

Institutional and Cultural Support

Prostitution and sex trafficking are deeply embedded in cultures, often with quasi-official support for sexual aggression. Farr (2005) traced cultural supports for prostitution across centuries and cultures (see also Goldstein, 2001). For example, to control sexually transmitted diseases during World War II in Hawaii, the Honolulu Police Department registered 250 prostitutes as licensed "entertainers."

The women were required to have regular medical exams, were not allowed to own property or a car, could not go out after 10:30 at night, and were not allowed to marry a member of the U.S. Army or Navy (see Bailey & Farber, 1992; Farr, 2005; Sturdevant & Stoltzfus, 1992).

Taxes and Profit Margins. The lack of taxes is only one reason that sex trafficking is a highly profitable business. An impoverished family may benefit by selling a daughter into prostitution, especially if she is a young virgin. Market forces put downward pressure on the age at which children are abducted into the commercial sex industry. But older sex slaves are also highly profitable commodities. Depending on the country to which they have been sold, each woman represents a profit of $50,000 to $150,000 per year.

Military Support. The culture often provides a knowing wink to sexual aggression, especially when the military is involved. For example, an odd form of entertainment evolved prior to the 1992 closing of the U.S. Clark Air Force Base in Angeles City in the Philippines. "Foxy boxing" required women to fight one another— and they were refused payment "until they drew blood or showed bruises" (Farr, 2005, pp. 190–195). Post–World War II military planners were aware of the volatile mixture of social forces around the Clark base: 25,000 (permanent) plus another 70,000 (rotating) troops in a small city. They were mostly young men, full of sexual energy, military minded, and far away from home. They were in a city with more than 1,500 registered bars, brothels, and massage parlors— and 55,000 Filipino girls and women working as "entertainers." After the base closings, the region became a vacation destination for sex tourism (Barry, 1995; Kluge, 1986).

Japanese Comfort Women. "Comfort women" was the positive-sounding euphemism that described the sexual enslavement of 200,000 Asian women by the Japanese military between 1942 and 1945. About 80% were Korean women, but there were also Filipina, Chinese, Burmese, and Thai women abducted from their homes and communities, beaten into submission, and forced to live in "comfort stations" near Japanese military bases. About 75% of these women "did not survive the violence they endured at the hands of the Japanese army" (Chai, 1993; Farr, 2005, p. 199). At war's end, the defeated Japanese opened their "comfort stations" to U.S. troops. The U.S. military asked that they build more.

Responses to Prostitution

Reynolds (1986) described four ways in which societies have responded to prostitution:

- Laissez-faire treats prostitution as illegal but tolerated.
- Regulation closely monitors legalized prostitution.
- A control approach legally suppresses obvious prostitution.
- Zoning accepts illicit prostitution within a particular geographic area (e.g., a "redlight" district).

Each approach has consequences in terms of aggression. For example, the laissez-faire, control, and zoning approaches all encourage a prostitute not to report any aggression because (a) authorities turn a blind eye to prostitution (laissez-faire), or (b) reporting aggression invites legal prosecution (control and zoning). Regulation, on the other hand, provides prostitutes with protection from aggression and reduces the transmission of STDs for both prostitutes and their clients. Within feminist circles, many people debate whether legalizing prostitution endorses the sexual objectification of women or provides safety and protection for women providing a consensual service that is simply never going away.

We opened this case study with the story of Doloreisa. Because of her trafficking victimization, she lost all contact with her family for several years. She reappeared in their lives about 15 years later, severely ill with an untreated sexually transmitted disease. She was shunned by them and died about a year later. This reaction from her former loved ones may have been one of the final forms of aggression she experienced during her shortened life.

DISCUSSION QUESTIONS

1. Prostitution has been called "the world's oldest profession." Should it be legalized, taxed, and regulated? This case provided just a start on the two sides of this debate. Discuss at least two advantages to legalizing prostitution, provide at least two disadvantages, and then state your opinion on the issue.

2. If sex trafficking follows the movement of armies, then what policies could military officers introduce that are likely to be effective at reducing the abuse of women by soldiers?

3. Create a typology—or use one that already exists in literature regarding aggression and

violence—to categorize each of the forms of aggression that were discussed in this case study. Identify at least two additional forms of aggression that you imagine victims of trafficking experience and add them to your typology.

4. Who should be given the harshest punishment when sex trafficking rings are brought down? Possible choices are the person who originally led the victim into trafficking (the kidnapper), the person who bought the prostitute (the owner), the customer who pays to have sex, the prostitute herself, or others.

11.2 The Great Train Robbery: Violence as Entertainment

First viewed in 1903, *The Great Train Robbery* (created by Edwin Porter and Thomas Edison; available on YouTube) was the very first moving picture to tell a story. Only 10 minutes long, the silent film begins when a stationmaster is beaten unconscious and then tied up by a gang who secretly board the train. Gang members exchange five shots with a guard before killing him, exploding a safe, and taking the loot. (The actor playing the dead guard wiggles around until he gets his arm in a more comfortable position, but he is *supposed* to be dead.)

Next, the gang takes over the steam engine by beating another man and throwing him off the train. They force the engineer to stop the train, rob the passengers, and shoot one man in the back as he foolishly tries to flee. That's one explosion, two beatings, two robberies, and three murders before history's first story film reached the 3-minute mark. The gang exits by shooting two more times into the air.

Cut to the unconscious, tied-up stationmaster's daughter, delivering his lunch. She discovers her father, prays that he is alive, cuts him loose with a large knife she happened to bring with her, and prays again. Finally, she throws water in his face. (She misses and actually throws the water over his shoulder, but he revives anyway.)

Cut again to a square dance of ordinary, happy citizens—who periodically shoot their guns to keep the dancing lively (three more gunshots). The stationmaster bursts in with news of the robbery and they form a posse. A chase scene produces 10 more gunshots and one more anonymous person killed. Cut once more to a forest scene in which the posse surprises the gang as they are splitting up their loot: about 25 gunshots and two more deaths.

But in the last 6 seconds, we come to the most famous scene in this historically important film. A rough-looking outlaw looks directly into the camera, slowly pulls out his gun, and fires directly at the camera! Twice! The first audience to see the film famously ducked in their seats and started to leave the theater—until they remembered that it was only a film. Then they demanded three more showings—and still didn't want to leave. Was the audience thrilled into increasing their own levels of violence, sparked by an **escalation of aggression**? Was there a **weapons effect** in which all the guns, knives, and violence primed the audience toward aggression? Or did watching fictional violence on film provide a cathartic experience that made them more peaceful and cooperative?

The 10-minute total is as follows:

- One explosion

- One man thrown off a train (fate uncertain, probably dead)

- Two beatings

- Two competing gangs of armed civilians

- Two robberies

- Five deaths

- About 50 gunshots

That averages to approximately one act of violence every 60 seconds and one gunshot for every 12 seconds during history's first storytelling film—plus one young woman who knows how to handle a large knife.

An article on CNN's website in 2013 stated that gun violence in movies has increased steadily since 1950, that gun violence in PG-13 movies is even worse than that seen in R-rated movies, and that "Americans love movies that depict violence" (Wilson & Hudson, 2013). The article cites several statistics from a study published in the journal *Pediatrics* that reviewed violence in PG-13 movies from 1950 to 2012 (see Bushman, Jamieson, Weitz, & Romer, 2013). But gun violence in movies started with *The Great Train Robbery* (1903). Aggression and gun violence have been part of film entertainment from the very beginning.

DISCUSSION QUESTIONS

1. Explain whether you believe that the modern film industry would have evolved into something with fewer violent storylines if they had started with a dramatic story of a mother rescuing her children from a house fire, a documentary of a sailboats, pictures of kittens playing, or some other nonviolent theme.

2. How might you devise an experiment (using random assignment to groups) that would test whether viewing this particular film encouraged viewers to act, think, or feel more aggressively. Would your procedures change from 1903 (when the film was released) to now—why or why not?

3. Identify and discuss how two different social psychological theories of aggression predict increased or decreased levels of aggression after viewing this film.

4. Propose a film plot that would be likely to *decrease* aggression among viewers.

KEY TERMS

Escalation of aggression effect 165

Weapons effect 165

11.3 "I Could Just Kill Them!" Fantasies About Murder

I could just kill them.

Almost everyone has said or at least thought something like this in a moment of anger. Fantasizing about getting revenge on someone who has wronged us can be a guilty pleasure—but most people don't actually go through with their wistfully wicked plans. Fantasizing about murder became the dissertation topic of Josh Duntley (2006), who worked with evolutionary psychologist David Buss. Buss had, just the year before, published a book called *The Murderer Next Door: Why the Mind Is Designed to Kill* (Buss, 2005).

When Duntley (2006) asked people about whether they had ever fantasized about murdering someone, the numbers of people who said "yes" were much higher than he expected: 91% of men and 76% of women reported having had one or more specific homicidal thoughts. Would you have said yes? Consider the following three examples of cases from his research. Once a participant admitted to having a murder fantasy, he asked them questions such as, Who did you think about killing? How would you do it? What could have pushed you over the edge to actually do it?

- CASE #273, *Male, Age 24:* [Who?] My ex-girlfriend's current boyfriend, who is 28 years old. [How?] Choked him, pummeled his face till he became unconscious, and then kicked his head in. I didn't see him for a few months. [What would have pushed you over the edge to kill him?] If I had seen him, and if I was drunk and he had provoked me. (p. 49)

- CASE #89, *Female, Age 19:* [Who?] I had known her for a couple of years and we were friends but the more I got to know her the more evil she seemed to be. She would get a kick out of making fun of my body which I was really insecure about at the time. She did this almost daily until I just couldn't take it anymore. [How?] The way I wanted to kill her was to hit her in the head with a large object until she was dead. (p. 57)

- CASE #F1, *Female, Age 38:* [Who?] My ex-boyfriend. He's a liar, a cheat, and a sponger . . . [How?] I hired an explosives specialist to blow him up in his car. [What prevented you?] It would be wrong and I could not afford it. [What would have pushed you over the edge to kill him?] Winning the lottery. [What did you actually do?] I reported him to IRS and arranged to have his property damaged. (p. 114)

Duntley's (2006) dissertation looked for patterns of aggression fantasy based on gender—did men and women have different plans, motives, and so on? He also examined people's theoretical victims, emotions, and hesitancies from an evolutionary perspective. His results showed some interesting trends. First, the person most often chosen as a fantasy murder victim was an "intrasexual rival," meaning someone who could take your place in a romantic relationship. Most fantasy victims were someone *not* genetically related to the participant, which Duntley and Buss interpret as evidence in favor of an evolutionary impulse to protect people who share our genetics. Interestingly, he also found that men were most likely to fantasize about murder after their partner cheated on them—but women were more likely to imagine killing someone who damaged their reputation.

Let's examine other interesting results regarding gender differences in aggression; aggression **typologies** and motives change for men and women, depending on the situation.

Male to Male: Direct and Physical. For the most part, it's men who challenge one another on the street, fight wars, take over governments, and kill rivals. But don't misunderstand this pattern. Men are also adept at sarcasm, put-downs, and other indirect and verbal forms of aggression. Some studies have found that boys are just as aggressive as girls in the stereotypically "girl ways" of hurting others (see Henington, Hughes, Cavell, & Thompson, 1998; Kim, Kim, & Kamphaus, 2010; Putallaz et al., 2007). But male aggression is more likely than female aggression to be direct and physical.

Female to Female: A Hidden Culture of Relational Aggression. Women are more likely to use exclusion and rejection to harm one another. But don't misunderstand this pattern, either. Some studies have found that in troubled marriages, women are more often physically aggressive than men (Lawrence & Bradbury,

2007). Overall, however, men are responsible for most physical aggression. Male homicidal fantasies tend to persist for weeks or even months. According to Buss's book, men spent about 15 minutes each day fantasizing about murder; women devoted only a few minutes (Buss, 2005, p. 115).

Rachel Simmons (2002) became interested in young girl-to-girl aggression after revealing to college friends how she had been bullied by her friend Abby in the third grade. Abby convinced their other friends to run away whenever Rachel drew near. **Relational aggression** occurs when someone abuses the trust in a relationship in order to hurt the other person. Relational aggression becomes more complex with age (Crick, Ostrov, & Kawabata, 2007), even though physical pain and social rejection are processed along similar neural pathways (DeWall & Baumeister, 2006; Panksepp, 1998). Linder and Gentile (2009) measured aggression on television shows popular with fifth-grade girls. They found that television's rating system for violence missed a great deal of relational aggression "hiding in plain sight" (see Putallaz et al., 2007).

Male to Female: Power and Dominance. Men who batter their wives tend to use gender roles and/or a **culture of honor** to justify their behavior. They may have objected to their wives questioning them about economic matters or failing to properly perform "wifely duties" (Stark & Flitcraft, 1996). Men who strongly believe in traditional gender roles are more likely to condone and cause partner violence (Finn, 1986; Vass & Gold, 1995). Hypermasculinity (being a "man's man") predicts more physical aggression toward all women (Parrott & Zeichner, 2003, 2008) but particularly toward those women who violate traditional gender roles (Reidy, Shirk, Sloan, & Zeichner, 2009). Consequently, male aggression toward females is usually understood within a framework of social power (Ahrens, Dean, Rozee, & McKenzie, 2007).

Female to Male: Maternal Aggression and Broken Promises. Sometimes, women will become more aggressive toward others when they have recently given birth. There is an easy-to-understand evolutionary logic to maternal aggression: Don't mess with my baby! Maternal aggression is regulated to some degree by hormones, especially during lactation (Flannelly & Flannelly, 1987; Flannelly, Kemble, Blanchard, & Blanchard, 1986; Nephew, Bridges, Lovelock, & Byrnes, 2009). Among humans, corresponding structural changes in brain regions are also associated with a mother's positive and protective thoughts about her baby (Kim, Leckman, et al., 2010).

But women are moved to aggression against men for many reasons. During the French Revolution's "Bread March," about 7,000 women murdered their way past male guards, entered the gold-encrusted rooms at the Palace of Versailles, and advanced toward the chamber of Marie Antoinette (see Cadbury, 2002; Tschudi,

1902, pp. 116–119). In this historical case study example, the threat of starvation stirred these women to aggression. But romantic entanglements are another trigger for female to male physical aggression.

For example, Buss (2005, pp. 69–74) described how former beauty queen Clara Harris confronted her husband, David, about his affair with Gail. David provided his wife with a feature-by-feature comparison of Clara's body compared to Gail's body, especially the size of Gail's breasts. He did admit, however, to preferring Clara's hands, feet, and eyes. So, Clara dressed more provocatively, agreed to expensive liposuction and breast implants, tanned in a salon, and lost 15 pounds. But after seeing David and Gail holding hands as they left a hotel elevator, she became strangely calm as she went to her silver Mercedes. She drove over her husband—three times—before parking on top of him.

DISCUSSION QUESTIONS

1. This case study discussed aggression in terms of gender differences and evolutionary impulses or motivations. Now, instead consider situational and personality factors that might have an influence on whether someone (1) fantasizes about murder or aggression and (2) actually goes through with the behavior. Identify at least three situational or personality variables or constructs that you think might predict more or less aggression, and explain why.

2. Explain at least one theory from social psychology that predicts fantasizing about murder will *decrease* the probability of actual aggression and at least one theory that predicts the opposite—that aggression fantasies will *increase* actual aggression.

3. Describe how men and women have been socialized in different ways to behave aggressively. In other words, consider how culture, media images, peers, parents,

teachers, and so on instill different values, skills, social norms, and so forth into boys versus girls as they grow up, or how adult men and women are socially rewarded or punished for acting differently.

4. This case identified a riot at the Palace of Versailles during the French Revolution. Identify another historic case study in which women were aggressive toward men and discuss the cultural, historical, evolutionary, situational, and/or personal psychological factors at play.

5. If you have one, write out a murder fantasy that you have had in the past and then conduct a brief class survey asking others to do the same thing. Are your results similar to those in this case study? Explain any differences about the frequency or types of murder fantasies between your findings and those reported by Buss and Duntley.

11.4 The Cinderella Effect

Many of us grew up with classic fairytales like *The Little Mermaid* and *Beauty and the Beast*. As children, we might not have questioned some of the implicit cultural messages that may become more salient to us as adults.

When Maria Tatar (2003) wrote *The Hard Facts of the Grimms' Fairy Tales,* she pointed out that the Brothers Grimm had to clean up the stories—a lot—before marketing them as nursery and household tales. The original versions were probably developed as adult entertainment in taverns and around campfires. These folk tales routinely featured murder, mutilation, cannibalism, infanticide, and incest. The violence often lies barely hidden beneath the disturbing plots made popular by the Disney Studios.

One of the messages sent in some classic legends and folk tales is that stepparents will not love their adoptive children as much as they would love their own, biological children. The "evil stepmother" theme is one carried out in many iterations across cultures and time. Modern social psychologists have even coined the term the **Cinderella effect**, referring to the increased risk of harm occurring from stepparents to stepchildren (compared to biological children).

Of course, most parents and stepparents do not physically harm their children. Nevertheless, Daly and Wilson (1985) found that stepchildren were 40 times more likely to be physically abused than biological children. Russell (1984) reported a similar pattern: Stepdaughters were seven times more likely to experience abuse than a biological daughter. Wilson, Daly, and Daniele (1995) even found some support for the idea of the "evil" stepparent, but it was often the stepfather rather than the stepmother who was to blame. Why might stepchildren be at higher risk?

Evolutionary Explanations

When a particular pattern of human behavior seems universal, regardless of particular cultures, it is often used as evidence of basic biological or evolutionary instincts or drives. Daly and Wilson (1998) pointed out that the template for the Cinderella story evolved independently across cultures. For example, Japanese culture evolved its own story about Benizara, a gentle, honest, and humble girl who is victimized by a cruel stepmother. Benizara's story is uncannily close to the Cinderella fairytale. First, Benizara's beauty and virtue win the hearts of those around her. Then, despite the trickery of an envious sister, Benizara eventually triumphs. How does she triumph? By winning the love of a wealthy nobleman. Why might such similar myths about evil stepparents emerge across cultures?

A stepparent has no genetic stake in a stepchild, so evolutionary psychology makes the chilling prediction that, on average, stepchildren will be more vulnerable to violence than biological children. In fact, **parental investment** in a child not biologically related to you could potentially take away resources from your own genetic offspring. Data from Canada and Britain about **familicide** (killing a spouse and one or more children) support this prediction; familicide was usually committed by a man, and stepchildren were *over*represented among the victims (meaning that stepchildren were much more likely to be killed than biological children). Furthermore, unlike other types of familicides, the male perpetrator rarely committed suicide afterward if he had killed a stepchild; suicide was more likely if he had resorted to killing a biological child (see Wilson et al., 1995).

However, there are more explanations than just an evolutionary psychology view. As usual, the best answer to the nurture-nature debate is that both forces are constantly at work. What insights could an examination of culture bring to this morbid phenomenon?

Cultural Explanations

There are subcultures in which violence toward children is more common (National Center for Child Abuse and Neglect, 1997). For example, D'Alessio and Stolzenberg (2012) found that rates of child abuse of stepchildren were more extreme when the family had scarce resources. But why should being poor increase any form of violence?

Possibly this is because merely witnessing violence creates violent expectations. Farver, Natera, and Frosch (1999) found disturbing patterns in the reports by mothers of 64 inner-city 4-year-old children. Most mothers heard gunshots on a *weekly* basis. More than half witnessed or experienced gang activity, drug deals, police pursuits, arrests, weapons, and being physically threatened, assaulted, robbed, or having their homes broken into. That's a lot of violence for any 4-year-old (or adult) to witness, and it was associated with personal distress and lower cognitive performance (see Attar, Guerra, & Tolan, 1994; Cooley-Quille, Turner, & Beidel, 1995; Farver, Xu, Eppe, Fernandez, & Schwartz, 2005; Raia, 1996; Taylor, Zuckerman, Harik, & Groves, 1994).

Social role theory proposes that social roles also create expectations that become self-fulfilling prophecies (see Eagly, 1997; Eagly, Wood, & Diekman, 2000). Boys, for example, are socialized to be overtly aggressive (Kim, Kim, & Kamphaus, 2010) while girls are more often socialized to be pleasant, passive, and dependent in ways that lead to "anxious expectations of rejection" (Downey, Irwin, Ramsay,

& Ayduk, 2004, p. 13) that lead to conflict (see Campbell, Muncer, & Gorman, 1993; Harmon, Stockton, & Contrucci, 1992; Underwood, 2004; Zahn-Waxler, 2000). Those social role expectations are formed, in part, by the many stories children hear about evil stepparents. The fairytales *Cinderella, Snow White,* and *Hansel and Gretel,* for example, all depict stepmothers as jealous, scheming, murderous opportunists of the worst kind. A stepdaughter usually threatens to steal desirable resources (such as a prince) from a mother's "real" daughters. Perhaps simply including stories like this in our culture makes the idea of weaker connections toward stepchildren salient, which may then become a self-fulfilling prophecy.

The Cinderella effect demonstrates how violence within families—and especially between parents and children—could be explained by an interacting combination of biological, evolutionary, and cultural points of view.

DISCUSSION QUESTIONS

1. This case study argued that at least some fairytales teach children the implicit lesson that stepparents will not love them as much as biological parents. Identify two other specific examples of messages about social relationships (in families, romantic relationships, friendships, etc.) that are taught in fairytales. Do you think these lessons are healthy for children to learn? Why or why not?

2. Some research has argued that "romantic myths" endorsed by mainstream culture through children's stories, television, movies, and books (such as, "Men will protect women" and "Women should be innocent and beautiful") glorify traditional, sexist, or out-of-date roles for men and women and set unrealistic expectations for modern intimate relationships. Do you agree or disagree—and why?

3. This case study mentions that across cultures, stepparents do engage in more violence toward children than biological parents do; however, there are other variables at play. One example is that growing up in poverty may also increase violence. What other situational or personality variables would affect familial relationships? How would you set up a research study to test your hypotheses?

4. Blended families (with stepparents and stepchildren) are becoming more and more common, as are "nontraditional" families such as those with single parents, two parents of the same sex, polyamorous arrangements, and so on. Do you think family dynamics will change as the definition of "family" changes? Why or why not?

KEY TERMS

Cinderella effect 170   Familicide 171   Parental investment 171

CHAPTER
12

Intimate Relationships

12.1 Religion and Marriage Counseling

It's not easy to peek inside a marriage. Experienced marriage and family therapists, however, are in a privileged position to observe the forces that influence intimate relationships. One of those influences is religion. Case studies (with the informed consent of the participants) are one useful way to understand the various influences of religion on a marriage.

But what if you are among the 15 million mostly young "new atheists"? Cragun (2015, pp. 195, 210) points to the widespread influence of three books: Sam Harris's (2004) *The End of Faith*, Richard Dawkins's (2006) *The God Delusion*, and David Dennett's (2007) *Breaking the Spell*. It may take some time for research to catch up to the growing base of atheists around the world, to see if marriage counseling needs to accommodate their cultural needs (see D'Andrea & Sprenger, 2007). It seems that, so far, atheists are just as likely to have marriage troubles as people of any given religion. So, the goal of using Steve Johnson's (2013) three case studies below is to extract, from a particular theoretical approach, any common benefits from marriage counseling to couples coming from three different religious traditions.

The Assumptions of Faith

Johnson (2013) used **rational emotive behavior therapy** (REBT; see Ellis, 2000) to "help address marital issues within couples counseling of religious individuals in a way that supports the couples' religious values but decreases disturbance associated with religious issues within marriage" (p. 84). He recognized that religion is much more than a particular set of private beliefs. Johnson's review clarified that religion is both an expression and a product of complex cultural expectations about the meanings of marriage. Those religious cultures create assumptions about what husbands and wives expect of themselves and of one another after they step inside the hidden intimacy of a long-term marriage.

Ira and Rachel: Jewish Expectations of Marriage. The geographical origin of American Jews is mostly from Eastern Europe. They represent a burst of immigration that began at the start of the 20th century. Many American Jews now represent the second to fifth generations living in the United States. Johnson (2013) explains the strong Jewish emphasis on marriage and family as partly a result of their history of extreme discrimination, a sense of their own history, the role of children as giving purpose to life, and religious commandments.

There are three major branches of modern religious Judaism (Orthodox, Conservative, and Reform); they all reinforce a strong Jewish identity. The Orthodox are the most visible and religiously traditional. The Reform movement is the most liberal. Many Jewish people, however, are "cultural" Jews, who do not identify especially with any organized religion but embrace a secular appreciation for Jewish life and culture based on their ethnicity.

Ira and Rachel were a conservative Jewish couple who had been married for 24 years and had one 22-year-old son. Their counseling revolved around their son's recent announcement that he was gay and had started a relationship with another man. Ira took an argumentative approach that damaged his relationship with both his son and his wife. Rachel exhibited several signs of depression and felt hopeless about her sense of loss regarding not having a grandchild. Ira and Rachel had grown more distant from one another.

Across eight sessions of REBT, the emerging pattern featured several concept-words prominent within REBT. Ira and Rachel displayed *demandingness* that their son *must not* be gay and *should* stop his relationship with another man. They believed that it would be *awful* for them not to become grandparents. Both parents displayed *self-downing* (like self-criticism) but also *downing of one another* as a way to blame the other's poor parenting skills for their son "turning out" gay.

The therapist first affirmed their Jewish values and desire to be grandparents. But the therapist also helped them tone down their extreme belief that life became meaningless if they did not become grandparents. The alternative was to express appropriate and authentic, but not exaggerated, disappointment. By the end of therapy, the couple was considering alternative ways to help disadvantaged children and leave a meaningful legacy.

Tom and Susan: Christian Expectations of Marriage. Like American Judaism, Roman Catholicism grew dramatically due to European immigration starting in the early 20th century. They were more likely to come from countries such as Ireland, Poland, and Italy. The earliest Protestant version of Christian faith in the Americas was Puritanism. Their belief in a divine calling to Christianize the native peoples helped precipitate the infamous Salem witch trials and two brutal wars with Native Americans: King Philip's War and King William's War. Many Puritans believed that dark-skinned people from anywhere, but especially the Native Americans who fought them, were actual devils (see Norton, 2002).

The Protestant churches continue to be subdivided into many denominations, sects, and independent churches usually organized around shared cultural values.

The traditional Christian view of marriage is that it transforms two people into one entity that models Jesus' relationship to the church. There are important distinctions between Protestant and Catholic views of marriage. Both emphasize that marriage is an institution created by God. However, the Roman Catholic view adds that marriage is a sacrament. The practical consequence for long-term marriages was that it was more difficult for Catholics to get divorced.

Tom and Susan had been married for 4 years and had a 2-year-old daughter and a 5-month-old son. They were in conflict over baptism. Tom had been raised as a Catholic, Susan as an evangelical Protestant. They had partially resolved their conflicting cultural and religious expectations by alternating attendance at a Catholic and conservative Protestant church. How to baptize their children was aggravating marital conflicts already stirred by the expectations of their disapproving families (Johnson, 2013).

The same word-concepts of REBT that helped Ira and Rachel were introduced by the therapist and helped them identify aggravating thought patterns. REBT therapists are trained to listen for words and emotions that express unreasonable demandingness about how other people should behave. Expressions such as *should, must, have to, ought, supposed to,* and *awful* signal a belief system that is probably self-harming. The therapist helped Tom and Susan to recognize that each was *demanding* that the other partner *must* accept their religious practices. They each made a *false inference* that the other's *unwillingness to change* over the baptism issue was a symptom of an insincere love. Each was, in fact, willing to change and compromise. The therapist helped them think about baptism as a preference rather than a demand.

Across four sessions, the REBT therapeutic approach affirmed their religious preferences. Therapy also focused on how their own demandingness was at odds with each one's religious views of how God viewed them. Their *demandingness* and *downing of the other* implied that God's decision to allow them a free will had been a mistake—each had the free will to make a different choice. Tom and Susan worked out another compromise by learning to assert their preferences without demanding that the other obey them. They reached a practical compromise. They could follow both the infant baptism advocated by Catholicism and the later baptism advocated by Protestantism.

Abdullah and Khadijah: Muslim Expectations of Marriage. There are two origins of Muslims in the Americas (Tweed, 2004). Muslims immigrated either by force (as part of the first slave ship, for example, in 1619) or by choice (predominantly Syrians) during the 20th-century migrations into the Americas. The second source is Muslim sects that developed among African Americans in the late part of the 20th century. The 2016 estimates by the Pew Research Center identify the total percentage of Muslims in the United States today at only about 1% (Mohamed, 2016). Nevertheless, the *New England Journal of Medicine* reported that recent efforts to restrict immigrants from Muslim countries have harmed American health care (Masri & Senussi, 2017). Like previous immigrants to the United States, many Muslims are fleeing desperate circumstances.

Muslims around the world, and especially in the United States, are facing significant strains. "Many Islamic countries are facing the challenges of modernity and social change" (Leeman, 2009, p. 743). The formal Muslim laws of marriage are different from traditionally Jewish and Christian marriages. Islamic law describes marriage as a contract between a man and a woman. A Muslim woman may only marry a Muslim man, but a Muslim man is free to marry a Jewish, Christian, or Muslim woman. A Muslim may, according to shari'ah law, marry four women but only if he can financially support all of them and treat them equally. In Islamic traditions, many marriages are **arranged** by male family members, but it is preferred that the woman consent to the marriage. Like other religious faiths, the marriage contract is central to preserving a sense of identity and the authority of the faith.

Abdullah and Khadijah were second-generation Arabs in the United States and had married 7 years earlier, in their early 20s. The marriage had not been arranged but their families had been influential in connecting them. Their emerging conflict was that Abdullah had decided that Khadijah should stop working and become a stay-at-home mother. She disagreed, believing that it would become an intellectually unsatisfying life (Johnson, 2013).

The REBT therapist was familiar with Islamic laws and customs and encouraged them to discuss their decision with an Islamic scholar. The scholar, for the most part, sided with the wife. Abdullah became worried that his reputation as a strong male leader would be stained. In short, he was experiencing a cascade of *irrational demands* made more severe by the cultural struggles of Muslims in America. For example, in keeping with Arab culture, Abdullah was *demanding* that his wife behave as he instructed, that it would be *awful* to have his peers think less of him, and that she *must* do what he said was right.

The therapeutic REBT approach affirmed the importance to Abdullah of being respected by his friends. But his demandingness was now moderated. He understood that others' beliefs did not—and could not—determine his manhood without his permission. Abdullah was able to tell himself that the goal of going to Mosque was to worship, not to gain the approval of his peers.

The Common Characteristics of REBT

You probably noticed that the theme of "demandingness" showed up across all three experiences of marriage counseling (Johnson, 2013). This was the product of looking at each case through the theoretical lens (and language) of REBT. Were you satisfied with the endings of these therapy sessions? They were all relatively brief, and they were able to apply the REBT principles to specific beliefs. The participants were all practicing religionists whose faith traditions and beliefs were important to them. On the surface, however, the three faiths appear to be quite different, and the therapy sessions are notable for what they did not address. For example, the therapists affirmed rather than challenged each one's beliefs, even though each couple's understanding of God was that their particular faith represented the one true God. Would there have been significant therapeutic gain by questioning their theologies?

Several studies have indicated positive benefits of religious participation on the quality of a marriage. One review by Mahoney, Pargament, Tarakeshwar, and Swank (2001) indicated small but reliable positive effects. But was it the actual religion or something else? Is this a case of "correlation does not imply causation"? Religious participation provides significant emotional, financial, and practical social supports that can increase **satisfaction** and **commitment**. However, as the authors (Mahoney et al., 2001) caution, there are many alternative (i.e., nondivine) explanations for a strong association between religious activity and marriage. In addition, there are many ways in which religious participation and subcultures may harm as well as help individuals and marriages.

These particular therapeutic interventions, based on REBT, appear to have been successful, at least in the short term. But is this a validation of REBT? Maybe the benefits were the consequences of troubled couples finally taking the time out to work on their problems and listen to each other's needs. Each couple had modest goals and achieved modest gains. Will they come back to therapy—or have they achieved their own "happily ever after"?

DISCUSSION QUESTIONS

1. Does thinking about marriage and counseling from a religious perspective help to consider the needs and motives of the clients involved—or does it only stereotype them and attempt to mold them into a relationship deemed acceptable by their religious perspective?

2. Do you think that your own religious or spiritual views affect the way you act in relationships or the people you prefer to have as partners? How do you plan to respond to things like family planning or relationship dynamics if your partner is of a different religious faith or culture than your own?

3. Some people have argued that *all* couples would benefit from occasionally visiting a couples counseling session—even couples who are not experiencing any major troubles. Theoretically, it offers a chance to check in with each other, air any grievances before they become resentments, and so on. Do you agree—or do you think that this type of session might only make a "mountain out of a molehill," meaning that people might bring up small issues they would otherwise simply let go?

12.2 Male Victims of Relationship Abuse

Perhaps the greatest contradiction in human relationships is when one lover abuses another. Within a committed relationship, your partner is supposed to be the person who supports and cares for you the most out of everyone in the entire world—so when that person becomes your abuser, it's hard to understand.

The stereotype of **relationship violence** is "wife battery," when a man controls a woman using both physical and emotional power tactics. This scenario is, unfortunately, more common than most people would like to admit; well-respected studies have estimated that as many as one in every three women will be victimized through abuse, stalking, or sexual assault by a man she is currently or was formerly dating at some point in her lifetime (National Intimate Partner and Sexual Violence Survey, 2010). Many antiabuse organizations and researchers argue that violence from men toward women within relationships is the most common form of relationship abuse, and thus attention toward any other form of violence takes attention (and potentially valuable resources) away from these terribly victimized women (see Campbell, 2002; Johnson, 2007; Kilpatrick, 2004; Klein, Campbell, Soler, & Ghez, 1997).

While it is true that prevalence rates of male-to-female relationship violence are extremely troubling—the ideal number of cases, of course, would be zero—it is also true that there *are* other forms of relationship violence. For example, violence within same-sex relationships is also much more common than anyone would like. Gay and lesbian victims may also fear that reporting violence will further enforce negative views of gay couples from outsiders as unhealthy or dysfunctional (Elliot, 1996; Hart, 1986). Still, violence in same-sex couples is prevalent; one study (Straus, 1979) reported the highest rates of violence within lesbian couples (48%), then gay male couples (38%), then heterosexual couples (28%). Note, however, that these numbers are several years old; more research and public attention must be given to relationship violence in all forms.

And violence does occur by women toward men. Denying the existence of female-to-male relationship abuse is disrespectful to the thousands of men who have to experience relationship violence every day. Research has also shown that the stigma and embarrassment that male victims of violence feel makes them less likely to report what's happening and therefore less likely to get any help (see Arnocky & Vaillancourt, 2014).

This case study highlights one example of a man who was abused by his wife over many years of marriage; their relationship qualifies as what Johnson (1995, 2007) calls "**intimate terrorism**." It includes emotional, psychological, sexual, and physical violence that increased over time in frequency and in severity. Eventually, the victim of the abuse sought help and was able to escape from his wife and very unhealthy marriage.

A Marked Man

Qualitative research expert Jacqueline Allen-Collinson published a case study of an "abused heterosexual male victim" (Allen-Collinson, 2009, p. 22). In the opening paragraph of her article, she noted that research on the experiences of female victims of abuse has provided valuable insights into their experience—but that research trying to show a man's perspective of victimization has been met with "controversy and hostility" (p. 22). Despite that hostility, the case she presents is of a man who kept a diary record of his wife's physical and emotional abuse of him over 20 years. In many ways, the man did not fit the common stereotype of victims of violence: He was White, was middle-aged, had a high-paying professional job—and of course, he was male. He started keeping a diary during the last 2 years of his 20-year marriage, as he attempted to confront what was happening to him and build up the courage to escape.

The man, who went by the initials NH to maintain his anonymity, wrote his diary in third person, "finding it too emotionally-charged and embarrassing to write in the first [person]" (Allen-Collinson, 2009, p. 26). So, instead of writing, "I woke up today," NH wrote, "He woke up today," referring to himself as a character in his own life. Writing one's story can be cathartic and therapeutic; doing so with the help of a mental health professional is called **narrative therapy**.

NH notes that over their long marriage, his wife's abuse and control tactics increased in severity. Often, her abuse took the form of emotional manipulation:

> He is lying in bed on Sunday morning feeling ill. His domestic situation is worrying him and his work situation is worrying him. He is feeling despondent because of these things. His wife enters the room. "Why are you still in bed?" "I'm just tired," he replies. "Yes," she says, "guilt does make you tired." She leaves the room. (Allen-Collinson, 2009, p. 30)

He also wrote about how he would often simply try to avoid his wife instead of dealing with her constant criticism:

> He finishes work by 11:30. Phew. Rings three times from the office . . . to see if he can bring anything home for Christmas. She tells

him off for having been at work. He brings home the turkey but gets into trouble because there is not the right stuffing at the butcher's. Once home, she tells him to "get out of the house" until [5:30 p.m.], when her parents are coming round. How does this fit with him never doing anything to help? He sits in the car on the common for three hours, getting more cold and more tired. What a way to spend Christmas Eve, he thinks. (p. 30)

Sometimes, his wife's physical behavior toward him could be interpreted in more than one way. If she pressures him for sexual intimacy, is that abusive? Does the answer change if it's a woman pressuring a man versus the other way around? In one diary entry, he writes that his wife began poking, scratching, and violently pulling on parts of his body (such as ears and genitals) in an attempt to get him to have sex with her. What happened next?

Then, when he is distressed by the aggression, she turns 180 degrees to feign comfort—attempts at stroking and cuddling . . . which are really only another form of aggression, invading his space when he needs it to recover. Along with this, dogged insistence on her part—"I won't leave you alone until I have had a cuddle." (Allen-Collinson, 2009, p. 28)

And at other times, her physical aggression is less subtle:

More beatings tonight and facial bleeding and cuts ready for his senior management away day tomorrow. He is finding it increasingly difficult to blame the dog. . . . She picks herself up and fists him in the face. . . . He goes upstairs to get out of the way. She follows, scratches, pokes, thumps and what he hates most now, puts both of her hands inside his mouth and pulls it open further than it will naturally go. (p. 32)

From Victim to Survivor

In her article about NH, Allen-Collinson (2009) notes that many male victims of heterosexual relationship violence are either not believed or are simply judged for being "wimps." Surely, a man who is physically bigger and stronger than his wife or girlfriend couldn't really be hurt, right? She notes that in many cases, the men struggle with how to defend themselves without physical retaliation that would, in turn, hurt their partner (Allen-Collinson, 2009, pp. 33–35). A common concern with male victims of female perpetrators is fear that if the violence comes from both parties, he will be labeled as the primary aggressor even in self-defensive situations.

Unfortunately, NH also had to deal with this struggle. In his diary, he writes,

He holds his arms up against his chest to defend himself. She loses her balance and falls back, hitting her head on the sofa. She accuses him of hitting her. This is significant as he is now [deemed to be] the violent party in the relationship. He has been waiting for this moment—that she will injure herself as a result of him defending himself and then he will become the guilty one. This point is now reached. (p. 34)

Escaping an abusive partner is much more challenging and complicated than many outsiders believe, sometimes leading to the victim-blaming question of, "Why don't they just leave?" Several studies have examined the psychological, social, and practical barriers to leaving, such as finding housing, access to finances, and overcoming social stigma (e.g., Kirkwood, 1993; Rosen & Stith, 1997). These barriers exist for almost every victim of violence, but they are especially challenging for victims who are low income, have religious reasons to stay in a marriage, believe they have to stay to protect children from abuse, or cannot access resources such as emergency shelters. Again, most shelters and government-provided services are intended to help women, and so men may have a harder time gaining access to them.

Fortunately, NH was eventually able to leave his abusive relationship safely. He divorced his wife and was able to rent a modest home and to maintain his professional career. Happy, safe endings need to be more commonly found for all victims of relationship violence, so that they can become survivors and begin to heal from their physical and psychological wounds.

DISCUSSION QUESTIONS

1. Many researchers and practitioners who work with victims of relationship violence debate over how serious the problem of female-to-male abuse really is. What is your opinion on this subject? Do you think that more attention and resources should be given to male victims (of either heterosexual or homosexual violence)? Or, do you agree that the problem is much greater for female victims and that they should be the focus of help?

2. Discuss how gender roles and stereotypes have influence in abusive relationships. How do perpetrators of violence—either male or female—use cultural norms, traditional values, the legal system, or any other institutional paradigms to their advantage?

3. People doing research to understand the dynamics of relationship violence have made use of both qualitative data (such as case studies and diaries) and quantitative data (such as statistics from police records or court cases). What are the advantages and disadvantages to each method when they are being applied to something so personal and potentially traumatic as relationship violence?

12.3 Happily Ever After: Ingredients to a Long, Happy Marriage

Happily ever after.

Most of us grew up on stories that ended with this phrase or a version of it, maybe in another language or specific phrasing. We're taught from a young age that concepts like "love at first sight" and "soulmates" exist, and that if we can only find the right person, then we'll reach the blissful point of never-ending love that leads to chirping birds and romps through fields of wildflowers. Unfortunately, for most people, intimate relationships aren't quite that simple. We struggle to find mutual attraction right at the beginning—and if we're lucky enough to find someone with whom to engage in a committed, monogamous relationship, it's often fraught with arguments, resentments, and hurt feelings.

So, can research help to explain the somewhat mysterious ingredients that make up happy, long-term marriages? Theoretical perspectives such as the **investment model** (Rusbult, 1980) state that **commitment** will be predicted by high **satisfaction**, high investments, and low alternatives. Most studies completed on the initiation, progression, and frequent dissolution of relationships have been done with college students or young people of about that age (between 18 and 30 years old), probably because of what science calls a **convenience sample**. Many researchers are faculty at colleges and universities, and they can easily ask students to participate in studies as a class assignment or for extra credit. But to really understand relationships that endure over decades, older samples are required—or researchers can attempt to summarize trends they've seen emerge.

Elements of a Happy Marriage

The latter approach was taken by clinicians and researchers who attended a conference in 1990 ("Healthy Families," 1990; see Kaslow & Robison, 1996). The theme of the conference that year was "basic dimensions of a strong, healthy family" ("Healthy Families," 1990, p. 8), and the attendees created a list of nine criteria they believed make up such happy families, based on years of research and working directly with clients in therapeutic settings. Their list of criteria was as follows:

- Adaptive ability (flexibility in dealing with stress)

- Commitment to family (recognition of individual effort and investment in the family as a group)

- Communication (honest and frequent exchanges)

- Encouragement of individuals (a sense of belonging, but not codependency)

- Expression of appreciation (consistent signs of positivity and caring)

- Religious or spiritual orientation (common to family members, but no particular type or sect of religion)

- Social connectedness (family participates in larger groups, such as the local community)

- Clear roles (each family member understands his or her responsibilities during both normal times and times of crisis)

- Shared time (simply being together; includes both quality and quantity)

Two researchers, Kaslow and Hammerschmidt (1993), tested this list against survey responses from 20 couples who had been married between 25 and 46 years. When their participants were given open-ended questions and asked about the essential ingredients to what made their relationships last over time, the list of eight criteria that emerged was similar but did include some differences to what the researchers at the conference had created. The list from their study (p. 35) was as follows:

- Trust in each other

- Good coping skills

- Permanent commitment

- Good communication

- Enjoy time together

- Shared value system and interests

- Mutual appreciation and reciprocity

- Deep love

Of course, another way to understand what helps relationships last over time is to understand challenges and conflicts that couples have. This approach was taken by a third set of researchers (Levenson, Carstensen, & Gottman, 1993). Here, they hoped to compare "middle-aged" couples—in which spouses were around 40 to 50 years old and had been married about 15 years—to "older" couples, in which spouses were around 60 to 70 years old and had been married at least 35 years. When these participants were asked about sources of conflict, younger couples were most likely to note disagreements about children (26% of the sample) or money (26%), whereas older couples were more likely to say they fought over communication (19% of the sample) or what to do for recreation (16%). Of course, it seems likely that the older participants might have fought about children and money when they were middle-aged as well—but note that all of the couples in this study were still married, despite their respective conflicts.

Generalization of Findings

Replication and generalization of findings from any single sample of participants is important, so that we know whether any results or patterns are limited in terms of external validity. Case studies are helpful here, as we can use detailed, qualitative analysis to see into the lives of a few individuals. The three studies summarized above were all conducted with heterosexual, American couples in mind. What about other people, other cultures, and other types of relationships?

Marriage in Pakistan. One case study that investigated happy marriage from a case study perspective conducted interviews with a woman from Pakistan who was 25 years old, became a wife as a result of an **arranged marriage**, and considered herself quite happy (Fatima & Ajmal, 2012). Did her experience mirror the types of "ingredients" researchers and clinicians had identified in American marriages, or did culture and religion have an influence?

Some of her interview showed the same essential components for a happy relationship. For example, both of the lists above noted that shared value systems or religious orientations make things easier. The woman in this case agreed, noting,

> Sectarian difference proves to be a hurdle . . . because you do not have
> to compromise with the habits and personality but with the whole set of
> beliefs of the person. . . . Also children of such parents remain confused
> throughout life. (Fatima & Ajmal, 2012, p. 39)

Another overlap was the need for mutual appreciation and shared caring for each other. While the woman in this case study might express caring for her husband in what is considered a very "traditional" way by some people in the United States and similar cultures, the motives behind her actions are clearly those of giving selflessness—and she expects the same from her husband:

Serving him food, being dressed according to his choice, taking care of his likes and dislikes . . . shows that you care for him and love him and in turn he is even more caring and loving for you. (p. 39)

The woman in this case study also emphasizes the importance of communication and trust, other criteria listed in both studies mentioned above:

I think good understanding lay the foundation for a happy marriage . . . it is really hard to live with the person who doesn't trust you because he/she makes your life like hell. So, partners should learn to trust each other. . . . If you communicate properly than your spouse would know better about you and effective communication makes your relationship stronger. (pp. 39–40)

So, many of the criteria did replicate in this particular case. Interestingly, the participant in this case study also pointed out additional elements of what made her marriage happy. These included forgiveness, that at least one of the members of the couple should be even-tempered, and that the happiest couples have children. She also reported that having happy, healthy relationships with one's in-laws are a large factor in a lasting marriage. These particular criteria didn't make it to the lists we saw earlier—but it's likely that many heterosexual American couples would agree with her.

Satisfaction in Gay Marriages. Another interesting way to test for generalization of findings from American heterosexual couples is to compare them to American same-sex couples. Now that marriages between two men or two women are legally recognized in the United States, more and more same-sex marriages occur each year.

One study explicitly set out to compare long-term heterosexual and gay relationships that had lasted an average of 30 years (the minimum to participate was 15 years; Mackey, Diemer, & O'Brien, 2004). Using a semistructured interview format, 216 participants answered a series of questions about what made them satisfied in their relationship. Again, there were many similarities found between the two types of couples.

One lesbian couple (who had been together for 25 years) talked about their conflict management; they acknowledged their ability to overcome disagreement and misunderstanding. This was one of the criteria listed earlier, so on this point, replication was found. One partner noted,

When there was something that needed to be talked about, that was a little hot, I would tend to retreat. . . . As we've been together over time, I've become more assertive about getting my opinion and my feeling out. (Mackey et al., 2004, p. 122)

And her wife followed up with,

> We were always very civilized with each other but our styles are vastly
> different. I am confrontational . . . in the middle of the most horrific, mud-
> slinging campaign, she was able to remain calm. . . . We learn one thing and
> we keep learning it again and again. There is no easy way. (p. 122)

Another lesbian couple talked about the importance of psychological intimacy, and one of the gay men in the sample discussed how over the 20 years of
his relationship, sexual intimacy had waned in favor of simple companionship.
These points had not been explicitly mentioned in the other studies—but again, it
is very likely that any two people who are in a relationship would be happier with
consistent psychological and physical intimacy.

The researchers of this study (Mackey et al., 2004) concluded that regardless
of sexual orientation, the couples in their sample said that quality of communication, conflict management, decision making, and physical affection were the most
significant predictors of happiness. When they did statistical testing on quantitative data they had collected with the same couples—comparing heterosexual couples, gay couples, and lesbian couples—they found that *neither* sexual orientation
nor gender of the participant had a significant influence on the results.

Conclusions

Several studies have tried to find the mysterious components to "happily
ever after" when it comes to love. While many of us struggle to find someone
with whom we can attain these components, the specific ingredients listed here
probably don't offer much in the way of surprises. We can logically understand
that things like good communication, consistent shows of love and support, and
mutual trust make us happy in love—but it always seems much harder to achieve
in the harsh light of day or the dark recesses of night. What may be most important to remember is that we should always hold out for someone who gives us the
kindness, love, and respect we deserve.

DISCUSSION QUESTIONS

1. When you look at the lists of criteria from
   "Healthy Families" (1990) and from Kaslow
   and Hammerschmidt (1993), are there any
   surprises? Are there important things left off
   of these lists that were either added by the
   two studies described later or that you can

identify yourself? Of the criteria on these two lists, which two or three "ingredients" do you think are the most important?

2. Here, you were asked to compare the two lists of criteria to two other studies that served, at least in some form, as replications. One comparison was an individual woman from another culture, and one comparison was with gay couples. Do you think these are appropriate comparisons? Why or why not? Does replication only really "count" if the samples are the same type of people? If an individual case study fails to find the exact same results, does that mean one or the other research attempt was invalid?

3. Levenson et al. (1993) compared couples who were middle-aged to those who were older and found some differences in what couple members said were most important in terms of leading to happiness. In this particular study, they did not include participants who were younger (high school or college aged). For younger participants who are just starting to form committed, long-term intimate relationships, what do you think are the two or three most important criteria for satisfaction and happiness? And, what do you think might be the two or three most common areas of conflict?

KEY TERMS

Arranged marriage 184
Commitment 182

Convenience sample 182
Investment model 182

Satisfaction 182

References

Agthe, M., Spörrle, M., & Maner, J. K. (2010). Don't hate me because I'm beautiful: Anti-attractiveness bias in organizational evaluation and decision making. *Journal of Experimental Social Psychology, 46*(6), 1151–1154.

Ahrens, C., Dean, K., Rozee, P., & McKenzie, M. (2007). Understanding and preventing rape. In F. Denmark & M. Paludi (Eds.), *Psychology of women: A handbook of issues and theories* (pp. 509–554). Westport, CT: Praeger/Greenwood.

Ajzen, I., & Fishbein, M. (1977). Attitude-behavior relations: A theoretical analysis and review of empirical research. *Psychological Bulletin, 84*(5), 888–918.

Allen-Collinson, J. (2009). A marked man: Female-perpetrated intimate partner abuse. *International Journal of Men's Health, 8*(1), 22–40.

American Academy of Pediatrics. (1998). Auditory integration training and facilitated communication for autism. *AAP News and Journals Gateway.* Retrieved from http://pediatrics.aappublications.org/content/102/2/431..info

American Psychological Association. (2003). *Facilitating communication: Sifting the psychological wheat from the chaff.* Retrieved from http://www.apa.org/research/action/facili tated.aspx

Ancel, P. Y., Goffinet, F., Kuhn, P., Langer, B., Matis, J., Hernandorena, X., . . . Dreyfus, M. (2015). Survival and morbidity of preterm children born at 22 through 34 weeks' gestation in France in 2011: Results of the EPIPAGE-2 cohort study. *JAMA Pediatrics, 169*(3), 230–238.

Appignanesi, L. (2008). *Mad, bad, and sad: Women and the mind doctors.* New York, NY: W. W. Norton.

Arnocky, S., & Vaillancourt, T. (2014). Sex differences in response to victimization by an intimate partner: More stigmatization and less help-seeking among males. *Journal of Aggression, Maltreatment & Trauma, 23*(7), 705–724.

Asch, S. E. (1946). Forming impressions of personality. *Journal of Abnormal and Social Psychology, 41*(3), 258–290.

Asch, S. E. (1951). Effects of group pressure upon the modification and distortion of judgments. In H. Guetzkow (Ed.), *Groups, leadership and men: Research in human relations* (pp. 177–190). Oxford, England: Carnegie Press.

Ashworth, T. (1980). *Trench warfare, 1914–1918: The live and let live system.* Basingstoke, UK: Pan Macmillan.

Attar, B. K., Guerra, N. G., & Tolan, P. H. (1994). Neighborhood disadvantage, stressful life events, and adjustment in urban elementary-school children. *Journal of Clinical Child Psychology, 23*(4), 391–400.

Axelrod, R. (1984). *The evolution of cooperation.* New York, NY: Basic Books.

Bailey, B., & Farber, D. (1992). Hotel street: Prostitution and the politics of war. *Radical History Review, 1992*(52), 54–77.

Balderrama, F. E., & Rodríguez, R. (2006). *Decade of betrayal: Mexican repatriation in the 1930s.* Albuquerque, NM: University of New Mexico Press.

Bamber, M. (2004). 'The good, the bad and defenceless Jimmy'—A single case study of schema mode therapy. *Clinical Psychology & Psychotherapy, 11*(6), 425–438.

Barry, K. (1995). *The prostitution of sexuality.* New York, NY: New York University Press.

Bartik, J. J., Rickman, J. T., & Todd, K. D. (2013). *Pioneer programmer: Jean Jennings Bartik and the computer that changed the world.* Kirksville, MO: Truman State University Press.

Bartlett, F. C. (1932). *Remembering.* Cambridge, England: Cambridge University Press.

Baumeister, R. F., & Leary, M. R. (1995). The need to belong: Desire for interpersonal attachments as a fundamental human motivation. *Psychological Bulletin, 117*(3), 497–529.

Becker, E. (1973). *The denial of death.* New York, NY: Academic Press.

Beer, J. S., John, O. P., Scabini, D., & Knight, R. T. (2006). Orbitofrontal cortex and social behavior: Integrating self-monitoring and emotion-cognition interactions. *Journal of Cognitive Neuroscience, 18*(6), 871–879.

Benjamin, L. J., & Simpson, J. A. (2009). The power of the situation: The impact of Milgram's obedience studies on personality and social psychology. *American Psychologist, 64*(1), 12–19.

Benjamin, L. T., & Crouse, E. M. (2002). The American Psychological Association's response to Brown v. Board of Education: The case of Kenneth B. Clark. *American Psychologist, 57*(1), 38–50.

Berman, T. & Balthaser, J. (2012, January 6). Michigan family alleges harrowing misconduct by prosecutors, police. *ABC News.* Retrieved from http://abcnews.go.com/Health/michigan-family-alleges-harrowing-misconduct-prosecutors-police/story?id=15299991

Best, J. (2013). *Social problems* (2nd ed.). New York, NY: W. W. Norton.

Biklen, D. (1990). Communication unbound: Autism and praxis. *Harvard Educational Review, 60*(3), 291–314.

Biringer, F., & Anderson, J. R. (1992). Self-recognition in Alzheimer's disease: A mirror and video study. *Journal of Gerontology, 47*(6), P385–P388.

Blass, T. (2004). *The man who shocked the world.* New York, NY: Basic Books.

Blomqvist, J. (2007). Self-change from alcohol and drug abuse: Often-cited classics. In H. Klingemann & L. C. Sobell (Eds.), *Promoting self-change from addictive behaviors: Practical implications for policy, prevention, and treatment* (pp. 31–57). New York, NY: Springer.

Bradbury, S., & Williams, J. (2006). New labour, racism and 'new' football in England. *Patterns of Prejudice, 40*(1), 61–82.

Brody, E. M., Kleban, M. H., Lawton, M. P., & Silverman, H. A. (1971). Excess disabilities of mentally impaired aged: Impact of individualized treatment. *The Gerontologist, 11*(2, Pt. 1), 124–133.

Brown v. Board of Education of Topeka, 347 U.S. 483 (1954).

Buchthal, S., & Comment, B. (2010). *Fragments: Poems, intimate notes, letters by Marilyn Monroe.* New York, NY: Farrar, Straus & Giroux.

Bushman, B. J., Jamieson, P. E., Weitz, I., & Romer, D. (2013). Gun violence trends in movies. *Pediatrics, 132*(6), 1014–1018.

Buss, D. M. (2005). *The murderer next door: Why the mind is designed to kill.* New York, NY: Penguin.

Cadbury, D. (2002). *The lost king of France: A true story of revolution, revenge, and DNA.* Basingstoke, UK: Macmillan.

Calamur, K. (2013, January 17). Lance Armstrong admits to using performance-enhancing drugs. *NPR.* Retrieved from http://www.npr.org/sections/thetwo-way/2013/01/17/169650077/lance-armstrong-to-admit-to-using-performance-enhancing-drugs

Campbell, A., Muncer, S., & Gorman, B. (1993). Sex and social representations of aggression: A communal-agentic analysis. *Aggressive Behavior, 19*(2), 125–135.

Campbell, J. C. (2002). Health consequences of intimate partner violence. *The Lancet, 359*(9314), 1331–1336.

Carrington, M. B., & Carnevale, P. J. (1984). Physical attractiveness and self-esteem: Attributions for praise from an other-sex evaluator. *Personality and Social Psychology Bulletin, 10*(1), 43–50.

CBS. (2012). 5 years later New York City subway hero Wesley Autrey is still the man. *CBS.* Retrieved from http://newyork.cbslocal.com/2012/02/21/5-years-later-new-york-city-subway-hero-wesley-autrey-is-still-the-man/

Chai, A. Y. (1993). Asian-Pacific feminist coalition politics: The chŏngshindae/jŭgunianfu ("comfort women") movement. *Korean Studies, 17*(1), 67–91.

Chang, S., Kenney, N. J., & Chao, Y. Y. (2010). Transformation in self-identity amongst Taiwanese women in late pregnancy: A qualitative study. *International Journal of Nursing Studies, 47*(1), 60–66.

Chessick, R. (1983). Marilyn Monroe: Psychoanalytic pathography of a preoedipal disorder. *Dynamic Psychotherapy, 1,* 161–176.

Claidière, N., & Whiten, A. (2012). Integrating the study of conformity and culture in humans and nonhuman animals. *Psychological Bulletin, 138*(1), 126–145.

Clifford, M. M., & Walster, E. (1973). Research note: The effect of physical attractiveness on teacher expectations. *Sociology of Education, 46*(2), 248–258.

Cohen, S. (2002). *Folk devils and moral panics: The creation of the Mods and Rockers.* Abingdon, UK: Psychology Press. (Original work published 1973)

Connell, S. D. (2000). Is there safety-in-numbers for prey? *Oikos, 88*(3), 527–532.

Cooley-Quille, M. R., Turner, S. M., & Beidel, D. C. (1995). Emotional impact of children's exposure to community violence: A preliminary study. *Journal of the American Academy of Child & Adolescent Psychiatry, 34*(10), 1362–1368.

Corbacho, A., Gingerich, D., Oliveros, V., & Ruiz-Vega, M. (2016). Corruption as a self-fulfilling prophecy: Evidence from a survey experiment in Costa Rica. *American Journal of Political Science, 60*(4), 1077–1092.

Cosmides, L., & Tooby, J. (1989). Evolutionary psychology and the generation of culture: II. Case study: A computational theory of social exchange. *Ethology & Sociobiology, 10*(1–3), 51–97.

Cragun, R. T. (2015). Who are the "new atheists"? In L. G. Beaman & S. Tomlins (Eds.), *Atheist identities—Spaces and social contexts* (pp. 195–211). Cham, Switzerland: Springer International Publishing.

Crick, N. R., Ostrov, J. M., & Kawabata, Y. (2007). Relational aggression and gender: An overview. In D. J. Flannery, A. T. Vazsonyi, & I. D. Waldman (Eds.), *The Cambridge handbook of violent behavior and aggression* (pp. 245–259). New York, NY: Cambridge University Press.

Critcher, C. (2008). Moral panic analysis: Past, present and future. *Sociology Compass, 2*(4), 1127–1144.

Crum, A. J., & Phillips, D. J. (2015). Self-fulfilling prophesies, placebo effects, and the social-psychological creation of reality. In R. A. Scott, S. M. Kosslyn, & N. Pinkerton (Eds.), *Emerging trends in the social and behavioral sciences* (pp. 1–14). Hokoken, NJ: Wiley.

Dalberg-Acton, J. (1887, April 5). Letter to Bishop Mandell Creighton. *Historical essays and studies*. London, England: Macmillan.

D'Alessio, S. J., & Stolzenberg, L. (2012). Stepchildren, community disadvantage, and physical injury in a child abuse incident: A preliminary investigation. *Violence and Victims, 27*(6), 860–870.

Daly, M., & Wilson, M. (1985). Child abuse and other risks of not living with both parents. *Ethology & Sociobiology, 6*(4), 197–210.

Daly, M., & Wilson, M. (1998). *The truth about Cinderella: A Darwinian view of parental love*. New Haven, CT: Yale University Press.

Damasio, A. (2010). *Self comes to mind: Constructing the conscious brain*. New York, NY: Pantheon/Random House.

D'Andrea, L. M., & Sprenger, J. (2007). Atheism and non-spirituality as diversity issues in counseling. *Counseling and Values, 51*(2), 149–158.

D'Avanzato, C., Joormann, J., Siemer, M., & Gotlib, I. H. (2013). Emotion regulation in depression and anxiety: Examining diagnostic specificity and stability of strategy use. *Cognitive Therapy and Research, 37*(5), 968–980.

Dawkins, R. (2006). *The God delusion*. New York, NY: Random House.

DeNault, L. K., & McFarlane, D. A. (1995). Reciprocal altruism between male vampire bats, Desmodus rotundus. *Animal Behaviour, 49*(3), 855–856.

Dennett, D. C. (2007). *Breaking the spell: Religion as a natural phenomenon*. New York, NY: Penguin.

DeWall, C. N., & Baumeister, R. F. (2006). Alone but feeling no pain: Effects of social exclusion on physical pain tolerance and pain threshold, affective forecasting, and interpersonal empathy. *Journal of Personality and Social Psychology, 91*(1), 1–15.

Dewing, J. (2007). Values underpinning help, support and care. In R. Neno, B. Aveyard, & H. Heath (Eds.), *Older people and mental health nursing: A handbook of care* (pp. 40–52). Malden, MA: Blackwell.

Dickar, M. (2006). Reading place: Learning from the savage inequalities at Erasmus Hall. *Educational Studies: Journal of the American Educational Studies Association, 40*(1), 23–39.

Doole, C. (2001). Albania blamed for human trafficking: Gangs use Albania to lure women into prostitution. *BBC News Online, 17*.

Downey, G., Irwin, L., Ramsay, M., & Ayduk, O. (2004). Rejection sensitivity and girls' aggression. In M. M. Moretti, C. L. Odgers, & M. A. Jackson (Eds.), *Girls and aggression: Contributing factors and intervention principles* (pp. 7–25). New York, NY: Kluwer/Plenum.

Dugatkin, L. A., & Mesterton-Gibbons, M. (1996). Cooperation among unrelated individuals: Reciprocal altruism, by-product mutualism and group selection in fishes. *BioSystems, 37*(1), 19–30.

Dugatkin, L. A., & Wilson, D. S. (1993). Fish behaviour, partner choice experiments and cognitive ethology. *Reviews in Fish Biology and Fisheries, 3*(4), 368–372.

Duntley, J. D. (2006). Homicidal ideations. *Dissertation Abstracts International: Section B. Sciences and Engineering, 66*(12-B), 6908.

Eagly, A. H. (1997). Sex differences in social behavior: Comparing social role theory and evolutionary psychology. *American Psychologist, 52*(12), 1380–1383.

Eagly, A. H., Wood, W., & Diekman, A. B. (2000). Social role theory of sex differences and similarities: A current appraisal. In T. Ekes & H. M. Trautner (Eds.), *The developmental social psychology of gender* (pp. 123–174). Mahwah, NJ: Erlbaum.

Elliot, P. (1996). Shattering illusions: Same-sex domestic violence. *Journal of Gay & Lesbian Social Services, 4*(1), 1–8.

Ellis, A. (2000). Can rational emotive behavior therapy (REBT) be effectively used with people who have devout beliefs in God and religion? *Professional Psychology: Research and Practice, 31*(1), 29–33.

EquaityNow.org. (2017). *Equality now: A just world for women and girls.* Retrieved at https://www.equalitynow.org/

Etcoff, N. (1999). *Survival of the prettiest: The science of beauty.* New York, NY: Anchor/Doubleday.

Farr, K. (2005). *Sex trafficking: The global market in women and children.* New York, NY: Worth.

Farver, J. M., Natera, L. X., & Frosch, D. L. (1999). Effects of community violence on inner-city preschoolers and their families. *Journal of Applied Developmental Psychology, 20*(1), 143–158.

Farver, J. M., Xu, Y., Eppe, S., Fernandez, A., & Schwartz, D. (2005). Community violence, family conflict, and preschoolers' socioemotional functioning. *Developmental Psychology, 41*(1), 160–170.

Fatima, M., & Ajmal, M. A. (2012). Happy marriage: A qualitative study. *Pakistan Journal of Social and Clinical Psychology, 9*(2), 37–42.

Fawkner, H. J., & McMurray, N. E. (2002). Body image in men: Self-reported thoughts, feelings, and behaviors in response to media images. *International Journal of Men's Health, 1*(2), 137–161.

Feingold, A. (1992). Good-looking people are not what we think. *Psychological Bulletin, 111*(2), 304–341.

Fenton, T., Nasser, R., Eliasziw, M., Kim, J., Bilan, D., & Sauve, R. (2013). Validating the weight gain of preterm infants between the reference growth curve of the fetus and the term infant. *BMC Pediatrics, 13*(1), 1–10.

Fernández-Cabana, M., García-Caballero, A., Alves-Pérez, M. T., García-García, M. J., & Mateos, R. (2013). Suicidal traits in Marilyn Monroe's fragments: An LIWC analysis. *Crisis: The Journal of Crisis Intervention and Suicide Prevention, 34*(2), 124–130.

Festinger, L., Riecken, H. W., & Schachter, S. (2008). *When prophecy fails: A social and psychological study of a modern group that predicted the destruction of the world.* Minneapolis, MN: University of Minnesota Press. (Original work published 1956)

Finkel, E. J., Campbell, W. K., Brunell, A. B., Dalton, A. N., Scarbeck, S. J., & Chartrand, T. L. (2006). High-maintenance interaction: Inefficient social coordination impairs self-regulation. *Journal of Personality and Social Psychology, 91*(3), 456–475.

Finn, J. (1986). The relationship between sex role attitudes and attitudes supporting marital violence. *Sex Roles, 14*(5–6), 235–244.

Fishbein, M., & Ajzen, I. (2010). *Predicting and changing behavior: The reasoned action approach.* New York, NY: Psychology Press.

Flannelly, K. J., & Flannelly, L. (1987). Time course of postpartum aggression in rats (Rattus norvegicus). *Journal of Comparative Psychology, 101*(1), 101–103.

Flannelly, K. J., Kemble, E. D., Blanchard, D. C., & Blanchard, R. J. (1986). Effects of septal-forebrain lesions on maternal aggression and maternal care. *Behavioral & Neural Biology, 45*(1), 17–30.

Fleming, J. S., & Courtney, B. E. (1984). The dimensionality of self-esteem: II. Hierarchical facet model for revised measurement scales. *Journal of Personality and Social Psychology, 46*(2), 404–421.

Flyvbjerg, B. (2006). Five misunderstandings about case-study research. *Qualitative Inquiry, 12*(2), 219–245.

Fransen, M. L., Fennis, B. M., Pruyn, A. T. H., & Das, E. (2008). Rest in peace? Brand-induced mortality salience and consumer behavior. *Journal of Business Research, 61*(10), 1053–1061.

Frieze, I. H., Olson, J. E., & Russell, J. (1991). Attractiveness and income for men and women in management. *Journal of Applied Social Psychology, 21*(13), 1039–1057.

Gagnon, J. H., & Simon, W. (1987). The sexual scripting of oral genital contacts. *Archives of Sexual Behavior, 16*(1), 1–25.

Gil, V. E., & Anderson, A. F. (1998). State-sanctioned aggression and the control of prostitution in the People's Republic of China: A review. *Aggression and Violent Behavior, 3*(2), 129–142.

Gilfoyle, T. J. (1999). Prostitutes in history: From parables of pornography to metaphors of modernity. *The American Historical Review, 104*(1), 117–141.

Global Witness. (2017). *Home.* Retrieved from https://www.globalwitness.org/en/

Goldstein, J. S. (2001). *War and gender: How gender shapes the war system and vice versa.* Cambridge, England: Cambridge University Press.

Goode, E., & Ben-Yehuda, N. (2009). *Moral panics: The social construction of deviance* (2nd ed.). Hoboken, NJ: Wiley-Blackwell.

Grabe, S., & Hyde, J. S. (2006). Ethnicity and body dissatisfaction among women in the United States: A meta-analysis. *Psychological Bulletin, 132*(4), 622–640.

Grey, D. J. (2013). 'Liable to very gross abuse': Murder, moral panic and cultural fears over infant life insurance, 1875–1914. *Journal of Victorian Culture, 18*(1), 54–71.

Gross, M. (2011). *Model: The ugly business of beautiful women.* New York, NY: HarperCollins.

Gunnell, J. J., & Ceci, S. J. (2010). When emotionality trumps reason: A study of individual processing style and juror bias. *Behavioral Sciences & The Law, 28*(6), 850–877.

Harmon, J. A., Stockton, S., & Contrucci, C. (1992). *Gender disparities in special education* (Research Rep. No. 143). Retrieved from ERIC database. (ED358631)

Harris, A. E., & Curtin, L. (2002). Parental perceptions, early maladaptive schemas, and depressive symptoms in young adults. *Cognitive Therapy and Research, 26*(3), 405–416.

Harris, S. (2005). *The end of faith: Religion, terror, and the future of reason.* New York, NY: W. W. Norton.

Hart, B. (1986). Lesbian battering: An examination. In K. Lobel (Ed.), *Naming the violence: Speaking out about lesbian battering* (pp. 173–189). Seattle, WA: Seal Press.

Harvard Business School. (2014). *The HBS case method.* Retrieved from www.hbs.edu/mba/academic-experience/Pages/the-hbs-case-method.aspx

Healthy families featured in Washington conference. (1990, July/August). *Family Therapy News,* p. 8.

Henington, C., Hughes, J. N., Cavell, T. A., & Thompson, B. (1998). The role of relational aggression in identifying aggressive boys and girls. *Journal of School Psychology, 36*(4), 457–477.

Hirschman, E. C. (1990). Secular immortality and the American ideology of affluence. *Journal of Consumer Research, 17*(1), 31–42.

Hoffman, R. R., Crandall, B., & Shadbolt, N. (1998). Use of the critical decision method to elicit expert knowledge: A case study in the methodology of cognitive task analysis. *Human Factors, 40*(2), 254–276.

Hughes, P. (1964, March 30). 'WILD ONES' INVADE SEASIDE—97 ARRESTS. *Daily Mirror,* p. 3D.

Isaacson, W. (2014). *The innovators: How a group of hackers, geniuses, and geeks created the digital revolution.* New York, NY: Simon & Schuster.

Jennings, N., Clifford, S., Fox, A. R., O'Connell, J., & Gardner, G. (2015). The impact of nurse practitioner services on cost, quality of care, satisfaction and waiting times in the emergency department: A systematic review. *International Journal of Nursing Studies, 52*(1), 421–435.

Johnsgard, P. A. (2005). *The nature of Nebraska: Ecology and biodiversity.* Lincoln, NE: University of Nebraska Press.

Johnson, J. M., & Pettigrew, T. F. (2005). Kenneth B. Clark (1914–2005). *American Psychologist, 60*(6), 649–651.

Johnson, M. P. (1995). Patriarchal terrorism and common couple violence: Two forms of violence against women. *Journal of Marriage and the Family, 57*(2), 283–294.

Johnson, M. P. (2007). The intersection of gender and control. In L. O'Toole, J. R. Schiffman, & M. L. K. Edwards (Eds.), *Gender violence: Interdisciplinary perspectives* (2nd ed., pp. 257–268). New York, NY: New York University Press.

Johnson, S. (2006). *The ghost map: The story of London's most terrifying epidemic—and how it changed science, cities, and the modern world.* New York, NY: Riverhead Books.

Johnson, S., Burrows, A., & Williamson, I. (2004). 'Does my bump look big in this?' The meaning of bodily changes for first-time mothers-to-be. *Journal of Health Psychology, 9*(3), 361–374.

Johnson, S. A. (2013). Using REBT in Jewish, Christian, and Muslim couples counseling in the United States. *Journal of Rational-Emotive & Cognitive-Behavior Therapy, 31*(2), 84–92.

Johnston, E. (2001). The repeated reproduction of Bartlett's Remembering. *History of Psychology, 4*(4), 341–366.

Jones, J. M., & Pettigrew, T. F. (2005). Kenneth B. Clark (1914–2005). *American Psychologist, 60*(6), 649–651.

Jussim, L., & Harber, K. D. (2005). Teacher expectations and self-fulfilling prophecies: Knowns and unknowns, resolved and unresolved controversies. *Personality and Social Psychology Review, 9*(2), 131–155.

Kane, J. (1998). *Sold for sex.* Farnham, UK: Ashgate.

Kaslow, F. W., & Hammerschmidt, H. (1993). Long term "good" marriages: The seemingly essential ingredients. *Journal of Couples Therapy, 3*(2–3), 15–38.

Kaslow, F. W., & Robison, J. A. (1996). Long-term satisfying marriages: Perceptions of contributing factors. *American Journal of Family Therapy, 24*(2), 153–170.

Kelley, H. H. (1950). The warm-cold variable in first impressions of persons. *Journal of Personality, 18*(4), 431–439.

Kilpatrick, D. G. (2004). What is violence against women? Defining and measuring the problem. *Journal of Interpersonal Violence, 19*(11), 1209–1234.

Kim, P., Leckman, J. F., Mayes, L. C., Feldman, R., Wang, X., & Swain, J. E. (2010). The plasticity of human maternal brain: Longitudinal changes in brain anatomy during the early postpartum period. *Behavioral Neuroscience, 124*(5), 695.

Kim, S., Kim, S., & Kamphaus, R. W. (2010). Is aggression the same for boys and girls? Assessing measurement invariance with confirmatory factor analysis and item response theory. *School Psychology Quarterly, 25*(1), 45–61.

Kirkwood, C. (1993). *Leaving abusive partners: From the scars of survival to the wisdom for change.* Thousand Oaks, CA: Sage.

Kirsch, I., & Sapirstein, G. (1998). Listening to Prozac but hearing placebo: A meta-analysis of antidepressant medication. *Prevention & Treatment, 1*(2), 1–16.

Kitwood, T. (1990). *Concern for others: A new psychology of conscience and morality.* Florence, KY: Taylor & Frances/Routledge.

Kitwood, T. (1997). The experience of dementia. *Aging & Mental Health, 1*(1), 13–22.

Klein, E., Campbell, J., Soler, E., & Ghez, M. (1997). *Ending domestic violence: Changing public perceptions/halting the epidemic.* Thousand Oaks, CA: Sage.

Klein, G. (2003). *The power of intuition.* New York, NY: Random House.

Kluge, P. F. (1986). Why they love us in the Philippines: The American naval bases provide cash and jobs. *Playboy,* 88.

Kozol, J. (1991). *Savage inequities.* New York, NY: Crown.

Krinsky, C. (2013). Introduction: The moral panic concept. *The Ashgate research companion to moral panics,* 1–14.

Krysa, J. (2012). 100 Notes, No. 055, Ada Lovelace. In *Documenta und Museum Fridericianum Veranstaltungs-GmbH.* Kassel, Germany: Kassel University Press.

Laumann, E. O., Gagnon, J. H., Michael, R. T., & Michaels, S. (1994). *The social organization of sexuality: Sexual practices in the United States.* Chicago, IL: University of Chicago Press.

Lawrence, E., & Bradbury, T. N. (2007). Trajectories of change in physical aggression and marital satisfaction. *Journal of Family Psychology, 21*(2), 236–247.

Le Bon, G. (1896). *The Crowd. Tr. fr. the French.* London, England: T. Fisher Unwin.

Leary, M. R., Kowalski, R. M., Smith, L., & Phillips, S. (2003). Teasing, rejection, and violence: Case studies of the school shootings. *Aggressive Behavior, 29*(3), 202–214.

Leary, M. R., Twenge, J. M., & Quinlivan, E. (2006). Interpersonal rejection as a determinant of anger and aggression. *Personality and Social Psychology Review, 10*(2), 111–132.

LeDoux, J. (1998). Fear and the brain: Where have we been, and where are we going? *Biological Psychiatry, 44*(12), 1229–1238.

Lee, C. W., Taylor, G., & Dunn, J. (1999). Factor structure of the Schema Questionnaire in a large clinical sample. *Cognitive Therapy and Research, 23*(4), 441–451.

Leeman, A. B. (2009). Interfaith marriage in Islam: An examination of the legal theory behind the traditional and reformist positions. *Indiana Law Journal, 84,* 743–771.

Levenson, R. W., Carstensen, L. L., & Gottman, J. M. (1993). Long-term marriage: Age, gender, and satisfaction. *Psychology and Aging, 8*(2), 301–313.

Lewin, K. (1951). *Field theory in social science: Selected theoretical papers* (D. Cartwright, Ed.). Oxford, England: Harpers.

Linder, J. R., & Gentile, D. A. (2009). Is the television rating system valid? Indirect, verbal, and physical aggression in programs viewed by fifth grade girls and associations with behavior. *Journal of Applied Developmental Psychology, 30*(3), 286–297.

Lovelace, A. (1843). *Sketch of the Analytical Machine Invented by Charles Babbage, Esq. With Notes by the Translator.* London, England: Richard and John E. Taylor.

Luciano, R., & Fisher, D. (1982). *The umpire strikes back.* New York, NY: Bantam.

MacCorquodale, K., & Meehl, P. E. (1948). On a distinction between hypothetical constructs and intervening variables. *Psychological Review, 55*(2), 95–107.

Mackey, R. A., Diemer, M. A., & O'Brien, B. A. (2004). Relational factors in understanding satisfaction in the lasting relationships of same-sex and heterosexual couples. *Journal of Homosexuality, 47*(1), 111–136.

Macmillan, M. (2000). *An odd kind of fame: Stories of Phineas Gage.* Cambridge, MA: MIT Press.

Mahoney, A., Pargament, K. I., Tarakeshwar, N., & Swank, A. B. (2001). Religion in the home in the 1980s and 1990s: A meta-analytic review and conceptual analysis of links between religion, marriage, and parenting. *Journal of Family Psychology, 15*(4), 559–596.

Mandeville, B. (1714). *The fable of the bees: Or, private vices, public benefits.* London, England: J. Roberts.

Marsh, H. W., & Richards, G. E. (1988). Tennessee self-concept scale: Reliability, internal structure, and construct validity. *Journal of Personality and Social Psychology, 55*(4), 612–624.

Masri, A., & Senussi, M. H. (2017). Trump's executive order on immigration—Detrimental effects on medical training and health care. *New England Journal of Medicine, 376*(19), e39.

Merton, R. K. (1948). The self-fulfilling prophecy. *Antioch Review, 8*(2), 193–210.

Merton, R. K. (1987). A simple model of capital market equilibrium with incomplete information. *The Journal of Finance, 42*(3), 483–510.

Merton, R. K. (1994). Durkheim's division of labor in society. *Sociological Forum, 9*(1), 17–25.

Milgram, S. (Director). (1962). *Obedience* [Documentary]. United States: Yale University.

Milgram, S. (1963). Behavioral study of obedience. *The Journal of Abnormal and Social Psychology, 67*(4), 371–378.

Milgram, S. (1974). *Obedience to authority: An experimental view.* New York, NY: Harper & Row.

Milinski, M., Pfluger, D., Külling, D., & Kettler, R. (1990). Do sticklebacks cooperate repeatedly in reciprocal pairs? *Behavioral Ecology and Sociobiology, 27*(1), 17–21.

Mohamed, B. (2016). *A new estimate of the US Muslim population. Pew Research Center.* Retrieved from: http://www.pewresearch.org/fact-tank/2016/01/06/anew-estimate-of-the-us-muslim-population

Montee, B. B., Miltenberger, R. G., & Wittrock, D. (1995). An experimental analysis of facilitated communication. *Journal of Applied Behavior Analysis, 28*(2), 189–200.

Moore, C. N. (2011). *"A diamond is forever": The construction of secular immortality and De Beers diamond advertising 1939–1958.* Las Cruces, NM: New Mexico State University.

Moulton, C., Regehr, G., Lingard, L., Merritt, C., & MacRae, H. (2010). Slowing down to stay out of trouble in the operating room: Remaining attentive in automaticity. *Academic Medicine, 85*(10), 1571–1577.

Muiño, R., Carrera, P., & Iglesias, M. (2003). The characterization of sardine (Sardina pilchardus Walbaum) schools off the Spanish-Atlantic coast. *ICES Journal of Marine Science, 60*(6), 1361–1372.

National Center on Child Abuse and Neglect. (1997). *Fifth forum on federally funded child abuse and neglect research: Fiscal year 1996 projects.* Washington, DC: Author.

National Intimate Partner and Sexual Violence Survey. (2010). *NISVS summary reports.* Retrieved from https://www.cdc.gov/violenceprevention/nisvs/index.html

Neill, S., & Cullen, J. M. (1974). Experiments on whether schooling by their prey affects the hunting behaviour of cephalopods and fish predators. *Journal of Zoology, 172*(4), 549–569.

Nephew, B. C., Bridges, R. S., Lovelock, D. F., & Byrnes, E. M. (2009). Enhanced maternal aggression and associated changes in neuropeptide gene expression in multiparous rats. *Behavioral Neuroscience, 123*(5), 949–957.

Nichol, F. D. (1944). *The midnight cry: A defense of William Miller and the Millerites*. Washington, DC: Review and Herald.

Nichols, M. (1993). Third-world families at work: Child labor or child care? *Harvard Business Review, 71*(1), 12–14.

Nietzsche, F. (1996). *On the genealogy of morals: A polemic*. Oxford, England: Oxford World Classics. (Original work published 1887)

Norton, M. (2002). *In the devil's snare: The Salem witchcraft crisis of 1692*. New York, NY: Knopf.

Nyman, L. (2010). Documenting history: An interview with Kenneth Bancroft Clark. *History of Psychology, 13*(1), 74–88.

Orjoux, A. (2005, August 26). Armstrong on newspaper's accusations: 'This thing stinks.' *CNN.com*. Retrieved from http://www.cnn.com/2005/SPORT/08/26/armstrong.lkl/

Oullier, O., de Guzman, G. C., Jantzen, K. J., Lagarde, J., & Kelso, J. S. (2008). Social coordination dynamics: Measuring human bonding. *Social Neuroscience, 3*(2), 178–192.

Panksepp, J. (1998). *Affective neuroscience: The foundations of human and animal emotions*. New York, NY: Oxford University Press.

Parrott, D. J., & Zeichner, A. (2003). Effects of hypermasculinity on physical aggression against women. *Psychology of Men & Masculinity, 4*(1), 70–78.

Parrott, D. J., & Zeichner, A. (2008). Determinants of anger and physical aggression based on sexual orientation: An experimental examination of hypermasculinity and exposure to male gender role violations. *Archives of Sexual Behavior, 37*(6), 891–901.

Pessoa, F. (2002). *The book of disquiet*. London, UK: Penguin.

Pitcher, T. J. (1993). Stewardship and sustainability of Pacific fishery resources: The need for critical insight and an encyclopedia of ignorance. In *Our common shores and our common challenge: Environmental protection in the Pacific. Proceedings of the Fourth International Symposium of the Conference of Asian and Pan-Pacific University Presidents*. Fairbanks: University of Alaska Sea Grant.

Pitcher, T. J., Misund, O. A., Fernö, A., Totland, B., & Melle, V. (1996). Adaptive behaviour of herring schools in the Norwegian Sea as revealed by high-resolution sonar. *ICES Journal of Marine Science, 53*(2), 449–452.

Porter, E. S. (Producer), & Porter, E. S. (Director). (1903). *The great train robbery* [Motion picture]. United States: Warner Bros.

Putallaz, M., Grimes, C. L., Foster, K. J., Kupersmidt, J. B., Coie, J. D., & Dearing, K. (2007). Overt and relational aggression and victimization: Multiple perspectives within the school setting. *Journal of School Psychology, 45*(5), 523–547.

Raia, J. A. (1996, March). Perceived social support and coping as moderators of effects of children's exposure to community violence. *Dissertation Abstracts International, 56*, 5181.

Raymond, J., Hughes, D., & Gomez, C. (2001). Sex trafficking of women in the United States: Links between international and domestic sex industries. North Amherst, MA: Coalition Against Trafficking in Women. Available at www.catwinternational.org

Reicher, S. D., Haslam, S. A., & Smith, J. R. (2012). Working towards the experimenter: Reconceptualizing obedience within the Milgram paradigm as identification-based-followership. *Perspectives on Psychological Science, 7*, 315–2324.

Reicher, S. D., Haslam, S. A., & Miller, A. G. (2014). What makes a person a perpetrator? The intellectual, moral, and methodological arguments for revisiting Milgram's research on the influence of authority. *Journal of Social Issues, 70*, 393–408.

Reidy, D. E., Shirk, S. D., Sloan, C. A., & Zeichner, A. (2009). Men who aggress against women: Effects of feminine gender role violation on physical aggression in hypermasculine men. *Psychology of Men & Masculinity, 10*(1), 1–12.

Reynolds, H. (1986). *The economics of prostitution*. Springfield, IL: Charles C Thomas.

Robins, L. N. (1993). Vietnam veterans' raid recovery from heroin addiction: A fluke or normal expectation? *Addiction, 88*(8), 1041–1054.

Rolls, J. A. (2010). Tales from broken hearts: Women and recovery from romantic relationships. *Storytelling, Self, Society: An Interdisciplinary Journal of Storytelling Studies, 6*(2), 107–121.

Roosevelt, F. D. (1933, March 4). *First inaugural address.* Washington, DC.

Rosen, K. H., & Stith, S. M. (1997). Surviving abusive dating relationships: Processes of leaving, healing and moving on. In G. Kantor & J. Jasinski (Eds.), *Out of the darkness: Contemporary perspectives on family violence* (pp. 170–182). Thousand Oaks, CA: Sage.

Rosenthal, R. (1994). Interpersonal expectancy effects: A 30-year perspective. *Current Directions in Psychological Science, 3*(6), 176–179.

Rosenthal, R. (2002). Covert communication in classrooms, clinics, courtrooms, and cubicles. *American Psychologist, 57*(11), 839–849.

Rosenthal, R., & Fode, K. (1963). The effect of experimenter bias on the performance of the albino rat. *Behavioral Science, 8*(3), 183–189.

Rosenthal, R., & Jacobsen, L. (1968). *Pygmalion in the classroom: Self-fulfilling prophecies and teacher expectations.* New York, NY: Holt, Rhinehart, and Winston.

Rusbult, C. E. (1980). Commitment and satisfaction in romantic associations: A test of the investment model. *Journal of Experimental Social Psychology, 16*(2), 172–186.

Russell, D. E. (1984). The prevalence and seriousness of incestuous abuse: Stepfathers vs. biological fathers. *Child Abuse & Neglect, 8*(1), 15–22.

Sabat, S. R. (1994). Excess disability and malignant social psychology: A case study of Alzheimer's disease. *Journal of Community & Applied Social Psychology, 4*(3), 157–166.

Sacks, O. (1970). *Migraine: The evolution of a common disorder.* Berkeley, CA: University of California Press.

Schell, J. (2014). *The art of game design: A book of lenses.* Boca Raton, FL: CRC Press.

Schmidt, N. B., Joiner, T. E., Young, J. E., & Telch, M. J. (1995). The schema questionnaire: Investigation of psychometric properties and the hierarchical structure of a measure of maladaptive schemas. *Cognitive Therapy and Research, 19*(3), 295–321.

Seligman, M. E. P. (2002). Positive psychology, positive prevention, and positive therapy. In C. R. Snyder, & S. J. Lopez (Eds.), *Handbook of positive psychology* (pp. 3–9). New York, NY: Oxford University Press.

Shryock, R. (1971). The medical reputation of Benjamin Rush: Contrasts over two centuries. *Bulletin of the History of Medicine, 45,* 507–552.

Siegel, S. C. (Producer), & Hawks, H. (Director). (1953). *Gentlemen prefer blondes* [Motion picture]. United States: 20th Century Fox.

Simmons, R. (2002). *Odd girl out: The hidden culture of aggression in girls.* Boston, MA: Houghton Mifflin Harcourt.

Solomon, S., Greenberg, J., & Pyszczynski, T. (1991). Terror management theory of self-esteem. In C. R. Snyder, & D. R. Forsyth (Eds.), *Handbook of social and clinical psychology: The health perspective* (pp. 21–40). Elmsford, NY: Pergamon.

Spoto, D. (1993). *Marilyn Monroe: The biography.* Lanham, MD: Rowman & Littlefield.

Stark, E., & Flitcraft, A. (1996). *Women at risk: Domestic violence and women's health.* Thousand Oaks, CA: Sage.

Sternberg, R. J. (2008). *An ethnographic approach to studying practical intelligence: A review of gang leader for a day.* New York, NY: Penguin.

Straus, M. A. (1979). Measuring intrafamily conflict and violence: The conflict tactics (CT) scales. *Journal of Marriage and The Family, 41*(1), 75–88.

Sturdevant, S. P., & Stoltzfus, B. (1992). *Let the good times roll: Prostitution and the U.S. military in Asia.* New York, NY: New Press.

Syracuse University School of Education. (2017). *Home.* Retrieved from http://soe.syr.edu/

Tatar, M. (2003). *The hard facts of the Grimms' fairy tales.* Princeton, NJ: Princeton University Press.

Taylor, L., Zuckerman, B., Harik, V., & Groves, B. M. (1994). Witnessing violence by young children and their mothers. *Journal of Developmental and Behavioral Pediatrics, 15*(2), 120–123.

Thomas, W. I., & Thomas, D. S. (1928). *The child in America.* Oxford, England: Knopf.

Thompson, K. (1998). *Moral panic*. London, England: Routledge.

Toledo, A. H. (2004). The medical legacy of Benjamin Rush. *Journal of Investigative Surgery, 17*(2), 61–63.

Tschudi, C. (1902). *Marie Antoinette* (E. M. Cope, Trans.). London, UK: Swan Sonnenschein & Co., Lim.

Turman, L. (Producer), & Nichols, M. (Director). (1967). *The graduate* [Motion picture]. United States: Mike Nichols/Lawrence Turman Productions.

Tweed, T. A. (2004). Islam in America: From African Slaves to Malcolm X. *National Humanities Center.* Retrieved from http://nationalhumanitiescenter.org/tserve/twenty/tkeyinfo/islam.htm

Twenge, J. M., & Campbell, W. K. (2003). 'Isn't it fun to get the respect that we're going to deserve?' Narcissism, social rejection, and aggression. *Personality and Social Psychology Bulletin, 29*(2), 261–272.

Twitchell, J. B. (2000). *Twenty ads that shook the world: The century's most groundbreaking advertising and how it changed us all*. New York, NY: Broadway Books.

Underwood, M. K. (2004). III. Glares of contempt, eye rolls of disgust and turning away to exclude: Non-verbal forms of social aggression among girls. *Feminism & Psychology, 14*(3), 371–375.

Van Vugt, M., & Van Lange, P. A. M. (2006). The altruism puzzle: Psychological adaptations for prosocial behavior. In M. Schaller, J. A. Simpson, & D. T. Kenrick (Eds.), *Evolution and social psychology* (pp. 237–261). Madison, CT: Psychosocial Press.

Vass, J. J., & Gold, S. R. (1995). Effects of feedback on emotion in hypermasculine males. *Violence and Victims, 10*(3), 217–226.

Venkatesh, S. (2008). *Gang leader for a day: A rogue sociologist takes to the streets*. New York, NY: Penguin.

Waddington, P. A. (1986). Mugging as a moral panic: A question of proportion. *British Journal of Sociology, 37*(2), 245–259.

Wampold, B. E., & Imel, Z. E. (2015). *The great psychotherapy debate: The evidence for what makes psychotherapy work* (2nd ed.). New York, NY: Routledge/Taylor & Francis Group.

Wang, S. S., Moon, S., Kwon, K. H., Evans, C. A., & Stefanone, M. A. (2010). Face off: Implications of visual cues on initiating friendship on Facebook. *Computers in Human Behavior, 26*(2), 226–234.

Waters, S., Edmondston, S. J., Yates, P. J., & Gucciardi, D. F. (2016). Identification of factors influencing patient satisfaction with orthopaedic outpatient clinic consultation: A qualitative study. *Manual Therapy, 25*, 48–55.

Wheeler, D. L., Jacobson, J. W., Paglieri, R. A., & Schwartz, A. A. (1993). An experimental assessment of facilitated communication. *Mental Retardation, 31*(1), 49–59.

White, L. (1990). *The comforts of home: Prostitution in colonial Nairobi*. Chicago, IL: University of Chicago Press.

Whitman, M. (1993). Removing a badge of slavery: The record of Brown v Board of Education. *Choice Reviews Online, 31*(1), 20.

Wilkinson, G. S. (1984). Reciprocal food sharing in the vampire bat. *Nature, 308*(5955), 181–184.

Williams, K. D., & Nida, S. A. (2011). Ostracism: Consequences and coping. *Current Directions in Psychological Science, 20*(2), 71–75.

Wilson, J., & Hudson, W. (2013, November 11). Gun violence in PG-13 movies has tripled. *CNN: Health.* Retrieved from http://www.cnn.com/2013/11/11/health/gun-violence-movies/index.html

Wilson, M., Daly, M., & Daniele, A. (1995). Familicide: The killing of spouse and children. *Aggressive Behavior, 21*(4), 275–291.

Wimo, A., Reed, C. C., Dodel, R., Belger, M., Jones, R. W., Happich, M., . . . Haro, J. M. (2013). The GERAS study: A prospective observational study of costs and resource use in community dwellers with Alzheimer's disease in three European countries—Study design and baseline findings. *Journal of Alzheimer's Disease, 36*(2), 385–399.

Woolley, A., & Kostopoulou, O. (2013). Clinical intuition in family medicine: More than first impressions. *The Annals of Family Medicine, 11*(1), 60–66.

Yin, R. K. (2009). *Case study research: Design and methods*. Thousand Oaks, CA: Sage.

Young, J. (1971). *The drugtakers: The social meaning of drug use*. London, England: MacGibbon and Kee.

Young, J. E. (1994). *Cognitive therapy for personality disorders: A schema-focused approach* (Rev. ed.). Sarasota, FL: Professional Resource Press/Professional Resource Exchange.

Young, J. E., Klosko, J. S., & Weishaar, M. E. (2003). *Schema therapy: A practitioner's guide.* New York, NY: Guilford.

YouTube. (2013). *19 sexiest women of Fox News.* Retrieved from https://www.youtube.com/watch?v=mjR_jv3uNlE

Zahn-Waxler, C. (2000). The development of empathy, guilt, and internalization of distress: Implications for gender differences in internalizing and externalizing problems. In R. J. Davidson (Ed.), *Anxiety, depression, and emotion* (pp. 222–265). New York, NY: Oxford University Press.

Zuk, M. (2011). *Sex on six legs: Lessons on life, love, and language from the insect world.* Boston, MA: Houghton Mifflin Harcourt.

Index